WHEN IS MARRIAGE NULL?

WHEN IS MARRIAGE NULL?

PAOLO BIANCHI

When Is Marriage Null?

Guide to the Grounds of Matrimonial Nullity
for Pastors, Counselors, and Lay Faithful

Translated by
MICHAEL J. MILLER, M.A.THEOL.

MARY'S ADVOCATES   ROCKY RIVER

Contents

Foreword

A common misconception, present even in some learned minds, is that the law of the Church is a more or less arbitrary imposition, upon the Body of Christ, of the unbending will of popes and bishops, and especially of the Roman Pontiff, throughout the Christian centuries. From this clearly positivistic point of view, the bonds of justice that exist within the Church and the mechanisms put into place to protect them are seen to be completely adventitious, foreign to the true nature of the Kingdom of God inaugurated by Christ the Lord.

This, however, is not the case. In a particular way, in what pertains to the reality of matrimony, the Church's law originates and flows from the very nature of marriage, instituted by God in the order of creation and raised to the dignity of a sacrament by God the Son Incarnate in the order of redemption. The foundation of the canonical discipline regarding Holy Matrimony is metaphysical or the objective reality of marriage. The essential properties of marriage—unity and indissolubility—belong to all valid marriages, whether sacramental or not. The essential goods of marriage—the *bonum fidei* or the good of fidelity, the *bonum sacramenti* or the good of indissolubility, the *bonum prolis* or the good of offspring, and the *bonum coniugum* or good of the spouses, which is the sum of the other three goods—are inherent to and inseparable from the nuptial relationship from the very moment of its coming into existence with the exchange of vows. God has made it so from the beginning, as our Lord teaches us in the Gospel (cf. Mt 19:8; Mk 10:6). The Church does not invent these essential properties and goods of marriage, but rather she recognizes and announces them as part of the Good News, protecting and defending them as the inalienable patrimony of marriage itself as it comes to us from the hand of God and as it has been endowed with divine grace by Christ the Lord.

Canon law, then, does not create the reality of marriage any more than it provides for a way of "annulling" a true marriage. The law of the Church states *in juridical terms* what marriage is objectively, in truth. The law, as an expression of justice, describes the minimum required for a marriage to be true or valid. Lack of respect for the juridical aspect of marriage does violence to marriage itself. However, the juridical aspect of marriage in no way exhausts the reality of marriage or of the Church's approach to this institution ordained by God for the good of husband and wife, and of their eventual children. The work of other disciplines, for example, of anthropology, ethics, sacramental theology, moral theology, spiritual theology and pastoral theology, is invaluable for the full appreciation of marriage. These other fields of knowledge, together and in harmony with the juridical science of canon law, offer a deepened appreciation of the "great mystery" that is marriage (cf. Eph 5:32).

The work of an ecclesiastical tribunal, then, when it treats the question of the alleged nullity of a marriage, is not to issue an affirmative sentence that declares the marriage null. Rather, the ecclesiastical tribunal has but one only concern: to seek the truth regarding the alleged nullity and to issue a sentence in conformity with the truth, for this is the indispensable service of justice, of which tribunals are preeminent instruments in the Church.

The faithful who approach the tribunals of the Church are asking an intimate and delicate question which touches on their very status in the Church and ultimately on their eternal salvation. The answer to the question is critical to how they live out their vocation to holiness: "Is it true that my marriage is null? Is it really the case that the sacrament of matrimony did not take place, even though I consented to marriage in good faith? Does there really exist, between my spouse and me, a nuptial bond that cannot be dissolved except by death?"

The final outcome of the marriage process, the decision whether the alleged nullity of marriage is established or not, is the sole concern of the judges who arrive at the decision. Other questions of the parties involved are ultimately of no concern to the judges as judges. This is not unfeeling harshness. Even less is it indifference to the plight of the parties and to the often difficult moral situation in which they find themselves. Still less is it insensitivity to the delicate pastoral challenges involved in the Church's ministry to the divorced and to those living in an irregular union. Rather, for the judge, it is the necessary impartiality that the faithful exercise of his office demands. The ecclesiastical judge knows that he can show true compassion and charity to the parties who seek a judgment regarding a claim of nullity only by giving a judgment in accord with the truth.

It will be helpful, here, to quote at length from Saint John Paul II's 2005 Allocution to the Roman Rota, the last one before his death:

> *The criterion that inspires* the deontology [i.e., ethical principles] of the judge is *his love for truth.* First and foremost, therefore, he must be convinced that *the truth exists.* The truth must therefore be sought with a genuine desire to know it, despite all the inconveniences that may derive from such knowledge. It is necessary to resist the *fear of the truth* that can, at times, stem from the dread of annoying people. The truth, which is Christ Himself (cf. Jn 8:32, 36), sets us free from every form of compromise with self interested falsehoods.
>
> The judge who truly acts as a judge, in other words, with justice, neither lets himself be conditioned by feelings of false compassion for people, nor by false models of thought, however widespread these may be in his milieu. He knows that unjust sentences are never a true pastoral solution, and that God's judgment of his own actions is what counts for eternity.[1]

The temptation to compromise or to be circumspect with the truth in such a delicate question—the claim that the *vinculum matrimoniale* or bond of marriage, despite appearances to the contrary, does not exist —out of fear of displeasing one's superiors or other interested parties is understandable, considering human weakness and the desire of those in the Church to come to the aid of others, finding solutions to the difficulties encountered in their moral and spiritual lives.

Such laudable pastoral goals notwithstanding, to deceive another, either deliberately or by negligence, regarding his sacramental status and the real reason for which his marriage has failed, is to deny him not only the truth, but also the occasion of grace that can lead to a conversion of life. The grace of the Lord Jesus will not be lacking to those who,

---

[1] William H. Woestman, ed., *Papal Allocutions to the Roman Rota 1939–2011* (Ottawa: Faculty of Canon Law, Saint Paul University, 2011), 283.

with good will, make difficult decisions to rectify their life situations so that they can live in a manner consistent with their baptismal dignity and Christian discipleship.

With these thoughts in mind, it brings me great joy to present to the reader Father Paolo Bianchi's work on the Church's process for the declaration of nullity of marriage. I have been blessed to enjoy the friendship of Father Bianchi from our years together in the study of canon law at the Pontifical Gregorian University in the early 1980s. Having observed the brilliance of his academic study of canon law during those years, I was also blessed, as an official and eventually as prefect of the Supreme Tribunal of the Apostolic Signatura, to witness his exemplary application of his canonical knowledge, first as a judge and eventually as judicial vicar of the Regional Ecclesiastical Tribunal of Lombardy, headquartered in his home diocese, the great Archdiocese of Milan. During my years of service at the Church's Supreme Tribunal, the ecclesiastical tribunal at Milan has consistently enjoyed the highest level of respect and esteem, thanks to the leadership of Father Bianchi and of his predecessor, Monsignor Giovanni Chierichetti, and to the excellent staff who have worked with them over the years. The Apostolic Signatura, in fact, has frequently recommended the Ecclesiastical Regional Tribunal of Lombardy to bishops who were seeking a tribunal at which priests and other tribunal staff members could do an internship, in order to be better prepared for service in the diocesan tribunal.

In his book *When Is Marriage Null?* Father Bianchi shares the fruits not only of his thorough and profound study of canon law but also of his practical application of canon law in response to the faithful who have come to him to seek the Church's judgment regarding an alleged nullity of marriage. What is more, Father Bianchi presents canonical doctrine and procedure in a way that is easily accessible to the faithful, especially to those who lack any special preparation in canon law. For that reason, his book, published some years ago in its original Italian edition and now happily published in English translation, has been a particular help to bishops, priests, students of canon law, and the faithful in general. Father Bianchi's scholarly work is marked not only by the fidelity of his thought but also by the readily accessible manner in which he conveys it.

Outside of rather confined academic circles, the demanding and painstaking work of professional canonists, as they apply the Church's law to the usually rather complex cases which are brought before them can seem, even to the reasonably well-informed Catholic or to the busy parish priest, a rather obscure exercise. One of the great strengths, then, of this present volume is that it presents the difficult and demanding concepts of canonical matrimonial law in a manner both accessible to those with only a general familiarity with the material and thought-provoking to those who are more expert in the field. There is no doubt that Father Bianchi's book, in correspondence with the author's own intentions, will be of tremendous benefit for those who work in the field of marriage law and tribunal praxis.

Father Bianchi's vast experience and expertise, both as an academic canonist and as judicial vicar for the Ecclesiastical Regional Tribunal of Lombardy, are manifest in his synthetic and practical treatment of each of the grounds of nullity of marriage. Each chapter follows the same basic pattern: an exposition of the substantive law in question, a section outlining the necessary considerations in developing a case on the ground, and finally a set of examples, drawn from actual cases, that highlight the points considered in the first two sections. The very methodology of the book greatly fosters the accessibility and serious consideration of its content.

Even though first published in 1998 and available only now for the first time in an English language edition, *When Is Marriage Null?* remains timely and relevant. It will prove to be a solid addition to any canonical library, a reliable and trustworthy point of reference for all those who, whether in parish work or in tribunal work, are cooperators of truth in the ministry of justice in the Church, and a sound and efficacious help for all who wish to understand better the Church's ministry of justice and love on behalf of those who claim the nullity of their marriage bond.

In presenting this important volume to your reading, I express the deepest gratitude to Father Paolo Bianchi for making more widely available the fruits of his priestly study and labor in the ecclesiastical tribunal. I thank also those who have labored to translate his book into English. In a particular way, I thank Ignatius Press for undertaking and guiding the publication of the English edition as a service to the Church and especially to her safeguarding and promotion of Holy Matrimony. May the reading of *When Is Marriage Null?* deepen our knowledge of the truth about marriage "from the beginning" and our fidelity in the service of that unchanging truth in ecclesiastical tribunals.

RAYMOND LEO CARDINAL BURKE
February 11, 2015
Feast of Our Lady of Lourdes

Foreword to the First Edition

In 1988, at the enthusiastic instigation of Father Beyer, a group of young Italian canonists founded the journal *Quaderni di diritto ecclesiale*,[1] an initiative that has proved to be very beneficial for maintaining the unity and the enthusiasm of that group of valiant collaborators—which incidentally has been continually reinforced with new recruits who hold doctorates in canon law—and also for the Italian Church, which found the journal to be an invaluable means of propagating the ecclesiastical discipline currently in force and canon law scholarship in general. As the journal begins its second decade, we anticipate that it will continue along the straightforward and productive line of renewal that it has followed until now.

Father Paolo Bianchi, who today [1998] is the adjutant judicial vicar of the Regional Ecclesiastical Tribunal of Lombardy,[2] was one of the founders of *Quaderni di diritto ecclesiale* and during those ten years was a contributor to the journal, especially though not exclusively on topics pertaining to contemporary marital problems. In particular in 1992 he began a series of articles about the grounds of nullity under the general title *The Pastor of Souls and Nullity of Marriage*, which are collected in this book. The original general title indicates for whom this book is primarily intended. Indeed, as his introduction emphasizes, the author takes his cue from article 56 of the November 5, 1990, general decree of the Italian Episcopal Conference, which lists examining the grounds

---

[1] The original Italian edition of this book, *Quando il matrimonio è nullo?*, is the first volume in a series of monographs that are the direct result of the first decade of experience of *Quaderni di diritto ecclesiale* (henceforth cited as *QDE*), the quarterly publication of Àncora Editrice, Milan.

[2] As of October 2013, the author is a monsignor and diocesan judicial vicar of the Archdiocese of Milan.

for a possible declaration of nullity among the forms of assistance that should be given by the ecclesial community to spouses in "serious difficulty". The decree notes that "initial assistance for such an examination should be ensured through the availability of discreet and prompt pastoral care, especially on the part of parish priests, employing also, if appropriate, the collaboration of a Christian counseling service rooted in the Christian faith and ethic." Therefore, the primary purpose of this book is to provide clear, well-founded information in sufficient quantity to parish priests and to all who act as counselors in these matters—either in formally organized counseling services or in other possible forms of collaboration with the parish priest or else in the ecclesiastical tribunals themselves—as a step previous to the possible introduction of a case.

This purpose determines the structure of each the following chapters: the first part, more or less extensive depending on the difficulty of the material and always entitled "Elements of Substantive Law", in which the kinds of evidence and the peculiar difficulties with that specific ground of nullity are noted. Then follows the part entitled "Guide for the Counselor", which gives very practical advice for those who assume the role of counselor, again taking into account the specific features of the ground of nullity in question. Finally, under the title "Examples" several real-life situations are presented, taken from judicial experience, which illustrate the peculiar aspects needing attention in evaluating the case within the framework of the problems presented by the ground of nullity under consideration.

This volume collects the work of Father Bianchi so as to make it more readily available—truly a very useful initiative not only for pastors of souls but also for professional canonists and, in particular, those who are called to perform the delicate ministry of judging cases of matrimonial nullity. Indeed, in these chapters the author presents a lucid, in-depth summary of the more characteristic structures of canonical marriage, and he focuses precisely on and gets to the bottom of the most complex problems and controversies related to each of the grounds of nullity he examines, while pointing out clear, thoroughly well-founded courses of action both to pastors and counselors and also to those responsible for administering justice in the Church.

The fact that Father Bianchi's work is aimed at pastors and counselors could arouse the suspicion that these are studies of a merely informative sort that make no attempt to examine in depth the swarms of problems implicated in each of the topics being treated. But such an approach is not in keeping with the author's seriousness and sense of responsibility. Indeed, he made the effort to present the complexity of the problems in simple form, purposely avoiding any hint of exaggerated scholarship, so that any pastor of souls who has studied the least bit of canon law might feel capable of forming a sure opinion about the various grounds of nullity and be able to give well-founded advice in the individual cases that may be presented to him.

Among the various problems that the author addresses I would like to call attention to two that are of particular importance and relevance: the incapacity described in canon 1095 and the error of fact described in canons 1097–98.

It is well known that in practice the ecclesiastical tribunals of some regions of the Church reduce all the grounds for matrimonial nullity to the inability to give valid marital consent and, more particularly, the inability to assume the essential obligations of marriage (can. 1095). Such jurisprudence is certainly oversimplified and has very negative consequences for the ecclesial community and for the faithful involved. The author earned a doctorate in 1988 with a dissertation, directed by Professor G. Versaldi, entitled *Inability to Assume the Essential obligations of Marriage: Analysis of the Jurisprudence of the Roman Rota, Particularly in the Years 1970–1982*.[3] This is a weighty volume with 350 densely printed pages that includes one of the most complete bibliographies on the subject available to date. In the book we are presenting now, the author returns to this topic and devotes two chapters to canon 1095: the first about nos. 1 and 2 of the canon, under the general title "Inability to Consent" (chap. 10); the other about no. 3, entitled "Incapacity to Assume the Essential Obligations of Marriage" (chap. 11). We do not hesitate to assert that the aforesaid chapters are without a doubt well grounded, indeed, probably among the best pieces published to date concerning a matter that is so complex and delicate.

Another topic to which I would like to call the reader's attention is the error of fact, concerning which the author offers an extremely well-reasoned presentation: "Error of Fact: About the Person, about a Personal Quality Directly and Principally Intended, or about a Personal Quality That Is the Object of Deceit" (chap. 3). On this matter it

---

[3] *Incapacitas assumendi obligationes essentiales matrimonii: Analisi della giurisprudenze rotale, particolarmente degli anni 1970–1982* published by Edizioni Glossa (Milan, 1992).

becomes necessary to recall how in the decade before the promulgation of the new Code of Canon Law, a certain jurisprudential trend, even of the Roman Rota, attempted to broaden the concepts of "error of person" and of "error of quality redounding to an error of person", thus departing from the meaning attributed to these expressions in the canonical tradition that had matured over the centuries. These tendencies, notwithstanding the significant change of the text of current canon 1097 §2 with respect to canon 1083 §2 of the Pio-Benedictine Code, have not yet been entirely overcome in quite a few lower tribunals, whereas little by little they have been almost entirely abandoned by the judges of the Rota, who have reaffirmed ever more forcefully the two fundamental criteria in this matter, namely the unequivocal concept of person (can. 1097 §1) and the evaluation of the invalidating relevance of the error about an accidental quality on the sole basis of the intention of the subject who is in error (can. 1097 §2). In dealing, however, with an error induced by deceit, in a scheme to obtain consent, the existing Code, by a positive decree of the legislator, requires, in order for that error to have invalidating force, not only that the quality be objectively such that of its very nature it can seriously disrupt the partnership of conjugal life but also that the deceived person subjectively consider the deceit about that quality, in his concrete case, to be incompatible with his marital consent. Indeed, it seems that there can be no doubts as to the irrelevance of the concomitant error ("I would have married you anyway even if I had known the truth"), even in the case of a deceitful error about a quality that by its nature can seriously disrupt the conjugal partnership. Father Bianchi subjects the individual questions involved to a keen analysis, comparing the law currently in force with the preceding law and offering well-grounded guidelines both in the more authoritative traditional and current teaching, and also in jurisprudence. The five real-life examples that he presents show a rigorous method of analysis and evaluation, combining the *criterium aestimationis* and the *criterium reactionis* in due proportion so as to arrive at the certitude required in order for the judge to be able to pronounce his sentence.[4]

---

[4] For the sake of completeness the author refers to another piece he wrote on the topic: "Esempi di applicazione giurisprudenziale del can. 1098 (dolo): casistica e problemi probatori", QDE 9 (1996): 357–78.

The author decided to collect in this volume only those essays on marital law that deal specifically with the more significant headings of nullity and to add a chapter dedicated to the problem of dispensation from a nonconsummated marriage. However, it should be stressed that, besides various essays on other matters, the author has published so many and such a range of articles on marriage in *Quaderni di diritto ecclesiale* that they could very well be collected in a second volume.[5]

We hope that the author will prepare as soon as possible a new collection with these studies, so as to continue along the same lines as the volume that I have the pleasure and the honor of presenting, a volume that offers a sound contribution to canonical scholarship and jurisprudence, with its clarity, depth, and thoroughness in discussing problems, and that seeks always to remain sensitive to the highest principles of canonical equity and faithful to the directives of the Church's Magisterium.

Urbano Navarrete, S.J.
Dean and Professor Emeritus
Faculty of Canon Law
Pontifical Gregorian University
Rome, March 1998

---

[5] "La preparazione al matrimonio, oggi, in Italia", *QDE* 1 (1988): 79–94; "Nullità di matrimonio e difetti nella sua preparazione", *QDE* 1 (1988): 126–32; "Commento a un canone: il luogo della celebrazione del matrimonio (can. 1118)", *QDE* 2 (1989): 188–96; "L'obbligo dei testimoni di collaborare nello svolgimento delle cause matrimoniali canoniche", *QDE* 2 (1989): 380–92; "È più facile, col nuovo Codice di diritto canonico, dimostrare la nullità di un matrimonio? I canoni 1536 §2 e 1679", *QDE* 3 (1990): 394–410; "Società secolarizzata ed esclusione della sacramentalità del matrimonio: un motivo di nullità matrimoniale in crescita?" *QDE* 4 (1991): 79–96; "Nota: La preparazione al matrimonio canonico nel decreto generale della Conferenza episcopale italiana", *QDE* 4 (1991): 197–200; "Nota: AIDS e matrimonio canonico", *QDE* 4 (1991): 370–75; "Matrimoni misti e scioglimento del matrimonio: l'art. 47 del decreto generale della CEI sul matrimonio canonico", *QDE* 5 (1992): 309–20; "Nullità di matrimonio non dimostrabili. Equivoco o problema pastorale?" *QDE* 6 (1993): 280–97; "Il 'diritto di famiglia' della Chiesa", *QDE* 7 (1994): 285–99; "Note in materia di 'forma straordinaria' della celebrazione del matrimonio", *QDE* 9 (1996): 257–67; "I Tribunali ecclesiastici regionali italiani: storia, attualità e prospettive. Le nueve norme CEI circa il regime amministrativo dei Tribunali ecclesiastici regionali italiani", *QDE* 10 (1997): 393–420.

Acknowledgments

The translator wishes to thank two colleagues who helped to prepare the English edition: Rev. Patrick T. Brannan, S.J., who drafted a translation of one of the chapters, and Rev. James Mercer, formerly a defender of the bond in the tribunal of the Diocese of Arlington, Virginia, who reviewed the complete English text, clarified several passages, and revised the terminology to conform to North American usage.

The publisher wishes to thank Rev. Joshua Guillory, a priest of the Diocese of Lafayette and an official at the Supreme Tribunal of the Apostolic Signatura, for his invaluable editorial assistance.

I

Introduction and Preliminary Considerations

The norm of the Italian Episcopal Conference

Article 56 of the general decree of the Italian Episcopal Conference (a decree promulgated on November 5, 1990, which has the force of law for the Italian Church [cf. can. 29] and went into effect on February 17, 1991) has a precise object and lays down a very clear precept: among those forms of assistance that should be given by the ecclesial community to spouses in "serious difficulty" should be included also an examination of "the possible existence of grounds that the Church considers relevant for a declaration of nullity of the marriage that was celebrated".[1]

The norm also specifies the individuals who are charged with providing this form of assistance to spouses in serious difficulty: it appears from the wording of the law that the Italian Episcopal Conference intended to oblige—at least in an initial phase of investigation—parish priests: "Initial assistance for such an examination should be ensured through the availability of discreet and prompt pastoral care, especially on the part of parish priests, employing also, if appropriate, the collaboration of a counseling service rooted in the Christian faith and ethic."[2] Hence, an obligation is imposed directly on parish priests (possibly supported by those institutions that by their nature propose to assist the family: Christian counseling services) to provide to spouses in serious difficulty initial guidance with respect to the examination of the possible invalidity of their marriage.

Only occasionally, on the other hand, and in relation to particularly

---

[1] Art. 56, par. 1.

[2] Ibid., par. 2.

difficult cases, is any intervention foreseen—in this phase of guiding the consciences of the faithful—by more technical organizations, such as the diocesan curia or the regional tribunal, which, in Italy are competent to deal with cases of a request for a declaration of nullity of a marriage. Indeed, Italian ecclesial law prescribes "It is good in any event that a qualified consultation and counseling service for causes of marital nullity be set up in diocesan curias and as part of regional tribunals, to which interested faithful can turn, especially in the event of complex situations or developments, on their own initiative or at the suggestion of their parish priest."[3] It is obvious, even from the wording of the norm itself, that although it is recommended, the establishment of counseling organizations as part of curias and tribunals is not binding, as is the obligation imposed on parish priests; rather it is presented as a helpful possibility "especially in the event of complex situations or developments".

One might ask the reason why the Italian Episcopal Conference in fact charged parish priests directly and primarily (with the help of Christian counseling services) with examining the possibility of introducing a canonical process for the faithful who are in serious marital difficulty, instead of requiring such an examination directly from more specialized authorities such as diocesan curias or tribunals. Hypothetically, we can suppose that the episcopal conference wanted to foster the "pastoral" moment, so to speak, of that initial discernment, when another primary concern is to make evident the reasons for a possible canonical proceeding and the importance of an ecclesial judgment on the couple's marital situation and on the actual existence of the obligations resulting from the sacramental bond: if so, then indeed parish priests are plainly the persons who can best ensure such pastoral attention.

Moreover, based on the author's personal experience, it seems appropriate not to burden tribunals directly and massively with the work of preliminary consultation about the advisability of marital cases. It is true that they could guarantee competence and experience in dealing with these questions, but—in light also of the scarcity of qualified personnel—consultations given by judges (especially if they are judicial vicars and adjutant judicial vicars) could cause difficulties later in

---

[3] Ibid., par. 3.

forming a panel of judges. Indeed, although it is true that consultation given is not a legal reason for a judge to abstain from judging or to recuse himself (cf. cann. 1448 and 1449), it seems logical that the consultation—especially if it was conducted in depth and actually resulted in responsible advice and not in a generic referral to another expert—suggests that it would be appropriate to abstain from judging that case, in order to safeguard the peace of mind of the judge himself and of the person who previously requested his counsel (who could, for instance, feel embarrassed to find himself being judged by someone who earlier had advised him not to initiate proceedings).

In order to resolve such difficulties, some tribunals in recent years have taken steps to nominate—pursuant to the optional provision of canon 1490 of the Code of Canon Law—a stable advocate to whom the work of preliminary consultation is generally entrusted as well. Others have made agreements with the advocates registered in their department, who have publicly pledged (e.g., through a declaration that appeared in the local diocesan newsletter) a consultation session free of charge to the faithful in marital difficulties in order to weigh the advisability of a canonical cause of nullity. It is well known that from now on all the Italian regional tribunals will have to nominate, within their own organization, at least two of the aforesaid stable advocates, as called for by article 6 of the norms of the Italian Episcopal Conference promulgated by the decree dated March 18, 1997,[4] that regulate some aspects of the administration of tribunals and also of the activity of the advocacy staff. One of the tasks of these stable advocates is precisely to offer qualified canonical counsel to the faithful concerning the possibility of promoting a canonical cause relating to their marriage, which could then lead the stable advocate to handle the case of the party in event of a judgment.

It must be noted, however, that even the appointment of such stable advocates throughout the national territory does not eliminate the need for some pastoral discernment, for a "filter" prior to their work of consultation, which could be carried out at the level of parish priests and the counselors: indeed, it is a good thing that cases that are manifestly unfounded in terms of the practicability of a canonical cause should not be allowed to reach as far as the stable advocates. Only

---

[4] Published in the newsletter of the same bishops' conference dated March 26, 1997.

those cases that, based precisely on nonsuperficial indications, would lead the first-level consultant to surmise the possibility of some further development. Otherwise there is the risk that the stable advocates might be swamped by a great volume of work related to the details of married life that require a sort of pastoral care different from what can be obtained by submitting the case to an ecclesiastical tribunal.

After pointing out the individuals obliged to provide the faithful with the consultation service described above, the 1990 norm of the Italian Episcopal Conference mentions two items of special care in performing this service.

In the first place, the general decree states that the examination concerning the possibility of a challenge to the validity of the marital bond must be carried out "when nonsuperficial indications" of possible nullity "are evident":[5] that is, when the presence of certain factual elements makes an in-depth study of the question reasonable, even though they do not yet present a full proof of nullity to be pleaded before the tribunal. Obviously, the norm leaves up to the individual designated to conduct and to propose the work of examination [a certain amount of discretion concerning the carrying out of the examination itself], inasmuch as it is conceivable that "nonsuperficial indications" are not always evident per se and are not already known to the counselor himself. This can also be one of the reasons why Italian particular canon law prescribes that parish priests should be the ones directly and primarily responsible for this work of consultation. Indeed, it is possible that the "nonsuperficial indications" that might justify further study along the lines of a potential declaration of nullity might emerge informally in the pastoral conversations that parish priests habitually have with the faithful and that the parish priests themselves can prudently examine informally, even before explicitly recommending the possibility of seeking a declaration of nullity. It is clear—in this connection—that, barring "nonsuperficial indications" already at one's disposal, the examination of the possible invalidity of one's own marriage will be that much more easily proposed, the more irremediable the situation of marital difficulty has become, or the more entrenched the situations objectively incompatible with marriage that prompt an examination of

---

[5] Art. 56, par. 1.

its possible invalidity (e.g., a new civil marriage after a divorce, with or without children).

The second provision called for by the guidelines of the bishops' conference is that "the research done to verify possible motives for marital nullity should always be conducted competently and prudently, taking care to avoid hasty conclusions."[6] Indeed, such hasty conclusions can, on the one hand, give rise to harmful illusions, for example presenting as possible or founded a cause that in reality is not, thus prompting the interested party to initiate faulty and disappointing procedures. On the other hand, they can discourage with superficial and hurried responses someone who is seeking counsel, thus ruling out—as the general decree also says—"a clarification that would be invaluable for ascertaining the freedom of a person's state of life and for the peace of mind that comes with a clear conscience".[7]

An aid to pastors and other priests who encounter spouses in difficulty

The Italian Episcopal Conference, in article 56 of its general decree of 1990 on canonical marriage, attributes the primary responsibility for counseling the faithful whether to seek a declaration of nullity not to legal experts but to priests who care for souls, especially to parish priests, requiring of them prudence and competence, recommending that they avoid hasty conclusions, and assigning to them the task of discerning the presence of possible nonsuperficial indications. Given this, the journal *Quaderni di diritto ecclesiale* decided to provide interested priests with a resource that would be as practical as possible, for the purpose of fostering greater care in carrying out this task of initial consultation enjoined on them by the particular law of Italy.

For this purpose, in the series of journal articles that are collected in this volume, the author explains the most useful concerns and suggestions to keep in mind in the course of the conversations of this initial consultation, with an eye to pointing out "the possible existence of

---

[6] Ibid., par. 4.

[7] Ibid.

grounds that the Church considers relevant for a declaration of nullity of the marriage that was celebrated".[8]

It is particularly important to stress the practical and didactic purpose of this work, a purpose that is reflected even in the structure of the articles that were first published in the journal and are now gathered together for the convenience of the intended readers. Specifically, after offering by way of introduction some general remarks about the spirit and the courtesies [*attenzioni*] to be shown in initial conversations, each chapter in the book suggests several ideas about the probative requirements described by canonical legislation for some of the most frequent grounds of nullity. This can help the priests to whom the Italian Episcopal Conference decree entrusts the first level of consultation with the faithful who are in serious marital difficulties, so as to bring into better focus the at-least-probable existence of a ground of nullity and the need for a useful more in-depth examination of the question.

All that remains is to explain that here we will limit ourselves to some of the most frequent "grounds of nullity", in other words, those that statistically more readily come to the attention of the tribunals, the specification of which may require greater care and more in-depth inquiry on the part of the advisor. Indeed, it is obvious that some grounds for nullity (except for perhaps a few particular probative difficulties) are per se statistically rarer and conceptually easier to identify. Think, for example, of the impediments to marriage resulting from Holy Orders (can. 1087) or from a public and perpetual vow of chastity in a religious institute (can. 1088). Moreover, it should be explained that this treatise will conclude with a chapter dedicated to dispensation from a ratified marriage that has not been consummated as well as with a chapter dedicated to validation and sanation, procedures that are another possible pastoral response to a marriage that there is reason to consider invalid.

In other words, the practical purpose of this treatise makes it possible to offer it not as a complete treatise on the canon law of marriage—either substantial or procedural—but only as a simple reference work for the use of pastors and those who counsel the faithful who have marital problems. Other articles in the journal *Quaderni di diritto eccle-*

---

[8] Ibid., par. 1.

siale or possible later editions of this work will be able to fill in any gaps and to incorporate any suggestions made relative to this first edition.

Preliminary general observations concerning the consultation interview for the purpose of determining a possible ground of nullity of a marriage

It seems appropriate to underscore several preliminary considerations that are generally useful in establishing pastoral rapport with the faithful, namely, considerations that help in examining the possible existence of a ground of nullity of a marriage that is in a serious, irremediable crisis. These considerations are as follows:

1. Especially at the beginning of the work of examination and when this inquiry is explicitly requested by the faithful (sometimes it is not, but the parish priest himself can anticipate the need for it, in light of the accounts that the interested party makes of his own conjugal life), it can be appropriate to recall the fact that the whole work of examination is based on the assumption of the utmost sincerity on the part of the interested party during the consultation.

This is so for two reasons: in the first place, because a possible declaration of nullity of a marriage is a problem that involves the conscience of the interested persons (in classical terms, also the area of the internal forum), since it relates to a law that is "beyond the control" of the free will of the spouses—in this instance a validly contracted marital bond. In other words, it is not merely about the external formalization of a personal situation but also about a fact that affects the conscience, with regard to which a finding of nullity would have no validity if it were based on statements that were deliberately falsified or that intentionally stretched the truth.

In the second place, honesty is necessary because the initial consultation, while it does have to address the problem of whether it is possible to prove the potential ground of nullity evidenced, does not yet allow the proof itself to be demonstrated. It is a matter of giving an opinion on the basis of facts that ordinarily come solely from declarations of the interested spouse or at most of both spouses. It is important to make them understand, if necessary, that stretching the truth or exaggerating can perhaps fool the advisor but will less readily be accepted by a tribunal, which will have to verify and compare the statements by the parties.

2. Anyone who must help the parishioner to determine the possible invalidity of his marriage must never forget the specific objectives of the work of examination itself, which can be summed up as follows: first, whether or not the case set forth by the person falls under one of the grounds of nullity foreseen by canon law; and second, whether it appears possible, generally speaking, to prove the ground of nullity that might be proposed.

This is because often the person, in his presentation, tends to relate facts that are not pertinent to the investigation or to express his own past and present feelings. Of course, the advisor must not interrogate the interested party with cold, bureaucratic efficiency—and nothing prevents him from sharing his feelings and showing human sympathy or empathy for the misfortunes experienced—however, he must not forget the specific purpose of the help that he seeks to give to the person, patiently getting him to disclose the truly relevant facts for the future canonical investigation and not letting emotional or sentimental considerations influence the opinion that he will have to offer. Often, as the norm of the bishops' conference also prudently points out, these considerations can give rise in the person himself to "harmful illusions",[9] causing the interested party to believe that he can resolve his own situation with a declaration of the nullity of a previous marriage on the basis of an opinion compromised by considerations not directly pertinent to the purpose, for example, that he is a good person, a practicing Catholic, that he was not responsible for the failure of the marriage that is being challenged, that he has suffered much because of said failure, or that he intensely desires to return to the sacraments while having placed himself in an objectively irregular situation from the Catholic perspective. Although the advisor obviously cannot disregard all these considerations, he must not lose sight of the specific object of the opinion that he is to offer to the interested party.

---

[9] Ibid., par. 4.

3. In order to avoid the danger pointed out in the previous paragraph, anyone who offers his own help as an advisor must also always remember that the future canonical inquiry has a precise point of view, that of the moment at which the marriage was celebrated. The presence of the possible ground of nullity must be demonstrated relative to that moment which gave rise to the marriage. Any fact, even a serious one (sickness, infidelity, etc.) that occurred after the wedding has no relevance with a view to a declaration of nullity of the marriage, unless it serves as evidence for a reason of nullity that was present at the moment of consent. For example, the resumption shortly after the wedding of a relation with another person who had already been a lover previously is a fact that can, under certain conditions, have relevance as an indication of the exclusion of conjugal fidelity.

4. Even though the actual course of the interview can go in very different ways, depending on the emotional conditions of the person who is challenging [the validity of the marriage], or on the fact that the consultation was requested expressly or else that it was conducted by the parish priest informally, examining in his own mind what the subject was telling him for other purposes (e.g., spiritual direction, confession, generic counsel), it is good for the advisor to keep in mind an outline of the principal grounds of nullity of marriage, so as to be able to make a complete examination on the points of interest relevant to the purposes of the consultation, without overlooking any. For example, the counselor could have in mind an outline like the following to help him in examining possible relevant facts. This is a thoroughly practical outline that nonetheless reflects what could be considered the most logical arrangements of the material, which should start with defects of consent, both involuntary (e.g., psychological incapacity) and voluntary (e.g., a "simulation"), and then turn to the examination of any factors that vitiate consent (e.g., errors of relevant fact), and also of the conditions for the juridical efficacy of consent (e.g., whether the subject is incapable of actually fulfilling any one of his essential obligations, as for example the obligation of conjugal physical union).

The outline proposed here for the counselor to keep in mind so as to be sure of the completeness of his own investigation is thoroughly practical and revolves around the following three concepts: freedom of

the person; his capacity; the correctness of his intentions. This outline
could be described thus:

FACTORS THAT VITIATE FREEDOM OF CONSENT

- Moral or physical constraint

- The presence of errors: concerning the person or concerning a
  quality of the person, directly and principally intended by the one
  in error, or an error induced by deceit

- Setting conditions on one's own marital commitment

Indeed, it is clear that if constraint directly vitiates freedom of consent,
then errors of fact also vitiate it indirectly (inasmuch as they substantially limit knowledge about the spouse, they inevitably influence the
freedom of the decision to accept the spouse as such), as do conditions
that make the consent itself less free, less pure.

INCAPACITY OF THE PERSON

- Impotence, that is, the inability to have sexual intercourse

- The inability to consent because of insufficient use of reason or
  because of a lack of discretion of judgment (lack of minimal critical
  estimation and of self-determination)

- The inability to assume any one of the essential obligations of marriage, for reasons of a psychological nature

VOLUNTARY DEFECTS OF CONSENT

- Simulation of marriage itself

- Exclusion of an essential property of marriage (unity-fidelity, indissolubility) or else of one of its essential elements (being ordered
  to children or to the good of the spouses)

This outline, or a similar one (we will come back to the contents of the
various grounds of nullity and analyze them), seems useful for inter-
rogating in an orderly fashion and for filling in what is freely disclosed

by the interested party. On the other hand, the grounds of nullity that are statistically rarer (e.g., the above-mentioned impediments resulting from a vow or from Holy Orders, but also abduction or consanguinity) normally tend to emerge spontaneously from the free disclosure of the interested party himself.

Before giving an opinion, even a provisional one (sometimes, indeed, several interviews are necessary, and it may prove possible and advisable to hear the other interested spouse as well), it is necessary to be sure that, by means of free disclosure and the counselor's questions, all the points that are pertinent to the consultation have been touched on. Having in mind an outline to follow in the investigation can facilitate the counselor's work and make it more effective.

5. As much as is possible at this phase of investigation, which is still preliminary, it seems very appropriate to offer reasons for the response that is given at the conclusion of the work of consultation, both as a sign of respect for the person and out of an educational concern. A declaration of the nullity of a marriage is in fact not a favor or an arbitrary action but [the result of] a search for the actual truth of things in light of the ecclesial discipline. [Offering reasons is helpful] as a consideration that fosters a better understanding of the response given, and hopefully also allows for further in-depth study or clarifications that were not examined thus far. Specifically, the reasoning for the response could be presented by explaining to the interested party the principal grounds of marital nullity (e.g., by following the outline discussed in the preceding point), helping him to apply to his own case the legislation currently in force. This can turn out to be a demanding task but one that is certainly productive, at least in terms of understanding the response given by the advisor, even when it may not favor the introduction of a canonical cause.

Having presented what seem to be several appropriate general concerns to keep in mind while helping the faithful with marital problems to identify possible grounds of nullity of their marriage, and keeping in mind, by way of example although with great freedom, the outline presented above, we can now begin the work of indicating the concerns that pastors or other priests who are interested in providing this pastoral care must take into consideration relative to the individual principal grounds of marital nullity.

II

Violation of Freedom of Consent

Elements of substantive law

Freedom of consent—which in canon law is the "efficient" cause of the conjugal bond, the factor that truly brings about marriage both as a juridic act and as a state of life—can be vitiated directly by physical violence or fear, as canon 1103 lays down.

Physical violence is any action performed by someone who physically forces others to do something unwillingly. This coercion represents a complete lack of consent, since the person being forced has no possibility of resisting the violent action (cf. can. 125 §1, on juridic acts in general). In the case of marriage, however, this reason for nullity does not occur very frequently, inasmuch as it presupposes simultaneous violence (or complicity in the violence) against the spouse, the sacred minister in attendance, the witnesses, and all present at the wedding.

Fear, on the other hand, which is much more common, is the consequence in the subject of a "moral violence" exercised by a third party, by dint of which someone feels coerced to perform an action (e.g., matrimonial consent) that he would not otherwise perform. In this second case, the contracting subject actually exercises his will to consent, but it is vitiated by the coercive action. Therefore, if the coercion was serious (given also the personal and social importance of the institution of marriage), canon law considers any consent given as a result of fear to be invalid from the start (cf. cann. 125 §2 and 1103), wishing to safeguard the subject's freedom in choosing his state of life. This freedom, moreover, is solemnly affirmed in the list of the rights belonging to the baptized (cf. can. 219).

Moral violence in marital matters can be exercised through the threat of physical harm (blows, expulsion from the household) or moral harm (defamation; loss of an affectionate, trusting relationship, the dread of which is "reverential fear"). Moral violence can also be exercised by an abuse of authority (e.g., by a parent who, even without any threat, imposed on his daughter the obligation to marry a particular man, considering it convenient for reasons of a financial or social nature).

This coercive action must come, according to the law, *ab extrinseco*, that is, from a free cause. To put it even more clearly: the action must come from a person and from his positive behavior, even though it may not be directly and intentionally aimed at extorting marital consent. Thus, based on someone's habitually domineering, despotic, or violent behavior, one can reconstruct the particular element that is termed *suspicio metus* (suspicion of fear, or one might say, "fear of fear"), which in canonical doctrine is equivalent to fear itself, according to the traditional axiom *suspicio metus pro metu sufficit* (the suspicion of fear is equivalent to fear). Even in this case, however, the reconstruction of the subjective situation of fear in the subject who experiences it will have to be made starting from an actual objective fact relative to the conduct of one or more specific subjects distinct from the one who experiences the fear. What cannot be maintained (and the law implicitly prohibits this by insisting on the "extrinsic" character of the fear) is an altogether subjective fear (fear *ab intrinseco*), in other words, one that is the product of mere self-persuasion by the subject at the wedding, without the presence of any external influence on his freedom by third persons. For example, the case of a young man who got his fiancée pregnant and decided to marry her, being driven by feelings of guilt and by a cultural heritage that favors "marriage of reparation", but without any decisive pressure by third parties at the wedding, would not be within the purview of canon 1103.

As will be clearer in due time, a grave lack of discretion of judgment —if it is such as to lead to a substantial defect of the will—constitutes a lack of consent, or an intrinsic inadequacy thereof (cf. can. 1095, 2°). This is a motive for nullity that is even more radical than that of fear. In this case, however, it would be a matter of the inability to consent, a situation that cannot be confused with the scenario of force that we are dealing with here. Indeed, whereas in the case of force the subject is per se capable of giving consent, in the case of a grave lack of discretion of judgment the subject himself, in contrast, is radically incapable of it. For this reason, these two scenarios of nullity must be carefully distinguished and thus can be taken into consideration only in a subordinate manner. In other words, it will be possible to talk about force only after having ruled out the possibility that the subject was per se incapable of giving consent. Certainly, the two scenarios cannot be considered "fungible", as though they were equivalent and interchangeable.

In order to vitiate consent, the fear described in canon 1103 must be, as stated by the same canon, "grave". (For example, moderate persuasion by a parent, without imposition or threat, in favor of a particular marriage, does not result in "grave fear".) Currently, to evaluate the seriousness of fear jurisprudence uses a standard that is subjective, so to speak: fear is considered grave when, in that concrete case, it was the effective reason why a particular person celebrated a marriage that was otherwise unwanted. This evaluation that we have called "subjective" takes into consideration the local (e.g., cultural) and personal (e.g., the character of the one threatening and of the one threatened, their reciprocal relations and the actual likelihood of the threat that was made) and the circumstances of the protagonists of the incident, in particular, logically enough, the circumstances of the person who claims to have been threatened. To summarize: the "gravity" is the ability of the coercive action to be the actual cause of the consent, by superimposing said action on the spontaneous will of the person who is coerced. At this conceptual level it is understandable why the law in force today no longer requires that the fear incurred be "unjust" (either as to its substance or as to the means by which it was incurred). Indeed, in matters such as the choice of one's state of life, any fear whatsoever that substantially determines consent should be considered unjust from any perspective.

From the probative perspective, the direct object of the judicial proof is the fact of the coercion. It may be proved by any method of proof, although normally the prevalent method is oral proof, derived from the deposition of witnesses who are informed about the fact or else by the admission of the subject who exercised the coercion.

Then, given the fact that fear—obviously within the parameters of "moral" and not physical violence—is a subjective feeling, and given the fact that often the coercion is exercised within the seclusion of home and family, great importance is given to the statements of the person who denounces the threat that he underwent, pursuant to cann.

1536 §2 and 1679. The subsequent importance of these statements for the proof of matrimonial nullity was already explained in *Quaderni di diritto ecclesiale* 3 (1990): 394–410.

The proof of force can be accomplished also by the indirect method, in other words, through circumstantial evidence. In the case of force, the principal indicator is aversion. Indeed, aversion is the logical and psychological presupposition of coercion: one can be forced to do only something that is unwanted, not something that one spontaneously already desires. Said aversion must be specifically directed toward marriage and to the other person as spouse, regardless of whether that person is pleasing or indifferent in other respects, for example, as a friend or even as a lover. It is clear that aversion is a strong element of circumstantial proof. The stronger and more evident the aversion to a specific marriage is in a person, the more likely it is that it could have been celebrated under constraint.

Guide for the counselor

In light of these brief remarks of substantive law relative to the theme of violence and fear as possible causes of matrimonial nullity, it becomes clear that the points on which to dwell in a consultation will be the following, drawn from article 56 of the general decree of the Italian Episcopal Conference on marriage:

1. It will be necessary first of all to investigate whether there was true aversion to the marriage in the following ways:

—One should clarify whether the person who claimed to have been forced was truly against that marriage, or merely unsure, not entirely convinced, or not very content.

—It is useful to understand the reasons why the person allegedly had been averse to the marriage. The more plausible the reason for the aversion, the more credible the aversion itself, which, as already mentioned, is the sole basis on which coercion can be exercised.

—Since the alleged aversion will have to be proved before the tribunal, it will be appropriate also to investigate how, when, and how many times that aversion was manifested and how it can be demonstrated. For example, are there persons who may be able to confirm what happened during the engagement (breakups, attempts to avoid the company of the person who was disliked), which prove the aforesaid aversion? Or are there credible persons who can report prenuptial statements of the person who claims to have been forced, expressing aversion to the marriage with that particular person?

2. It will then be necessary to identify whether there was any true coercion to marry. From this perspective it is necessary to bring to light the following:

—Above all for what motive the person who was averse decided to marry anyway: in particular whether besides the alleged threat, there were other motives or reasons that could lead to a reassessment of the weight of the supposed force (e.g., whether the subject who claims to have been forced, while not feeling attracted to the spouse, nevertheless hoped to benefit from her dazzling economic and social status, something that he was advised and urged to do for his own interests and those of his family).

—Whether the coercion that is alleged was exercised by one or more specific persons. Indeed, canon law now in force requires that the coercion come from without, that is, from one or more persons.

—What relations there were between the one(s) threatening and the one threatened and what their respective personalities were. Indeed, it is intuitively obvious that the prospect of a marriage imposed by a brusque command on a rebellious son who habitually ignored the admonitions of his weak parents will not be very probable, whereas it could be a plausible thesis that an authoritarian parent who was habitually and blindly obeyed might have committed an abuse of authority with regard to a timid daughter who was accustomed to rendering the utmost obedience.

—Whether the threat made or the command given was truly effective, that is, whether it was the true cause of a marriage that otherwise would not have been celebrated. In this connection it will be important to clarify what type of threat was made to the interested party and whether that threat was plausible for him and such that it forced him to accept what he did not want, namely, the marriage. Thus, for example, the threat of being thrown out of the house (if plausible) can be effective with regard to a young adolescent without an alternative place to live or personal income, whereas it cannot so easily be considered effective for a man in his forties who is established professionally and has the wherewithal to live on his own.

—Whether there is some way of demonstrating the fact of the coercion itself. For example, are there persons who know about the coercion or the threats made, persons who are also willing to give confirmation thereof? Or are there persons who can at least shed light on the relations between the one threatening and the one threatened and their respective characters? Indeed, we must not forget that proof in the judicial forum is constructed by the overall presentation of many pieces of evidence and testimonies. Not every witness can know all the aspects of an incident, but each one can contribute toward clarifying with certainty some aspect of it and, together with the others, to help the advisor to arrive at conclusive certainty about what must be proved.

3. It must be determined whether there are circumstances in support of the claim of true coercion. Some circumstances, indeed, can be pieces of circumstantial evidence which show that genuine coercion took place with respect to a subject who was truly averse. The following should be considered as possible circumstantial evidence:

—How the subject sought to resist the constraint. Did he stress his opposition and, above all, seek all reasonable help, in keeping with the options reasonably available to him to escape the unwanted marriage? If a person who claims to have been forced in fact had reasonable and possible means of escaping the threat or the imposition (e.g., the possibility of leaving the sphere of influence of the one who was threatening him, of turning for help to individuals who could have protected him from the imposition, of complaining about the pressures to which he was being subjected to someone who, by his own authority, could have called off the marriage) but did not have recourse to them, one may doubt the reality of that person's aversion and therefore of the actual extent of the alleged coercion.

—What were the attitudes of the person who claims to have been forced with respect to the preparations for the wedding, and on the day of its celebration. The refusal to participate in the preparations or the fact of having done so with obvious reluctance and, also, a manifestly sad and unloving attitude toward the spouse during the marriage ceremony and on the wedding day can contribute as circumstantial evidence toward a proof at least of the aversion to that marriage.

—How the person who says that he had been forced dealt with married life. Did he seek to escape from it? Did he neglect its duties? Did he complain about it to others? Behavior during married life certainly must not be considered a conclusive indication (a woman who submits under constraint to a wedding often submits also to conjugal life, thinking that she is now definitively obliged to do so), but the consideration of how the parties lived their married life (duration, children, reason for separation) can nevertheless be of not insignificant interest.

Examples

We think it useful to report—as we will do for every cause of matrimonial nullity that we investigate—several examples that illustrate concretely several cases in point in which the validity of the marriage is challenged. This is done so as to make even more practical the service that this book is intended to render to canonical marriage advisors, whether priests or other qualified counselors, enabling them to understand, albeit summarily, the argument developed by the tribunal in evaluating the various cases. Knowledge of this, indeed, helps one better to investigate and to probe the case even in the previous advisory phase, for the benefit of the lay faithful in marital difficulties.

First example

Ann fell in love during the 1950s with John, whom she met while he was voluntarily enlisted in the military. To her sixteen-year-old eyes, his uniform was an attractive, fascinating feature. Both of them were southerners who had moved to the north: Ann with her large family,

John alone. At first Ann's parents opposed their daughter's romantic feelings, but then they grew to like the young man. For several years they welcomed John as a guest at their house for meals and invited him to stay overnight at a house they owned next door to the father's workplace.

Over the course of those years Ann's love dimmed and was actually extinguished when unexpectedly her father, on his own initiative (and also for reasons of thrift) decided to combine the wedding of the two young people with the wedding of three other siblings of Ann who had decided to marry. Ann, however, no longer loved John and tried to explain the matter to her parents. Her father, though, an authoritarian man who had toiled to improve the family's lot and to make the best possible arrangements for his children, would hear no more of it when Ann began to speak. He silenced her and imposed the marriage on her. She submitted, although she complained about it to other persons, both before and after the wedding. She became pregnant and continued her married life for many years, although it caused her suffering that led to disturbances of a psychosomatic nature.

Proving the invalidity of the marriage was not easy. On the one hand, there were the contraindications, consisting of Ann's initial infatuation, the long duration of their married life, and the fact that not all the persons who were then closest to Ann had noticed the change in her feelings toward John or become aware of the father's imposition. On the other hand, the father admitted, at least to some degree, the fact that he had imposed on his daughter, which was also known to some of the witnesses by virtue of the contemporaneous confidences of Ann and of her mother, now deceased. Moreover, strong testimonies brought to light the habitual authoritarianism of Ann's father in the family and the practical impossibility of her resisting or contesting her father's imposition.

This example means to emphasize two aspects of the complex problem: (1) that even an imposition made without any threat, and on only one occasion (Ann's father wanted to hear no more on the subject of marriage after her first timid mention of her feelings against it), can amount to coercion to marry; (2) that it is necessary to reflect carefully and prudently on the difficulty of distinguishing between marriage caused by coercion and one resulting from simple acquiescence to the parent's will, albeit reluctantly and without full conviction.

Second example

Martin, a young man accustomed to a wealthy, freewheeling lifestyle, even from the romantic perspective, met Claudia, with whom he started a relationship. Claudia became pregnant, and their marriage was celebrated. When it failed shortly afterward, Martin complained that he had been forced to marry by Claudia, who had threatened not to acknowledge him as the father of the child she was carrying and to refuse him contact with the child if he did not marry her. To strengthen his case, Martin said that he was then really in love with another young woman, Laura, with whom he had had relations even as the wedding day approached. It seemed to be a rather clear-cut case, but a serious investigation brought to light his complete unreliability.

In fact, Claudia, before the tribunal, forcefully challenged Martin's statements. Not only did he not prove convincingly that he had been threatened, but it was also denied by mutual friends who corroborated the wife's story. The pregnancy was something that he and she had agreed on so as to confront Martin's parents with a fait accompli and thus proceed more easily to the wedding. Moreover, Martin's story about Laura being his true love did not stand up to scrutiny. The young woman existed and had truly been in love with him, but for Martin (who said so to his friends at the time), she was only an amusement. In fact, Martin no longer saw Laura after his wedding with Claudia, except years later so as to induce her to testify, at which point he once again despicably deceived her—leading her to believe that if the outcome of the case was favorable, it would be possible for them to marry, whereas he had already become involved with a third woman, Joanne.

Therefore, not only was there no sign of true aversion on Martin's part to the marriage with Claudia, but there was no proof of her threats either (even if they were to be considered practicable and therefore capable of frightening someone). Martin's lies about important points during the case called into question his credibility—a rather important element of proof, as we have seen, in causes of nullity by reason of force.

And that is precisely what this example means to underscore. Although on the one hand, the statements of someone who has undergone constraint cannot fail to play an important role in the evaluation of the case (the fear must be "measured", as we said, in relation to the subject), it is also true that a tribunal (and therefore someone who advises spouses who are in difficulty) must seek—albeit with different degrees of thoroughness—to examine at the very least the consistency and trustworthiness of the story of someone who declares himself to be the victim of coercion.

Third example

Cynthia and Mark lived on a farm, in an economically depressed area. When Cynthia was a teenager the two began occasionally to go out in the company of friends, and they were automatically considered engaged. As the years passed they made preparations, with the help of their respective families, for their own house and for their wedding.

Several months before the wedding, however, Cynthia met a co-worker at the factory, Philip, with whom she fell in love. She told her fiancé, and he related the news to his own relatives and to the young woman's family. She was scolded severely and insulted as a frivolous girl and vehemently exhorted to continue her engagement, while Philip was waylaid and intimidated on several occasions by members of Cynthia's family. She, frightened by the reactions of her relatives and fearing for her beloved (therefore on the basis of conduct that strongly pressured her and objectively and maliciously aimed to harm Philip), went through with an unwanted wedding, manifesting obvious sadness on the day of the celebration and little enthusiasm in the few months of her married life. During those months she continued to see Philip, whom she considered her true love from whom she had been unfairly separated, until, at the cost of breaking off relations with her family, she definitively left her husband.

Appearances notwithstanding, the proof of force was not easy. Mark and even Cynthia's relatives denied the young woman's version of things and their own responsibilities. The latter could be reconstructed with certainty, however, through the depositions of friends and colleagues who had seen in the factory or who had been told at the time by Cynthia and Philip what was happening. These friends and colleagues —persons whose seriousness and reliability had been certified—made it possible to prove Cynthia's love for Philip antecedent to her marriage, her intention not to marry Mark after all, and the reactions of Cynthia's family, including one of the ambushes to intimidate Philip.

This example is meant to emphasize that, although an admission on the part of the person who forced someone to marry is an important element that facilitates the proof of the coercion, the proof itself is not impossible even if such collaboration in the truth is absent. Before giving an opinion, the advisor should find out whether the perpetrator of the alleged coercion is able and willing to confirm it in the judicial forum, while also examining the possibility of compensating in some other way for the possible absence of that evidence.

Fourth example

Mary Ellen, at the age of fifteen, allowed herself to be seduced by the promises of a playboy who, when she got pregnant, lost interest in her. The girl wanted to keep the child and by necessity had to rely on her relatives, who helped her, although they made her feel the full weight of the dishonor to the family that she had caused. In that small, traditionally-minded rural area, even Mary Ellen's movements were limited. The less that people saw her around, especially with her baby, the better. In one moment when she was particularly depressed, the young mother even made an attempt on her own life.

When Mary Ellen was around nineteen years old, a young man from the same region, Peter, came forward declaring that he was in love with her and was willing to marry her and to adopt her child, look after him, and contribute to his support and his education. Mary Ellen did not like Peter and did not intend to accept his proposal. At that point some of Mary Ellen's relatives began to pressure her insistently to accept the marriage. They repeatedly exhorted her and tried to arouse in Mary Ellen a sense of guilt for the mistake she had made in her adolescence. There were no threats, but there was rather an insistent and high-pressure campaign to persuade her, based on an implicit moral blackmail, which burdened Mary Ellen with the weight of the mistake she had made, the displeasure it had caused her parents, and the help given her through the years during and after her pregnancy and the birth of her child. Mary Ellen gave in to the pressures and celebrated a wedding that she did not want, with a man whom she did not love. Their married life did not last long, and it was characterized by Mary Ellen's attitude of rejection toward Peter (who was aware from the very beginning of her aversion to the wedding), which was manifested also by her avoidance of conjugal relations as much as possible, thereby denying Peter the heirs he desired.

This example means to highlight first of all the fact that even a series of pressures, exhortations, and insistent requests by persons who are considered authoritative by the subject (for reasons of affection and gratitude) can be—even without true threats in the strict sense—the basis for morally forcing the subject into an unwanted marriage. The behavior of the persuaders should be considered abusive in its insistence and because it was dressed up in pseudo-moral reasons. In this case, the greater respectability that Mary Ellen personally, and consequently her family of origin, would regain by the marriage proposed to her by Peter. This must also be deemed to contain an implicit threat, consistent with the claim of a probable attitude of disappointment, on the part of someone who insistently persuades, toward the person who does not accept his ''advice''. In this case, young Mary Ellen, by refusing a marriage with Peter, would face the prospect of continuing her life in her family, where the thick clouds created by her extramarital pregnancy would probably grow darker.

Secondly, the example is meant to draw attention to the fact that sometimes the pressures that drive someone into an unwanted marriage awaken in the victim a sort of rebellion, by which the person excludes a true marital commitment, feeling precisely that the marriage is something imposed unjustly. In this case, for example, Mary Ellen, whether as a reaction to the coercion, or out of fear that Peter might prefer his own child to the one she had while still an adolescent, resolved to deny Peter himself the possibility of procreating by denying him the right to have, with her, acts suitable for the generation of children. We recall this not out of a concern with canonical classifications and juridic logic (i.e., not with the question of whether Mary Ellen's case should be judged in terms of the exclusion of children or in terms of force); that will be instead the job of an advocate and of the tribunal. What is important to note for the priest who advises spouses about their marital situation is the need to make a complete survey of the situation. In this case, examining how Mary Ellen had reacted to pressures from her family made it possible to find evidence of a possible (further) reason for the invalidity of her matrimonial consent.

III

Error of Fact: About the Person, about a Personal Quality Directly and Principally Intended, or about a Personal Quality That Is the Object of Deceit

We will now consider the defect of consent consisting of the error of fact, that is, the error that concerns not the institution of marriage in general and its essential juridic characteristics (which is called instead the error of law and is regulated in cann. 1096 and 1099) but rather the particular person with whom the wedding is celebrated. More precisely, we need to determine under what conditions it is possible to maintain that this type of error results in invalid consent, since it limits the freedom of the contracting party. Indeed, one intuitively grasps how an error of great significance about the person himself or some important characteristic of his personality might be regarded as a limitation of freedom of choice, which depends on correct knowledge of what actually is the object of the pact, of the marital self-gift. And, as is well known, the persons of the contracting parties are precisely the object of the marital pact inasmuch as they formally assume the rights and duties of the marital state: canon 1057 §2 is quite eloquent in this regard.

In keeping with the practical and didactic purpose of our study, we will not go into questions of a speculative nature concerning the juridic structure of error: for example, whether all errors of fact are defects or whether one of them (error about the person) is a true and proper lack of consent; or what the ultimate basis is for the prescriptions of the Code. What was mentioned a little earlier on this subject should suffice.

Nor will we seek to propose or even to discuss in depth innovative interpretations of the canonical norm that are not yet commonly accepted

47

(either in canonical scholarship or especially in jurisprudence). We will seek only to clarify what rules are to be applied to matrimonial cases in which the faithful report an error about the person or the qualities of their own spouse, and what the usual interpretation of those rules is. As will become clearer further on, in the present matter, the canonical norms, jurisprudence, and scholarship have undergone a remarkable development in recent decades, and therefore the usual interpretation is itself not always easy to determine.

According to the outline followed by each chapter of our study, after some information about substantive law, we will offer some guidelines for the questions that the advisor can ask the lay Catholic so as to investigate the case, as well as several concrete examples that may serve to clarify the set of problems more fully.

Elements of substantive law

In order to understand the existing legislation concerning the error of fact, it is necessary to refer briefly to the discipline of the 1917 Code, among other reasons because it is still applicable to marriages celebrated while it was in force, and therefore as late as November 26, 1983.

The 1917 Code and the problems of interpreting it

The 1917 Code, in applying to marital matters the general discipline with respect to error contained in canon 104, provided in canon 1083 that error about the person rendered marriage invalid (§1). However, it stated that error about a personal quality did not render marriage invalid, even in cases where the quality was the reason for the contract, with the exception of two extraordinary cases. The first consisted of the possibility that said error about the quality "redounded" to an error about the person (§2, 1°); the second consisted of the possibility that one of the future spouses was considered by the other to be a free man, whereas instead he was in servitude, a slave, strictly speaking (§2, 2°). Some explanations are necessary with regard to this norm.

What "error about the person" consisted of is not difficult to understand. This is a truly substantial error, inasmuch as it foresees that the intended spouse is different from the physical person with whom marriage is contracted and with whom one agrees on the essential object of consent: the perpetual and exclusive right to acts ordered to procreation. In other words, to cite the example used by the classic canonists, it is the case of the patriarch Jacob, who intended to contract marriage with his beloved Rachel (who was a person known and desired precisely in her individuality) but found himself instead married to Leah, whom he did not desire. It goes without saying that such a case is unique (and perhaps today would be even more so), inasmuch as it presupposes entirely exceptional circumstances—which are often ceremonial as well (e.g., procured marriage). Indeed, it is not easy to substitute the physical person in the normal conditions of celebrating marriage.

As we saw, the second paragraph of canon 1083 of the former Code considered instead the error about a personal quality of one of the contracting parties, most importantly establishing a general rule: error about a quality does not render marital consent invalid even if that quality "is the reason for the contract". What does it mean to be the reason for the contract? It means being the motive or one of the motives that move the will of the future spouse to marry a specific person. For example, I am marrying Martin because he is rich; I am marrying Charlotte because it seems to me that she is a decent young lady, etc. And why then can the error that is the reason for the contract not be considered as rendering the marriage invalid? Because it, so to speak, precedes or accompanies the act of will that is consent, as a prerequisite for it or a motivating element, yet it leaves it intact in its essential structure, which is the choice of a particular person with whom to establish the partnership of marital life through the exchange of that essential title, which is the perpetual and exclusive right to the acts that are in themselves ordered to procreation. Error motivated the consent, was the reason for it, and prompted the contracting party to give it, but the consent was full and complete in itself and therefore produced its juridic effects. This is the general rule prescribed by the 1917 Code in matters of error relative to the quality of the person of the spouse.

As we mentioned, however, the 1917 Code foresaw two exceptions to this general rule. Let us address the second one first, since it did not survive in the legislation currently in force and is easier to explain. The second clause of paragraph 2 of canon 1038 established that in the case of a spouse who is enslaved, an error about that quality results in the nullity of the marriage. Why is this? The reason is the fact that a slave, in the proper sense, cannot freely dispose of himself and, consequently, cannot bind himself to convey the particular right that constitutes the essential object of marital consent. With this norm the 1917 legislator basically wanted to safeguard anyone who erroneously had celebrated marriage with a person who could not dispose of himself or guarantee an effective recognition of the essential right to marry. Today it seems that it is no longer possible for this situation to occur, at least not formally (given the disappearance of slavery in the modern legal systems with which the life of the Christian community comes into contact), and therefore the new legislation was able to drop it without hesitation from its legislative provisions.

The first exception to the general rule concerning errors about quality was contained in clause 1 of paragraph 2 of canon 1083 of the 1917 Code. It established that an error about a quality of a person that redounds into an error of person results in nullity of marriage. But what is the significance of this "redounding"? For centuries, the canonical tradition (which the 1917 Code had intended to compile and organize; cf. can. 6) had interpreted this redounding as follows: an error about a quality of a person redounds into an error of person when that quality makes it possible to identify him as a physical person, since he was known to the erring individual precisely through that quality. Thus, for example (citing classical examples here too, at least in part), someone who said, "I intend to marry the daughter of the king of France", or else "I intend to marry the eldest daughter of Sir Peter", and then found himself married to a daughter, but not the king's, or else to the second or third daughter of Sir Peter, would have fallen into an error about a quality that redounded to an error about the person.

Although for centuries it was subject to the interpretation just mentioned, there was no lack of debates and questions, both among scholars and in practical jurisprudence, as to how this concept of a redounding quality is to be understood in terms of its formality. Saint Alphonsus Maria Liguori, the great moral theologian of the eighteenth century, had sought to clarify the concept of an error about a quality redounding into an error of person, maintaining that it occurred in three cases. It is useful to recall his reasoning, inasmuch as one of the interpretative rules of Saint Alphonsus is at the basis of the 1983 Code of Canon Law that is in force today. According to Saint Alphonsus, an error about a quality redounds into an error of person in the following ways:

- A designated quality is the object of a condition: for example, "I marry you, but provided you truly are the daughter of the king of France"; "I marry you on the condition that you really are rich"; etc.

- It is an individual quality proper to a specific person, not shared by others and hence identifying that specific person in relation to others: for example, "I want to marry the daughter of the king of France, and I marry the woman who is presented to me specifically as the daughter of the king of France; however, my consent pertains to the former woman."

- A designated quality is intended directly and principally with respect to the person: for example, "I want to marry a rich man, and it is wealth that I desire above all, and I marry Martin because it appears to me that he is rich."

As the reader may have noticed, the second rule of Saint Alphonsus is nothing but a reiteration of the traditional interpretation of the concept of redundant error: an error about quality is redundant when the quality identifies the person in his physical individuality, since the person himself was known to the erring individual by way of that quality. The first and third rules foresee, so to speak, that the redundancy of the quality into the person is willed by the erring subject himself, who either makes the presence of a designated quality (or the absence of negative qualities) a sine qua non condition for his own consent, or else seeks that quality *first* (logically) from the person and chooses the person only secondarily, that is, because and inasmuch as he has judged that the person is the bearer of a designated quality (or devoid of certain negative qualities).

Insofar as the 1917 Code is in force, it can be said that all three interpretations of the concept of "redundant" qualities offered by Saint Alphonsus would be applicable. The first applies because it can be traced back to the general rule about a sine qua non condition in a legal act (see cann. 104 and 1092.4); the second as a traditional interpretation that has been implicitly codified (see the aforementioned canon 6 of that Code); and the third inasmuch as it is utilized by the jurisprudence of the Rota, even though not all scholars agreed with that utilization.

However, in order to have a complete picture of this set of problems concerning the significance of the concept of the redundancy of an error about a quality into an error about the person, we cannot fail to take into consideration an innovative jurisprudential trend that started after the Second Vatican Ecumenical Council.

Based on the presupposition that the Council—especially in the pastoral constitution *Gaudium et spes*, On the Church in the Modern World —had developed a more integral and complete view of the human person, including also his moral, religious, psychological, and social identity, this jurisprudential trend proposes that attention be paid to these qualities also, some of which can characterize the person so intimately as to change his very identity. In other words, it is a matter of paying attention to the objective value of certain qualities and to their role in shaping a more complete and integral vision of the person to whom they appertain. In a certain sense, it could be said that we are invited to shift our attention from the concept of "person" as a definite physical individual to the concept of "personality", in which the individual is substantially characterized, for better or for worse, by his moral, religious, psychological, and social qualities.

By way of example, we can recall the rotal decree that started this jurisprudential trend—decision April 21, 1970, written by the rotal judge Canals, who, besides what he described as a "very strict" interpretation of the concept of redundant quality (the quality as the sole feature individuating the physical person) and another that he described as "less strict" (the quality understood primarily with respect to the person; compare the third rule of Saint Alphonsus), proposed that a third concept be taken into consideration, whereby an error about a quality redounding into an error about the person would occur also when the mistaken quality is a moral, legal, or social quality so closely connected with the physical person that, if that quality were to be lacking, the physical person himself would have to be considered different.

What can be said about this innovative jurisprudential trend? And, most importantly, does it appear prudent to apply it to marriage cases that may arise, with a view to proposing a canonical process for marital nullity? Very briefly, and with the utmost respect for anyone who believes that he should maintain the contrary position, this author thinks that he must uphold a negative opinion—that is, that the extensive interpretation of the concept of person is neither admissible nor practicable—and for the following reasons.

On the one hand, the motivation for developing the extensive interpretation seems clear: to provide for possible cases of marriages that failed because of serious personal characteristics of one of the spouses —characteristics unknown to the other before the wedding—that cannot be classified under the traditional headings of marital nullity. Such is the case with the above-mentioned sentence by Canals, which had to do with the case of a man who had concealed his own previous civil marriage, which was canonically invalid yet revealed much about his overall character. Although this appears to be the praiseworthy intention of the interpretation that we have called extensive, namely—to be perfectly clear—the interpretation that extends the concept of person as the object of a factual error in marital cases to include the concept of personality, it must nevertheless be noted that the type of interpretation thus proposed, if subjected to careful consideration, raises bigger problems than the ones that it generously intends to resolve.

The first problem has to do with the interpretation's very foundation: historical, conciliar, and systematic. Indeed, from the historical perspective, the interpretation of the concept of person in the proper sense—in other words, as physical person—is altogether traditional in canon law, and even Pope John Paul II, in his 1993 allocution to the Roman Rota, urged the judges not to assign to the words of the law meanings that are not consistent with the canonical tradition, particularly in matters of an error of fact pertaining to marital cases.[1]

From the conciliar perspective, it is by no means evident that *Gaudium et spes* had intended to formalize a new concept of person, much less a juridical concept. Indeed, it is well known that the conciliar constitution (appropriately described as "pastoral" and not dogmatic or definitional) intended simply to present to the world, among the other topics that it addressed, the Christian vision of the person in a dialogic and proactive way but not to transform the contents of Christian anthropology itself.

From the systematic perspective, then, it is not clear why in the same juridic and normative system the term "person" (referring to the physical person) should in a case of error in a marital matter have a different meaning from the one it has in its other occurrences.

A second problem has to do with the theoretical sustainability of the

---

[1] Cf. *Acta apostolicae sedis* 85 (1993): 1259 (hereafter cited as *AAS*). [The addresses of John Paul II to the Roman Rota can be found on the Holy See website: http://vatican.va/holy_father/john_paul_ii/speeches/index_spe-roman-rota.htm.]

equivalence between the concept of person and the concept of personality. Certainly no one intends to maintain that qualities having obvious moral, juridic, and social significance are not important characterizations of a person or that suitable juridic safeguards cannot be found against errors with regard to them. However, if the concepts of person and personality were interchangeable—in other words, if a quality having the aforesaid significance were to be understood as characterizing the person substantially—this would mean the disappearance of the possibility of the person's own identity over the course of his life. In other words, a person remains the same even though at a certain point in his life he comes down with an illness or commits an action (e.g., a serious crime) that will indelibly mark the rest of his days. Such a thing, on the other hand, would not be among the qualities that define the person himself in a downright "substantial" way.

The third problem is related to the fact that this innovative interpretation of the concept of person with respect to the error of fact in marital cases was not derived unequivocally from scholarship, nor has it become common jurisprudence (i.e., the common way of judging similar cases) at the rotal level. Certainly there have been some rotal sentences that have taken into consideration and also applied this concept of person, defined as something more integral and complete, but there have also been many verdicts that have not admitted it, even rather recent ones that were argued with special care (e.g., a decision by the dean of the Rota dated February 6, 1992).[2] In any case, this has never become the constant and common criterion of the Rota in deciding cases of marital nullity predicated on an error about a personal quality. Now—since in the canonical system neither individual rulings nor a certain number of similar decisions sets a precedent in law, but only constant jurisprudence—it cannot be said that this innovative interpretation has been sanctioned by the Rota, one of whose functions is to contribute to the unity of canonical jurisprudence.[3] Furthermore, anyone who has had the patience to study those rotal decisions from 1970 onward that also have allowed for this innovative interpretation could observe that many of them oscillate between an "objective" consideration of the quality, which would correspond to the new, more

---

[2] Apostolic Tribunal of the Roman Rota, *Decisiones seu sententiae* 84: 49–62.

[3] Cf. the apostolic constitution *Pastor bonus* on the Roman Curia, at art. 126.

integral consideration of the human person, and a rather "subjective" consideration, which essentially reduces the question to the first and third rules of Saint Alphonsus. (What did the subject really seek in celebrating marriage? What weight did he attribute to that quality? Did he make his marital commitment conditional upon it? Did he use the person of the other spouse as a means of obtaining that personal quality?) Although we cannot present a point-by-point argument for the conclusion here, one that we believe is in keeping with a careful reading of the jurisprudence, it must be said that not even the jurisprudential trend that accepted the "innovative" concept of error about a quality of the person has always applied it consistently.

A fourth problem can perhaps be described as having to do with "legislative politics". Indeed, it should be recognized that the extensive interpretation of the term "person" poses even greater practical difficulties in applying the norm than the traditional interpretation did. When does a quality make someone an entirely different person? In other words, when is it so important that its absence (or presence) objectively forms an individual different from someone who does (or does not) exhibit that quality? It is easy, in other words, to understand how identifying qualities that objectively achieve a different personal reality is by no means an easy task and also presents the occasion for debatable or abusive interpretations. Even though more serious scholarship has sought to clarify criteria for distinguishing between the truly substantial qualities and those that are accidental, it is not possible to say with certainty, either at the level of jurisprudence or at the level of scholarship, that there is agreement and common vision.

The reasons just set forth make it impossible to accept the extensive concept of error about the person that has been developed in jurisprudence and scholarship since 1970. Perhaps we should view in this light also the decision of the 1983 legislator that the new canonical norms concerning error about a personal quality of the spouse should abandon the concept of "redundant error" that in a certain way had given rise to the problematic interpretation. It is possible, even though not supported by elements directly deducible from the work of revising the Code, that the legislator, in abandoning that concept, had intended to set a limit to the speculations that it had ultimately generated, reorganizing the whole matter in such a way that those speculations would no longer have any reason to exist (by making other provisions for the cases that had produced that elaboration) or any occasion to develop (by abandoning concepts that are difficult to define, such as the notion of "redounding"). Moreover, in other points of matrimonial canon law the legislator also proceeded analogously. This, for example, is what happened with the concept of the "ends" of marriage and the qualifiers "primary" and "secondary", the previous Code used and the new one did not adopt, precisely to avoid reductive interpretations thereof.

The 1983 Code

The topic of error of fact in marital matters is treated in the revised Code in canons 1097 and 1098. In light of the explanation made concerning the legislation previously in force, it is possible to clarify the current Code more easily and more briefly.

Canon 1097 § 1 regulates the case of error of person. What this means has already been explained in the exposition of the earlier law. All that can be added is that some authors, who also base their argument on a (not officially motivated) terminological variation—the 1917 CIC [*Codex iuris canonici*] spoke about error *circa personam*, whereas the current CIC speaks about error *in persona*—speculate that we should understand this paragraph to include not only the error about the physical identity of the person but also the concept of error "redounding" into an error of person, in which case, furthermore, "person" would have to be understood in the more integral and comprehensive sense proposed by the developing trend of jurisprudence originating in the 1970s.

By virtue of the reasons already explained, however, we reiterate that it appears reasonable and prudent to abide by the classic interpretation of paragraph 1 of canon 1097, understanding the error *in persona* as error about that person's physical identity. Nor can there be much relevance in the remaining argument offered by the proponents of the extensive interpretation of the norm, namely, that if interpreted in the traditional way, the norm itself would be applied very rarely. Such an argument loses much of its persuasive force as soon as we recall that the nullity of a juridic act can be only the exception and not the rule. Moreover, there seems to be no problem with the fact that the legislator provided other clear-cut norms for the validity of marriage that also are very rarely applied—think of the impediments of the abduction and detention of the woman referred to in canon 1089 and the two forms of the impediment of crime referred to in canon 1090.

Canon 1097 §2, addressing the topic of error concerning a personal quality, repeats first of all the general rule that error concerning a quality—even if it happens to be the reason for the contract—ordinarily does not render the marriage null. What is to be understood by the expression "is the cause for the contract" has already been explained above.

However, the legislation currently in force, like the previous Code, foresees two exceptions to this general rule. They no longer involve the state of slavery and the redundant error. With regard to their content they are different and are regulated by canons 1097 §2 and 1098.

The first exception is the one contained in canon 1097 §2, which considers an error concerning a personal quality that is directly and principally intended as vitiating consent. It is easy to see that this norm reiterates the third rule proposed by Saint Alphonsus Maria de Liguori to explain the concept of "redundant" error.

What does it mean specifically, though, to intend "directly and principally" a quality with respect to a person? It means that the quality is the direct object of the will, whereas the person is intended only secondarily, since he was valued as the personal bearer of the desired quality. Therefore, it will not be enough for the person to desire a certain quality intensely, or that one of the reasons that prompted him to marry was the fact that he saw a particular quality in the future spouse. In these examples we would have a case in which the quality is simply the cause of the contract. Rather, it will be necessary to prove that the person was seeking that particular quality above all ("I want to marry a rich man";"I want to marry someone from Milan like me"; "I want to marry someone who is not a drug addict, because my previous fiancé was one, and he caused me so much grief") and that the presence of this particular quality (or the absence of the dreaded negative quality), having been verified, was the decisive reason for the marriage.

Only if the present legislation is understood in this way are we not only being faithful to canon law but also grasping in practical terms the *ratio*, or reason, for the ordinance under consideration. The consent given under these conditions is invalid inasmuch as the person was, so to speak, "used as means to an end" with respect to a particular quality, which was the direct and principal object of the erring person. And thus, when the principal object of the will fails, so does the consent of the will. In other words, error concerning the quality vitiates the marital consent because, so to speak, the quality itself plays a "pathological" role in the consent and not the "physiological" role of a quality that simply "provides a reason". And the invalidity of a juridic act is such a serious event or thing that it must be possible to trace it back to something "pathological" or abnormal in human acts.

In contrast, understanding the concept of a "quality directly and principally intended" in a broader sense (for example, by assigning importance to instances such as the following: "I married because I wanted very much to have children, and now I find out that my husband is sterile"; "I married thinking that my wife was a decent woman, and now I see that she is an immoral person", etc.) would perhaps mean providing an apparent solution for cases of failed marriages but at the cost of forcing the meaning of the canonical provision. Canon law calls not for a simple presupposition but for a true act of the will directed toward the quality—an act of positive will that is quite obviously required by the fact that the quality was "intended", directly and principally, with respect to the person.

Therefore, from the perspective of judicial proof, it becomes rather difficult to demonstrate that ordinary qualities and qualities that are ordinarily desired were intended "directly and principally". Indeed, everybody usually wants to marry a decent, sincere person who is able to contribute to the support of the family and is capable of having children, without that being set as the immediate and principal object of one's own will. This is not to say that a quality like one of those just mentioned could not, absolutely speaking, be intended directly and principally. It does mean, however, that such qualities normally are merely presupposed in the future spouse without being the object of a precise act of will and without being the decisive reason for the choice of that particular person as one's own spouse. At this point one might inquire as to the extent of the applicability of this revised norm regarding error concerning a personal quality. This extent, according to a strict interpretation of the norm, must be considered somewhat limited, surely more restricted than what was allowed by the concept of "redundant" error understood in the sense of the evolving interpretation that arose in the 1970s. This has been noted even by some rotal judges (see, e.g., the July 22, 1985, ruling by the judge and later dean of the Rota, M. F. Pompedda). In fact, however, this is the norm in force. In order to allow for a broader application thereof, the ruling just mentioned assumes that it can consider as implicit—even if not subjectively elicited by the subject—the direct and principal intention concerning those qualities that within a particular context of place and time are especially valued as prerequisites for marriage (e.g., the woman's virginity in some cultures). But this, as the decision itself notes, is an objectively forced interpretation of the current norm that can be upheld only in the presence of somewhat peculiar cultural and personal circumstances.

The second exception to the general principle that an error concerning a personal quality of the spouse does not render marital consent invalid is found in canon 1098, which regulates error that is deceitfully induced about a personal quality of one of the parties for the purpose of obtaining the marital consent of the other.

This is a true and proper legislative innovation, inasmuch as deceit as a ground of nullity in marital cases was not contained in the previous legislation, even though some of the scholarship in recent decades suggested including it in the system of matrimonial canon law.

What is foreseen in canon 1098 is ultimately founded on a precept of natural law, namely, freedom of marital consent (which is indirectly vitiated by deception). Since it is concretely a prescription of positive law, insofar as the law defines the case in point[1] in minute detail, it is considered by the prevailing scholarship and jurisprudence as applicable only to marriages celebrated after the new Code went into effect, that is, from November 27, 1983, onward, based on the common principle that positive laws are not retroactive (cf. can. 9).

The norm of canon 1098 is rather articulated and complex, and its contents can be explained as follows:

a. One of the two contracting parties must be at the moment of consent in a state of error, that is, of incorrect judgment concerning a particular reality, since it is at least debatable that mere ignorance involving no judgment would suffice in this matter. On the contrary, it is certain that the error in question must be the reason for the consent. In other words, it must be an error that was the determining factor in

---

[1] Parameters of deceit.—ED.

the utterance of the consent itself. If in fact that was not the case, then the error could not be a defect of the consent.

b. This reality must be a quality of the other contracting party and hence a stable characteristic of the person directly belonging to him, not a mere circumstance relative to him. For example, a chronic illness is a quality in the sense intended by the canon, whereas the fact that the subject presently has no job is a mere circumstance. Such a quality must furthermore concern the person of the other party specifically and not third parties. For example, the fact that a person can be considered a habitual delinquent is a quality in the sense intended, but not the fact that he may have a brother imprisoned for having committed a serious crime. In the second case the delinquency pertains to the aforesaid brother and not to the person who is contracting marriage.

c. The quality that is the object of error must be by its nature capable of seriously disrupting the partnership of married life. It is not easy to say when a quality is of this sort. From a general perspective, arguing from the fact that marriage is a perpetual and exclusive partnership of life ordered to the procreation and upbringing of children and to the well-being of the spouses, one may surmise that among the qualities capable of seriously disrupting the partnership of life are those that cause the subject to act in contempt of the unity and faithfulness that belong to marriage (e.g., the morally invincible propensity toward infidelity), of its permanence over time (although it is less easy to give examples), of its being ordered to the good of offspring (whether physical: e.g., deceitfully concealed sterility [cf. can. 1084 § 3]; or lavish spending or an addiction to gambling that constantly puts the support of the children at risk; or else moral: e.g., an inclination to seriously harmful habits that make the person gravely unsuited, or even incapable, of carrying out the educational duties belonging to a parent), and of the well-being of the spouses (e.g., contagious diseases, drug addiction, AIDS, which either destroy the relationship of trust between the spouses or else have an extremely burdensome effect on their relations, e.g., on their sexual relations). It should be noted that what is required is not so much an actual disturbance of marital life but rather the fact that the quality, the object of the deceit, could be considered potentially such as to cause it.

d. The inducement to error must have been made deceitfully, that is, deliberately and with the knowledge of the significance of one's own action. Hence, for example, not by a subject incapable of a human act, even only at that moment. It must be stated also that, since the norm does not specify that the deceitful action had to be necessarily committed by one of the future spouses to the detriment of the other, it could in principle be committed also by a third party, although it is difficult to imagine that if someone were plotting to deceive one of the future spouses to his detriment, the other would not be aware of it.

e. Finally, this deceitful action must be performed with the purpose of securing the marital consent of the other contracting party and not for other reasons. In other words, it is necessary to prove the presence of a specific fraud.

As one might guess, this second exception to the general principle of the irrelevance of error about a personal quality is not easy to apply either. Whether from the perspective of identifying the "objective" legal requirements, which aim to verify the aptitude of a particular personal quality for seriously disrupting the partnership of life; or from the perspective of identifying its subjective requirements—if in fact, according to the common rule, once the deception has been ascertained, one must presume that there was fraud (i.e., the will to deceive)—it is not so easy to prove, even with circumstantial evidence or presumptively, that the deceiver's action was aimed at the marriage, nor can his mere confession as a matter of principle dispense from the burden of seriously verifying the same. Hence, before speaking about deception and suggesting to the Catholic who is in marital difficulty a cause of nullity on the basis of canon 1098, the pastor of souls who is consulted will have to evaluate the situation very prudently and in great depth.

Guide for the counselor

In light of the somewhat complex canonical scholarship set forth in the previous paragraphs, it is evidently not very easy to propose sample points or questions for the advisor. In order to simplify the task, we will not take into consideration the case of the error of person strictly speaking, among other reasons because it is sufficiently easy to understand what the objects of the proof are: Tim wanted to marry Kathy and then found himself in fact married to Samantha. Nor will we propose guidelines concerning an error of quality that "redounds" into an error of person, the latter being understood in a "more complete and integral" way. Indeed, as we have explained, this interpretation of the legislation concerning error is not commonly accepted. We will focus instead on illustrating the two cases foreseen by the current legislation regarding an error concerning a personal quality: the case of error concerning a personal quality that is directly and principally intended, and the case of a deceitfully induced error concerning a quality of the spouse. Additionally, the first case is applicable—although for formally different reasons—to marriages celebrated not only while the present Code has been in force but also under the old Code. In the 1983 Code it is a motive for nullity positively established by the law, and in the 1917 Code it was an accepted explanation of the common jurisprudence in relation to the concept of an error concerning quality that "redounds" into an error of person.

Error concerning a personal quality directly and principally intended

Let us recall briefly the explanation of the instance given above: one of the contracting parties desires to marry a person having one or more specific qualities and decides to marry his own future spouse precisely because he finds that the person corresponds to this desire. He has found the person to be, so to speak, the personification of that desired quality, which is the reason for his choice to marry that person. He then finds himself obliged to admit that his own judgment had been wrong.

To verify whether an error concerning quality has actually occurred, it is necessary to investigate the following points:

1. What sort of quality did the one who regrets his error have in mind? Was it a well-defined quality or set of qualities? Indeed, someone who does not have clear ideas cannot will anything, much less do so "directly and principally".

2. What weight did the person assign to that quality? This is the *criterium aestimationis*, which measures the subjective importance attributed to the quality. Indeed, it is logical that the more important a person considers a particular quality to be, the greater the role that the presence or absence of said quality can play in his choice of spouse. In order to investigate this, one could inquire as to whether the subject often spoke of that particular characteristic, whether he had even broken off his own previous engagements because the persons involved were lacking from that point of view, whether he had ever said, for example, that he would never marry someone who did not have that quality, etc.

3. Moreover, it must be ascertained whether the subject was in a state of error, that is, of false judgment, concerning the presence of that quality. Thus, for example, one would have to verify whether the interested party had made inquiries or asked for reassurances in order to establish the presence of a particular quality. For example, if a young woman of humble origins wanted to marry a rich man, convinced that that would substantially improve her living conditions, it seems logical that she would give her own assent to the marriage only after having been able to appraise somehow the wealth of her future spouse. Alternatively, it seems logical that a man who wanted as his wife a woman who would assure him of having descendants would seek information about his fiancée's health and physical condition with a view to the possibility of motherhood, even suggesting that she undergo a physical examination to certify her fitness. The absence of such inquiries not only raises doubts about the state of error but also casts doubt on the actual importance of that quality in the subject's choice of a spouse. Indeed, it should be recalled that, under this scenario, the parties are in a rather extraordinary situation, in which the person of the future spouse is subordinated to a particular quality. Therefore, the manner of behavior on the part of the subject in this regard must also be in keeping with the uncommon character of the canonical case that one is trying to establish.

4. One would then have to ascertain whether what the subject desired was truly a personal quality, that is, a stable characteristic directly belonging to the person. Thus, to stay with the examples just mentioned, wealth or fitness for motherhood can actually be considered

qualities. On the other hand, the fact of owning a house, or of presently having a job, or of not currently being in a sentimental relationship with others cannot be considered qualities. It would be different if a formal condition were stipulated concerning such factors, but then the condition and not the error concerning the quality would have to be taken into consideration as the cause for the possible nullity of marriage.

5. One would also have to highlight the role of motivating cause played by the presence of a particular quality in the subject's decision. It is logical that, in the case of a quality intended directly and principally, the quality will have to be the principal (albeit not exclusive) motive of the decision, and it will have to be proved that the subject's will was directed toward that motive. Thus, a woman who said, "I am marrying Martin, whom I love and from whom I want children", would not will the future spouse's fertility directly and principally. On the other hand, a woman who said, "I want a child, and I want one right away" (e.g., because of problems of age or health) and "I am marrying Martin because he seems fit for procreation and willing to give me a child soon", would intend directly and principally his fertility (among the other factors).

6. Obviously, one would also have to verify that the judgment made was false, in other words that the quality thought to have been present was not—for example, in relation to the examples just mentioned, that in reality the future spouse was not rich or that Martin was sterile and therefore incapable of procreation.

7. Finally, the reaction of the person who discovers that he had fallen into error must also be investigated. This is the classical *criterium reactionis*. From the intensity of the reaction one can deduce circumstantially the importance that a particular quality had for the subject and the role that it played in his choice of the person. Thus, for example, a man who noticed that his wife was sterile but continued to have conjugal relations with her, without conflicts related to the error that he had made, would deny by his deeds that he had wanted primarily—more than the person—the quality of the spouse's fertility.

Deceitfully induced error about a quality

We should recall here in outline form deceit as a ground of nullity: one of the contracting parties is deliberately deceived about a personal quality of the other party, a quality that by its nature can seriously disrupt the partnership of life, and this deception is done for the purpose of obtaining the marital consent of the victim of the deception.

It is obvious that the requirements for proof in this case are different from those in the preceding case. The following points will have to be verified:

1. The subject was in error from a subjective point of view—in other words, that he had mistakenly thought that a particular quality (e.g., that the other held a university degree) was present or that a negative quality (e.g., that the other was addicted to drugs) was absent. The error is easier to prove, the more active the subject was in desiring a particular quality and in seeking to verify it. In the case of deceit by omission (that is, the concealment of negative qualities), however, it is sometimes difficult to distinguish completely error from ignorance, that is, from merely not knowing a fact. It is certain, though, that if it is possible to prove some act of misinformation on the part of the one inducing error (which sometimes can also be inferred circumstantially, as in example no. 4 below), then this aggravates ignorance. The latter is still essentially a not-knowing but is rendered such by the omission of information that ought to have been given. In practice, the consultant must try to discover exactly what the person who erred in assessing the qualities of the future spouse knew at the moment of the wedding and what he may have done in order to substantiate his own judgment. For example, did a woman who suspected that her fiancé was sterile suggest that he be examined by a physician? Another a posteriori proof of the error, in the subjective sense, will be the reaction to the discovery thereof, which will also have to be investigated.

2. The subject was in error also from the objective point of view. In other words, it will be necessary to prove that in fact the judgment did not correspond to reality: for example, not only did Patricia think that Gary was a physician, but Gary was not really a physician.

3. The error was truly relative to a personal quality of the other future spouse. In this respect we refer back to what was said above,

when we tried to distinguish between a quality and an accessory circumstance. Thus, for example, having used drugs several times or having had occasional homosexual experiences cannot be considered a personal quality. In contrast, drug addiction or long-term homosexual inclinations or behavior can be.

4. The quality was apt to disrupt the partnership of life seriously. In the exposition of the substantive law, the general criteria for this evaluation were already given. We simply recall here that an actual disruption is neither sufficient proof nor necessary per se. What is required, rather, is that the quality was by its nature so important as to be able to disrupt the marital communion of life. This is therefore a rather general and objective evaluation, even though one may often encounter also an actual disruption of the relationship of trust and harmony between spouses as a result of a deception concerning important aspects of the personality of one of them.

5. The person who was mistaken was led into error, in other words, the error was caused by behavior on the part of someone (normally the future spouse but possibly also a third person) who had simulated something (e.g., that he was a physician when he was not) or else dissimulated something (e.g., that he was not homosexual when he was). Therefore, the behavior of the one who allegedly deceived will have to be investigated: What did he say about himself? How did he answer questions about himself? How did he behave in the sight of his future spouse (e.g., did he act in misleading ways that suggested the erroneous judgment)?

6. The deception was deliberate. This point is difficult to prove, because the deceived party is often the one to turn to the advisor (and to the tribunal), rather than the party who caused the deception. Ordinarily—based on the principle that one is responsible for his own actions—it is presumed that, once the deception is proved, the will to deceive must also be considered present. The latter, however, can also be proved from circumstantial evidence—for example, the care that the one who deceived may have taken to keep the deceived party from coming into contact with persons who could have helped him detect the intrigue.

7. The purpose of the deception was the marriage, in other words, strictly speaking, the marital consent of the deceived party. This too is a difficult point to prove for the reason mentioned in the previous point, that it is often difficult to obtain a confession from the one who plotted the deception because he is not interested in the case or because he does not want to admit his responsibility. Moreover, even in the case of a confession—and also because one wants to avoid a priori judgments—someone who has already deceived once in such serious matters as marriage may not always be overly reliable. However, as in the case of fraudulence per se, the fact that the deceptive action was aimed at marriage could also be proved circumstantially—for example, by bringing to light how much the deceiver cared about the marriage or by considering whether, besides marriage, he had other motives that could explain his deception. The stronger the proof of the desire for marriage on the part of the deceiver, the more certainly one can deduce from circumstantial evidence that his deception was aimed at the marriage itself.[2]

Examples

Here we offer several examples that may help to illustrate more clearly the legal interpretation and the investigatory suggestions just presented. The first three examples relate to cases of error about a personal quality directly and principally intended; the last two, to cases of deceitfully induced error.

First example

Catherine maintains that she married Claude intending directly and principally—because of her great desire for children—her husband's fertility. Evidence of this is the fact that their common life allegedly began to falter when, in the course of tests administered three years

---

[2] Readers who would like to study in greater depth the problems of proof associated with cases of deceptive error may consult an article published by this author, which includes case studies related to several dozen tribunal cases: "Esempi di applicazione giurisprudenziale del can. 1098 (dolo): Casistica e problemi probatori", *QDE* 9 (1996): 357–78.

after the wedding specifically to explain why they had no children, it was ascertained that Claude was sterile as a result of testicular retention in the abdomen. Furthermore, there was the fact that, having separated from him after about eight years of married life, she had finally had two children by a man whom she had married civilly.

The instruction carried out by the tribunal, however, brought to light the following facts, which prove that Catherine's demand was baseless.

In the first place, before her wedding and in the early years of her married life, Catherine did not speak particularly about children, although she manifested a general desire for them. The *criterium aestimationis* therefore does not appear to be very highly developed in this case.

In the second place, the instruction shows that it is not true that Claude's sterility was discovered three years after the wedding and within the context of examinations as to why they had no children. As the treating physician testified, the sterility was discovered a few months after the wedding and in relation to other health problems Claude had. Aside from casting doubt about the sincerity of the parties (Claude had affirmed Catherine's false account of the time and manner of the discovery of his sterility), the doctor's testimony proved that there was no strong demand for children on Catherine's part since the sterility was in fact accidentally discovered.

Moreover, and in the third place, the instruction shows not only that their common life continued for almost seven years after the discovery but also that during the whole time practically no inquiries were made into Claude's sterility and, more importantly, there was no treatment, since both spouses quickly resigned themselves to the opinion of the aforementioned physician. Therefore, the *criterium reactionis* also appears to be extremely weak.

Among the other pieces of circumstantial evidence, two in particular weighed heavily in deciding the case. The first circumstance was prenuptial. Having had intimate premarital relations, Catherine had noticed Claude's anatomical defect but had not worried much about it, much less sought proofs of his fertility. In light of this, it appears not very credible that her husband's fertility could have been intended by her directly and principally.

The following circumstance, on the other hand, was post-nuptial: the lack of children and his sterility were not what caused the end of their married life, but rather their mutual infidelity that started after several years of married life.

This example is meant to highlight how the advisor—even though obviously he must not and cannot anticipate the instructional phase of the case and even though he must assign reasonable weight to what the interested parties tell him—must not accept passively whatever story is told. In light of the probatory criteria already detailed, the consultant must investigate the facts generally so as to verify that they do not contradict the reconstruction of events that is presented to him. Furthermore, he must warn the interested parties themselves that possible half truths, besides essentially vitiating the canonical process, could be discovered by the tribunal in the course of the trial (e.g., in this case, the time and manner in which Claude's sterility was ascertained), with serious consequences for the credibility of their proposed theory of nullity.

Second example

The second example is only partially similar to the first. It illustrates —even in the reliability of the facts narrated—the difficulty of proving the actual existence of a direct and principal intention aimed at a quality rather than at the person of the spouse. Indeed, the case from which this example is drawn had contrary responses at various levels of judgment, namely, a negative response in the first and third instances and an affirmative response in the second.

At the age of nineteen, Gina, greatly desiring to have children, married Carl. Just one month after the wedding she went to a gynecologist, worried about not being pregnant. The gynecologist started to laugh at the young woman's concern, given her age and the fact that she had been married for only a month. But for Gina the matter was so serious that she took offense and changed her gynecologist. She underwent various tests which proved that she was fit for motherhood until, with great persistence, she convinced Carl to undergo testing also. The results showed that he was almost entirely sterile and incurably so. For Gina the news was a very heavy blow. Nevertheless, she continued their married life for several years, although she became more troubled.

Moreover, she asked her own relatives not to mention the topic of the lack of children in her family so as not to grieve Carl, who had become embittered by the discovery of his own sterility.

As one can see, the case appears to be difficult: the strong desire for children on Gina's part (that is, the *criterium aestimationis*) is proved, since it prompted her to consult a doctor frantically even in the first few weeks of her marriage, although in truth the young woman had not asked her fiancé before the wedding for any sort of guarantee of his fertility. On the other hand, it appears that there was much less of a *criterium reactionis*: the circumstantial evidence that she had chosen Carl as a man fit to make her a mother, even more than as a husband in the more generic and complete sense of the term. Moreover, her request to her own relatives not to mention her lack of children so as not to upset Carl would lead one to think that Gina liked him in the first place as a person, even though he was unfit for procreation.

Precisely because of these difficulties, the case met with contrary judgments at various levels of the ecclesiastical courts. In particular, the tribunal that judged in favor of nullity maintained that Gina's intention with regard to her husband's fertility, directly and principally intended, should be considered implicit in her behavior showing a frantic concern about children after the wedding. The other judgments, in contrast, highlighted the absence of prenuptial inquiries by the young woman regarding her future husband's fitness, the weak *criterium reactionis*, and the meager proof that for Gina children were more important than Carl. According to the judges of the first and third instances, this showed only that Gina wanted children very much, whereas it appears hasty to assert that her desire for children implied that she "principally" intended Carl's fertility and willed solidarity with him as her husband only secondarily.

What the case of Gina and Carl can teach the consultant is precisely the difficulty that is often encountered in understanding what the principal object of the subject's will was. For this reason any advice must be given with great caution. This does not mean refraining from any initial advice. Rather, it means considering it and proposing it only as an initial recommendation that may possibly be investigated with a view to obtaining a definitive recommendation from professional experts—an investigation that requires, however, very careful reflection on all aspects of the case.

Third example

Albert had broken off two earlier engagements because the young women to whom he was planning to get married had both exhibited serious health problems, which were worrisome also with regard to procreation. Having become acquainted with Carla, he decided to marry her, but he demanded precise guarantees about her health and was reassured by her relatives, some of whom were physicians. Certainly he felt attraction to and affection for Carla, but the principal reason that prompted him to marry her was the positive judgment that he arrived at by means of the information that he had requested about his fiancée's good health. Yes, he did want to get married, but to a healthy woman, and he had chosen Carla, whom he also liked, because it appeared to him from the information that he had obtained that she was in perfect health. His desire for the quality was therefore not only general (every man wants to marry a healthy young woman) but actual and positive (he had broken off two engagements for that reason and had requested the aforesaid assurances about Carla).

After the wedding it became clear that Carla had a predisposition to nervous disorders attributable to a condition that ran in her family, which the young woman had actually manifested previously (even before her acquaintance with Albert). This discovery was for Albert reason enough to decide to separate. Not only did he feel deceived by Carla's parents, but he maintained that his marital pledge was rendered invalid inasmuch as it was in fact made to a person who did not correspond to the qualities that he principally desired. If he had known about Carla's condition, Albert would have broken off that engagement too, as he had the previous ones. The desire for the specific quality and the reaction to its absence are very clear in this case.

The purpose of this example is to show how even a quality that is ordinarily presupposed by someone who gives marital consent may be desired as the direct and principal object of the will, even though proof of this desire requires particular circumstances that show that it was the object of a true act of the will (whereas usually it is a simple presupposition). In this case, there was proof positive of a specific intention on Albert's part with regard to the optimal health of Carla (his subjective motive was very strong, given the unfavorable outcome of his previous plans for marriage). Equally certain was the proof of the error, since Carla's previous mental health problems could be proved by documentation. It should be noted that it is not enough to demonstrate that a quality of the person of the future spouse was taken by the subject as the essential object of his own consent. It must also be possible to verify that there was an error in this regard, in other words, that the reality was substantially different from what the subject had supposed it to be.

Fourth example

Mark, a former drug addict, was in a rehabilitation community. He was officially detoxified and even holding a job as an instructor-moderator within the community.

Jeannie became pregnant as a result of sexual relations with Mark, and accordingly they decided to marry. At that point Mark left the community. He did not want Jeannie to have any more contact with it, and not one of its members was invited to the wedding. Mark explained his departure from the community to Jeannie by saying that he had been expelled for the bad example he had given by impregnating his fiancée. At the same time, he reassured Jeannie that he had by no means relapsed into drug abuse. Jeannie believed Mark, and the two were married. Only two weeks after the wedding, Jeannie took Mark's automobile to go shopping, since her own needed repairs. As she rounded a curve the glove compartment opened, and drug paraphernalia fell out. When she confronted Mark about it, he admitted that he had started using drugs again during his final months in the community (and this was the real reason why they sent him away). He had said nothing about it to Jeannie so as not to give her cause to cancel the wedding, thinking that he would be able to stop using drugs. He had not succeeded, however, and confessed to his wife that in two weeks he had already spent on drugs all the money friends and relatives had given them as wedding gifts. Jeannie found a place for Mark in another rehabilitation community, telling him that she would let him back in the house only after she had proof of an actual recovery —a recovery that had still not occurred several years later at the time of the canonical process.

In this case, it is necessary to check for the existence of the essential elements of the matter of error induced by deceit that are described in canon 1098. Jeannie was led into error by Mark's prenuptial assurances, which were aimed at concealing the truth of his state of drug addiction. She was led into error deceitfully, that is, deliberately, inasmuch as there is no evidence that Mark was incapable of comprehending the significance of his actions and inasmuch as there is a series of suspicious circumstances (e.g., his concern that Jeannie should have no further contact with the rehabilitation community that he had left) that attest to an action that was premeditated and carefully planned. Furthermore, the fraud perpetrated by Mark was specific, because the purpose of his action was marital, as Mark himself confessed at the nullity trial (he knew that by admitting his situation to Jeannie he might have lost her and that surely the wedding would not have taken place in the meantime), and because he had no other motive for concealing the truth from Jeannie. The object of the deception, that is, actual chemical dependency, can be considered a personal quality, inasmuch as it is a condition that over a long time characterizes a person's whole life. It must also be considered—if it is true and serious addiction, as in Mark's case—a quality that by its nature is apt to disrupt seriously the partnership of marital life, whether from the perspective of the good of the spouses (just think of how the situation would affect normal sexual relations, since Mark was taking drugs intravenously, with the real risk of contracting AIDS) or from the perspective of the good of the children, with regard to his ability to support them, as well as with regard to their upbringing, since a habitual drug user is incapable of forgoing behaviors and attitudes that can seriously and negatively influence the upbringing of children.

Thus, in similar cases, whether it is a matter of fraud by omission (the concealment of the truth) or a matter of simulation of a nonexistent quality, the advisor will have to seek to clarify the at-least-probable existence, in each specific case, of all the elements of fact that make up the components of fraud as outlined by canon 1098 before proposing to the interested parties the prospect of a canonical trial for declaring the nullity of their marriage.

Fifth example

Barbara was a young woman of eighteen who lived in an unhappy family. Her father was a good man but indulged excessively in alcohol.

Her mother suffered from a serious psychiatric ailment that required long periods of rehabilitation in specialized settings. At home there was therefore little harmony, irregular work, and little income. Barbara herself had to count pennies every time she bought something, even the most personal and necessary items of clothing.

She had a passing acquaintance with a local man, Christopher, a thirty-year-old physician who made a show of his personal success and drove around in a high-class car of foreign make. Although unfortunate in other respects, Barbara was a pretty young woman. Christopher noticed her and began to court her. However, Barbara was not at all attracted to the man, who was so much older than she and perhaps less physically attractive as a result. Nevertheless, she grew fond of him and decided to marry him because she pictured him as a successful doctor just starting his career and also hoped to improve her own life in economic terms. Barbara had confided in Christopher extensively about the miserable conditions of her own family, including their financial difficulties, and her fiancé had always reassured her, holding out to her the hope of a calmer future from an economic perspective as well.

After the wedding was celebrated, however, the reality appeared to Barbara quite different from what she had imagined. The couple had to leave the rental apartment where they had gone to live because it was not up to the local building code. The newlyweds therefore had to move in and adjust to living with Christopher's parents. The luxury car turned out to be leased, and Christopher was not making the payments. Even his activity as a surgeon starting a prestigious career was not only not producing income but seemed to be falling through. At a certain point Barbara became suspicious, and she looked up an old schoolmate who was a nurse at the large hospital where Christopher worked and asked her to make some inquiries. The upshot was that nobody at that hospital knew Dr. Christopher. Cornered by Barbara, Christopher had to confess that in reality he was not a physician. He had been only a student and had not passed his exams and—for the moment, he told her—had found a job as an assistant to an orthodontist friend. Barbara saw that she had been beguiled and deluded in all her expectations of a calmer, less harried life, in economic terms as well, and decided to leave Christopher, initiating also a cause of nullity because she had been misled deceitfully.

The instruction phase of the trial was able to prove through witnesses the fact that Barbara's conviction that Christopher was a physician had been for her an important reason for her decision to marry. Through witnesses, through documents (reconstruction of Christopher's curriculum vitae, showing that he had scarcely begun his university studies), and also through Christopher's own admission it was possible to prove not only that he was not a physician but also that for the approximately two years of their prenuptial relationship he had deceived Barbara almost daily concerning his profession and his activity, with the specific motive of not losing her, given that he was perfectly aware both that this "qualification" of his was important to the young woman and also that he had little else to offer her. The tribunal held that such a deception should be considered apt by its very nature to disrupt the partnership of married life, as in fact happened.

This example is meant to emphasize that the quality that is the object of the deception must have been important in the choice of the spouse. In other words, it was the reason for the consent. Only in that case can the error under consideration be held to vitiate the consent itself and to affect its validity. In probative terms, then, the example illustrates well how circumstantial (e.g., personal and familial) facts can contribute toward honing in on a precise ground of nullity.

IV

Simulation of Consent

General Notions

While deposing witnesses in matrimonial nullity trials, one often hears the following questions, especially from zealous pastors who carefully prepared the engaged couple for their wedding and scrupulously completed the prenuptial investigation: How could you ever declare null the marriage of someone who now contradicts what he declared solemnly during the preparation and in the wedding ceremony? Does it not run the risk of rewarding someone who changes his own statements whenever convenient? Does it not also run the risk of endangering the stability of the institution of marriage? And what point is there to the careful work of pastors in marriage preparation if the tribunals then contradict that work?

This prompts us to embark on a very complex subject in matrimonial canon law, both substantive and procedural: the topic of simulation of consent.

Before entering into this difficult subject, however, it seems appropriate to repeat very clearly several premises.

This very simple study, in keeping with its title, *When Is Marriage Null? Guide to the Grounds of Matrimonial Nullity for Pastors, Counselors, and Lay Faithful*, is intended as an aid to pastors (and to other counselors) who provide assistance to couples experiencing difficulty, so as to offer them an initial checklist to evaluate the appropriateness of examining in greater depth and in the competent forum the possible nullity of their marriage. Therefore, care is taken here to give a simple presentation devoid of technicalities, limited to common jurisprudence and to the common interpretation of matrimonial law, without presuming to go into debated interpretations of the law that are not yet

77

commonly accepted. For that purpose there are many very fine scholarly journals that present recent research of a doctrinal and jurisprudential character, where anyone interested in particular problems and in the study of the development of jurisprudence or in prospects *de iure condendo* can find considerable material.

In keeping with this practical purpose of our study, as we address the phenomenon of the simulation of consent, instead of beginning with a discussion of total simulation, we will start—after some general information about the phenomenon of simulation—with one of the cases in which this phenomenon occurs most frequently, at least in Italy and in the Western world, namely, the case of the exclusion of children.

Elements of substantive law

1. First of all, we should recall one of the "cardinal" principles of matrimonial canon law, a principle derived from Roman law and incontestably introduced over the course of the twelfth and thirteenth centuries: matrimony is produced by the consent of the parties. Consent is, as the classical authors put it, the "efficient cause" of marriage. The current legislation as well repeats this principle in canon 1057 § 1, solemnly declaring, *matrimonium facit partium consensus*, that is, "the consent of the parties makes marriage." Note that this is not only a legal principle; it also has profound theological and spiritual implications. It is enough to reflect that it is at the basis of the common statement that the spouses themselves are the "ministers of the sacrament" of matrimony. Since they are the protagonists of the marriage "contract" —precisely through their consent—and since the marriage of baptized persons has been raised by the Lord Jesus to the dignity of a sacrament, it follows that the "ministers" of the contract, of the marital covenant, are also the "ministers" of the sacrament.

But what is consent? The Code itself gives a definition in canon 1057 § 2: consent is an act of the will by which the contracting parties mutually make a gift of themselves for the purpose of establishing a marital relationship between them. This definition is dense with meaning and fraught with consequences, which we do well to elucidate briefly.

In defining consent as an act of the will, the Code establishes first of all that the canonical legal system requires, in order to contract marriage, the performance of a human act, that is, of an act based on the adequate functioning of the natural faculties of intellect and will. In order to marry, it is therefore necessary, with regard to the intellect, to have sufficient use of reason (can. 1095, 1°), a minimal awareness of the essence of marriage (can. 1096), and a sufficient ability to appreciate concretely the obligations of marriage itself (can. 1095, 2°). With regard to the will, it is necessary to have sufficient freedom, both internal (again can. 1095, 2°) and external (can. 1103).

But what is the matrimonial will of the spouses directed toward? In other words, what is the object of matrimonial consent? Canon law defines very clearly that the direct object of matrimonial consent is the gift of self. Those who contract marriage, the law says, *sese mutuo tradunt et accipiunt*; that is, they mutually give themselves to and accept one another. This normative expression was chosen by the legislator to express the profound personal significance of marriage and of matrimonial consent. It is an expression that is perhaps not so easy to delineate legally, but it certainly indicates a tendency and a line of "policy" that the new legislation is pursuing. This can be documented by comparing the definition that the legislation previously in force gave to matrimonial consent, specifically in canon 1081 §2 of the 1917 Code. There, from the subjective point of view, consent was defined as an act of the will; from the objective point of view, though, consent was presented as directed toward the exchange between the spouses (or more precisely, to the establishment between them) of "a perpetual and exclusive right over the body, for acts that are in themselves suitable for the generation of children".

It would be incorrect to develop a reductive interpretation of this norm, for example, by asserting that it was aimed solely at the procreative act (in reality it establishes a right that is well defined and delineates the limits of the extent of its exercise), or by asserting that it is proof of a "biologistic" concept of marriage (which would mean isolating the norm from its context and from the canonical tradition). It would be even more inaccurate to present this definition of the object of consent as though there were a rupture—instead of continuity—between it and the definition currently in force. Indeed, the right mentioned in the 1917 Code (the perpetual and exclusive right to acts that are per se suitable for procreation) is no doubt part of the legal analysis of the meaning of the "gift of self" discussed by the present legislation. It is certain, however, that the 1983 legislator, in choosing not simply to replicate the formula of the earlier codification, intended to draw attention to the interpersonal context within which the physical gift of self must also be situated.

Our analysis of the object of matrimonial consent must not stop, however, at its "material" object, (i.e., what is given being the persons of the spouses); rather, it must also extend to the consideration of its formal object (i.e., for what purpose, to what end, this self-donation comes about). The canonical norm states that the end of the conjugal interpersonal donation is to establish marriage. As canon 1057 §2 emphasizes, the contracting parties give themselves to each other *ad constituendum matrimonium* (for the purpose of establishing a marriage). This clarification concerning the object of the consent is of fundamental importance for the topic that we intend to address in this chapter. Indeed, to prescribe that matrimonial intent must be directed toward establishing marriage implies—at least in the canonical system—that the essential elements of that institution cannot be different from the ones normatively foreseen by the legislation itself. Therefore, in intending to bring a marriage into being, the will of the contracting parties must assume (at least implicitly), and therefore cannot positively reject, the pivotal points of the concept of marriage as the law itself defines it: the establishment of a perpetual and exclusive partnership of life, ordered to the procreation and upbringing of children and to the well-being of the spouses, which for baptized persons has the dignity of a sacrament (cf. cann. 1055 and 1056).

2. In light of what has just been said, we come to understand another cardinal principle of the canonical matrimonial system and of the topic we wish to explore: namely, the presumption established by canon 1101 §1.

This canon codifies a general rule of experience, which rises to the level of a juridical principle of interpreting the facts and of guaranteeing the certainty of legal relations: namely, what someone says he wants corresponds in truth to what he really wants. More concretely, when a person says he wants canonical marriage, goes through the required examinations, and celebrates the nuptial rite, it must be maintained that he truly wants to marry and to make his own all the elements and all the essential properties that describe marriage as understood by the law. (At least he accepts them implicitly as the contents of the canonical concept of marriage.)

The presumption that the declared will corresponds to the real will within the subject can be appreciated more fully in terms of the deeper reason for it. This presumption is a guide derived from experience for understanding one another in human relations ("I must maintain that so-and-so really wants what he asks me for"). It also is a legal rule to guarantee the certainty of the law within the community ("I consider to be truly married those who have celebrated a wedding"). It also exists, if not most importantly, to affirm and to instantiate the sense of respect and trust that the Church cultivates toward the human person, especially when he solemnly commits himself and in relation to decisive choices in life, for example, the choice of the vocation to marriage and the consecration of that choice in the nuptial rite.

3. Given what is explained in the preceding point, it is necessary, furthermore, to consider that the primary interest of the Church, in her juridical system as well, is to guarantee that individuals and communities can orient themselves toward their own supernatural end, accepting their own responsibilities and the objective truth of their own condition.

The final provision of canon 1101 §2 can be explained along these lines: to absolutize the presumption discussed in paragraph 1 (i.e., that someone's declared will corresponds to his real will) would mean achieving a merely formal certainty of human relations, and from this perspective even marriages that in reality were not valid would have to be considered as though they were irremediably so. Objective reality, rather, must prevail over purely formal certainty. Therefore, the law establishes that the presumption in paragraph 1 of canon 1101 must be considered a "simple" presumption, as is customarily said—in other words, one that admits for the direct proof of the contrary.

This is precisely what is laid down in paragraph 2 of the canon, which states that it is possible to prove that—notwithstanding the declarations made at the moment of marriage—in that same moment, and with a positive act of the will, one of the contracting parties rejected marriage itself as a whole, or one of its essential elements (the fact that it is ordered to children and to the well-being of the spouses), or else one of its essential properties (unity, fidelity, indissolubility, and if one wants to consider it as such, sacramentality).

In the case of a will positively contrary to one of these essential aspects of the institution of marriage, the same marital covenant would be null, inasmuch as it was not founded on an authentically conjugal consent. Such a will would in fact not be directed toward the establishment of marriage as understood by canon law (recall the points made in the commentary on canon 1057 §2 concerning the "material" and the "formal" object of the marital covenant) but rather to something essentially different from it.

4. This possible motive for matrimonial nullity that has just been briefly described is generally called (not by the law but in forensic practice) simulation. This term does not necessarily indicate "bad faith" on the part of the person who makes the marriage null by his own act of the will (bad faith is not always present in this scenario of nullity; e.g., the subject could act prompted by an invincible error, which eliminates moral guilt). Rather, it indicates the objective and substantial discrepancy between what is declared externally (the acceptance of canonical marriage) and the subject's real will, which, in this instance, is to reject it—either totally or in one of its essential aspects.

Therefore, from a systematic perspective, simulation is classified among the defects of consent, precisely to indicate the intrinsic non-conjugality of the act of will in which it consists. This pseudo-consent is in itself naturally insufficient to create the marriage and is not simply vitiated by a fact that is "external" to it, as happens, for example, in the case of fear, which we have already dealt with.

One requirement that the canonical norm formulates carefully must be emphasized strongly, namely, that in order for there to be simulation of consent, there must also be a positive act of the will. What do these words mean? They intend to point out that the act of simulation must be a true decision, a "counterconsent"—that is, a voluntary act having the same force as the consent. Only in this case, indeed, could the counter consent oppose the true consent and "paralyze" its efficacy. Even Pope John Paul II, in one of his allocutions to the Roman Rota (an allocution having at least a general indicative value, given the role assigned to the Rota to contribute to the uniformity of canonical jurisprudence),[1] stressed the need for a positive act of the will in order for a simulation of matrimonial consent to be possible.[2]

In trying to explain this concept more fully, we can use several illustrations that are commonly adopted.

In the first place, the content of the legal prescription can be expressed as follows: a mere lack of will cannot be considered a positive act of will, nor can a merely negative will (for example, the will of someone who said, "I do not want to get married"; "I am marrying reluctantly"; "I am not thinking of having children"; etc.) A positive act of will consists in an intention that could be expressed approximately as follows: "I want not to marry (despite the ritual)"; "I want not to have children (notwithstanding the fact that I declare that I accept them)"; etc. Many times it is certainly difficult to distinguish in practice among the various degrees of intensity of the will, but on a general level what the canonical norm intends to require emerges with clarity.

In the second place, by way of differentiating, we can try to elucidate the positive act of the will by distinguishing it from phenomena that belong to another faculty of the person, for example, errors in the intellect (e.g., "I think that marriage can be dissolved") or the imagination ("I fear that my marriage might go badly and that we will end up splitting"), or else feelings or moods ("I am getting married, but I am not very much in love"; "I am not sure about getting married"). All these phenomena can certainly influence the will, but they do not necessarily determine it. Obviously, what has just been said is not meant to deny the anthropological principle of the unity of the human person or the common rule of experience that normally someone acts according to his own thought and his own feelings. Nevertheless, it appears possible—and sometimes, as in this case, useful and proper —to distinguish between the various aspects and the different functions of human action and to assign a serious phenomenon such as the simulation of matrimonial consent to the sphere of full legal and moral responsibility, in other words, to the sphere of deliberate consent.

---

[1] Cf. *Pastor bonus*, art. 126.
[2] Cf. *AAS* 85 (1993): 1259.

5. Anyone who has attentively considered the text of paragraph 2 of canon 1101 will surely have asked himself the question: How many forms of simulation are there? Indeed, the norm indicates, albeit generically, several possible objects of the act of the will to simulate.

The current text of the law highlights above all the possibility of excluding *matrimonium ipsum*, or marriage itself. This is what the scholarly and jurisprudential tradition calls total simulation. This is, in itself, the most radical form of simulation, and we will deal with it further on, given also the statistical infrequency of this particular case. Jurisprudence has pointed out various forms in which this total simulation can manifest itself. Let it suffice here to state that most times it boils down to the intention not really to get married, excluding the total acceptance of the other person as spouse, and excluding the fact that binding obligations on the moral and juridical level result from the celebration of marriage.

The norm then considers the possibility of voluntarily excluding an "essential element" or an "essential property" of marriage. These particular cases are commonly referred to as partial simulation. This is because the person per se would still have the intention to marry yet would not completely accept the canonical concept of marriage and would instead exclude one aspect or "part" of it. Hence the qualifier "partial" reserved for these forms of simulation.

We recalled earlier what is to be understood by *essential properties* of marriage: indissolubility, unity-fidelity (unless fidelity is included in the "well-being of the spouses"), and sacramentality (unless classified under total simulation). The journal *Quaderni di diritto ecclesiale* has already dealt with this particular problem of the exclusion of the sacramental dignity of marriage and of its possible systematic classification;[3] therefore, we will not take up this question again.

We also recalled earlier what is to be understood by the *essential elements* of marriage: the fact that it is ordered to the procreation and upbringing of children and to the well-being of the spouses. It is well known that this latter concept was recently introduced into canon law and that judges and scholars have not yet finished reflecting on what its juridically binding contents are. It appears sufficiently certain that

---

[3] Cf. *QDE* 4 (1991): 79–96.

this concept should include the secondary ends of the legislation previously in force (cf. can. 1013 §1 of the 1917 Code), that is, mutual assistance and the remedy for concupiscence. The latter concept could be understood to include the possibility of leading a sexual life that is ordered according to nature and morality, which leads to a minimal psychosexual integration, as is maintained by at least one jurisprudential trend. Concerning other possible contents of the concept of the well-being of the spouses ("essential interpersonal relations", "right to the communion of life"), the debate is still open and does not appear to have arrived at conclusive results.

As for the possible forms of simulation of matrimonial consent, some scholars and practitioners of canon law, basing their argument on the fact that the effect of all simulation is to render the consent inadequate and therefore the marriage null, have tried to deny the distinction between total simulation and partial simulation or, at least, the usefulness of continuing to refer to it. For both traditional and substantive reasons, however, the distinction is still generally accepted and utilized. Suffice it to recall, by way of example, the fact that in total simulation the simulator cannot fail to notice his own will not to marry and therefore the nullity of his marriage (even though it is probably not expressed mentally in legal terms), whereas in partial simulations the will to exclude an essential element or property (e.g., children) can be accompanied by the intention to contract marriage, whereby the interested party does not manage to grasp the matrimonial inefficacy of his defective consent. This, however, is an academic question, with little relevance to the pastoral character of these reflections.

6. Before proceeding to an analysis of the most frequent types of simulation of matrimonial consent, it is necessary to address the problem of whether it is possible to prove it judicially.

This is a delicate problem, which applies to all possible forms of simulation and which we will discuss here only this once.

The delicate nature of the problem results from the very concept of simulation. Simulation is an intention that is positively contrary to marriage itself, to an essential element of it, or to an essential property of it. Now, as an act of choosing, an intention is an interior fact, known directly and completely only to God and to the interested subject. The object of the proof of a simulation of consent, in other words, is a fact that is indeed real but internal, which in its most intimate reality eludes the perception of third parties, and also of those who must judge.

Although this assertion is true, it is also true that a person's will is often manifested externally. And this normally happens in two ways: either by words, through which the person expresses what he intends, what he wants; or else by actions, which, as jurisprudence in its wisdom teaches, are often *verbis eloquentiora*, more eloquent than words themselves.

The possibility of proof is structured along these two lines, one that is commonly called direct and the other, indirect.

The direct proof is the one that reconstructs the intention of the interested person at the moment of the marriage by inquiring into his verbal manifestations. The person may have indeed spoken about his decisions—for example, concerning children or marital fidelity—to others, and they can then report the statements in their depositions. It is clear that the testimonies that are obtained by the tribunal must not be evaluated in material, quantitative terms but rather in relation to other parameters, such as the time relative to the testimony (which is that much more important the closer it is to the wedding), the depth of the conversations that can be reported (indeed, it is one thing to have caught bits and pieces of sentences, and another to have had in-depth discussions with the interested person), the possibility of comparing the testimony of fellow witnesses, that is, of other persons who were present at the same conversations and can confirm them, and the credibility, even extrinsic, of the witness, who may be well known by certain persons (especially priests or religious) who can testify positively about the reliability of the witness himself.

The indirect proof, in contrast, is one that logically reconstructs the intention of the interested person, deducing it from facts and circumstances that have the value of circumstantial evidence. There is hardly any need for a reminder that such presumptive proofs must be based, as the law itself requires (cf. can. 1586), on certain and determinate facts having a direct connection with the object of proof. In other words, it is not enough that something is asserted by one of the parties or by a witness to consider it proved and therefore to be the basis of the construction of judicial presumptions. It is necessary that it be truly certain, well circumstantiated, and pertinent to the contractual intention that is to be reconstructed. But what sorts of facts can have this possible value as circumstantial evidence?

What has particular value in cases of simulation is above all the *causa simulandi* (cause of the simulation), that is, the reason why a specific person would have acted in that particular way. In other words, particular probative importance is attached to the presence of a plausible motive for the behavior that one intends to demonstrate. The stronger the motive is, even if only subjectively, the more probable it is that the simulation actually occurred. To give an example: a person who knew that he was affected by a serious hereditary illness would have a strong, specific, and credible motive not to want children. It is necessary to emphasize here that the presence of a motive produces, in and of itself, the possibility and not the complete proof of simulation, unless one wants to adopt a deterministic, mechanical view of human action, to the detriment of any acknowledgment of personal responsibility. This would happen if a tribunal—in the absence of other true findings— reasoned, for example, in the following way: "It is proved that so-and-so was egotistical and irresponsible and that he had had a difficult childhood and unloving parents; hence, he could not have wanted children and therefore excluded them." Allow us to make a comparison, which is not meant flippantly but only clarifies and facilitates our presentation: even in detective novels the one with the strongest motive does not always turn out to be the guilty party.

Another thing that is usually considered circumstantial evidence is the so-called *causa contrahendi* (cause of contracting), that is, the motive for which the alleged simulator contracted the marriage. The "weaker" the reason (from a moral, Christian perspective) for which the person married (e.g., financial or social advantage, "reparation", pressures from third parties or from the social environment), the stronger the possibility of simulation. On the other hand, the more genuine the reason for the marriage (e.g., mutual love, although not in the sense of mere sentimental attraction), the less probable the simulation.

Circumstances then play a special role, whether previous to the wedding, or at the time of its celebration, or relative to the couple's actual day-to-day married life. For example, if during the engagement there were quarrels, break-ups, arguments, or doubts, then reservations concerning the indissolubility of the marriage will be more plausible than if the engagement had been idyllic. Alternatively, if on the wedding day one of the spouses displayed impatience or sadness, that could be evidence (albeit per se generic) consistent with his amorous affection for someone else, within the framework of proving a possible exclusion of fidelity. Finally, if during the course of their married life the couple systematically used artificial contraception, or if there were voluntary abortions, this would be evidence consistent with a declared refusal of procreation.

To clarify, it should be recalled that the two modes of proof—the direct and the indirect—normally are pursued conjointly, in the sense that the judge usually draws his own conclusion about the case to be resolved both by weighing the tenor of the direct testimonies as a whole and also by considering evidence and circumstances.

It is good also to emphasize that this method of proof is just a method to help the judge and is not a rigid formula to be applied mechanically. Every human case, and therefore every marriage case as well, has its own uniqueness and special features. For this reason too, there can be widely different combinations of the various elements of the traditional method of proof. In some cases a few witnesses will suffice (if they are reliable and well informed), while in other cases many will be necessary (e.g., because they know only particulars and the situation can be reconstructed only by examining many witnesses). In some cases the circumstances will appear unambiguous; in others ambiguous, while not entirely devoid of factors in favor of nullity; and so on.

Finally it should be recalled that the procedural law currently in force, in order to promote the greatest possible conformity of the "procedural truth" to the "effective truth" of things, allows the application of the moral argument of proof, derived from canons 1536 §2 and 1679 to all causes. This revolves around the credibility of the parties themselves and the finding of evidence and circumstances that corroborate irrefutably (*omnino*, totally) their statements in court. The journal *Quaderni di diritto ecclesiale* has already dealt explicitly with this probative scenario; hence, for a more in-depth study the reader can refer to that article.[4]

---

[4] Cf. *QDE* 3 (1990): 394–410.

V

Exclusion of Children

Elements of substantive law

Of the various possible forms of simulation, we will deal first of all with those that are statistically the most widespread in our society, starting with the exclusion of children. The same data reported by journalists concerning the demographic trend of the Italian population serve as a social and cultural background with regard to the field of canon law.

For Catholic doctrine, it is a precept of natural law that marriage is ordained to procreation. Canon law stresses this precept in canon 1055 §1, and it is explained in an enlightening way by the most authoritative expressions of the Magisterium in recent decades: *Gaudium et spes*, the pastoral constitution of the Second Vatican Ecumenical Council (especially in nos. 50 and 51) and *Familiaris consortio*, John Paul II's post-synodal apostolic exhortation on the duties of the family in the modern world.

The constant teaching of the Church has been consistently translated into her discipline. Thus, the 1917 Code asserted in canon 1013 §1 that the primary end of marriage is the procreation and upbringing of children. In canon 1081 §2 it declared that the object of matrimonial consent is the perpetual and exclusive right over the body for acts that are in themselves suitable for the generation of children. And finally, in canon 1086 §2, it declared that a marriage is null if one of the spouses, with a positive act of the will, excludes *omne ius ad coniugalem actum,* in other words, radically denies the other spouse's right to ask for and to obtain an opportunity to actualize the gift of self in this way.

For decades this rigorous and consistent legislative system regulated the canonical discipline in matters of the exclusion of children. However, jurisprudential application and scholarly reflection on it did not fail to bring to light several problems of interpretation. Let us recall the chief problem here: What, precisely, is the possible extent of simulation?

The norm that directly regulated this particular case, the aforementioned canon 1086 §2, was indeed expressed in a very precise way: anyone who radically excludes the right to conjugal acts contracts marriage invalidly. The question that followed from this norm, in a properly rigorous interpretation of the canonical prescript—justified by the fact that it is an invalidating law, that is, one that foresees the conditions of possible invalidity of a juridical act that, as a rule, should be presumed to be valid once it is placed—was this: Is a marriage null when one of the spouses grants to the other the right to acts suitable for procreation yet intends to render them ineffective with forms of contraception that do not modify the natural performance [in Italian, *svolgimento*] of the acts themselves? Or [is it null when one of the spouses] expects to take no interest in any children who may be born and to allow them to die, for all he cares?

One part of canonical scholarship and jurisprudence had sought to resolve the difficulty by hypothesizing that there was a twofold normative source of matrimonial nullity on account of the exclusion of children: one explicit (can. 1086 §2), which declares the denial of the right to acts per se suitable for procreation to be a reason for nullity; and one implicit (derived from can. 1031 §1), which would include any denial in principle of the procreative end of marriage, however that denial was achieved, as invalidating. This solution was challenged, however, for several reasons. One was the consideration that it presupposed an invalidating norm not expressly foreseen by the positive legislation (the one derived from the procreative end of marriage described in can. 1013). As we will see momentarily, the revised Code adopts a manner of expression that seems to resolve this interpretative problem.

Indeed, the 1983 Code, in delineating the juridical structure of the institution of marriage, abandons the terminology of the "ends" of marriage. With respect to children, it prefers to declare that the institution of marriage, *indole sua naturali*—by its very nature, by its structure within the natural order of things—is oriented to the procreation and upbringing of children (cf. can. 1055 §1). The definition of the object of consent is different too. It is no longer the perpetual and exclusive right over the body for acts suitable in themselves for procreation, but as we saw while commenting briefly on canon 1057 §2, it is the gift of self with a view to the establishment of the marital relationship. Finally, another difference is the formulation of the provision for possible simulation with regard to children. The provision no longer has recourse to the *omne ius ad coniugalem actum* but foresees, somewhat more generically and comprehensively, the exclusion of an "essential element" of marriage.

These expressions of the current Code lead us to think that the principal object of the simulation, in the case of exclusion of children, must be understood as the natural ordering of marriage to procreation, the "structural fecundity" inherent in marriage and sexuality, however it may in fact be frustrated—by denying to the other spouse intimate acts; by granting the other spouse acts that are intimate but not conjugal, because they are systematically rendered contraceptive; by proposing recourse to abortion in case of pregnancy; or by killing newborns, or else abandoning them.

As it may already be evident from the concepts just set forth, we must not forget that not just any abuse of the exercise of sexuality results in nullity of the marriage, nor any lack whatsoever of responsibility toward the new life that is conceived or born, but only the principled exclusion of the structural fecundity of marriage and of the right of the other spouse to the acts corresponding to it. As classical Christian thinkers (e.g., Saint Thomas Aquinas) had already remarked, the only relevant exclusion of children is that which concerns the *intentio prolis*, one's intention, one's fundamental disposition toward children; or else that which is related to children *in suis principiis*, as a matter of principle.

There is little need then to remind the reader that, in order to be a cause of nullity of a marriage, the exclusion of offspring as a matter of principle and the refusal to engage with the spouse in the acts that bring about conception must be at work in the will of the subject at the moment of the marriage, at least virtually (i.e., in the form of a true decision already made and not withdrawn). Any decision made subsequent to the marriage, even if it were a true preclusion in principle (e.g., "Our marriage is going badly, and therefore I want to have no children, so as not to involve them in the suffering when it fails"; "My husband has become incurably ill, and therefore I rule out the possibility of having children by him, so as not to bring into the world children who will soon be orphaned''), has no relevance to the validity of the marriage inasmuch as it does not affect the consent that was given correctly and integrally at the moment when the wedding was celebrated.

This distinction helps us to orient ourselves in some concrete cases, which present quite a few difficulties in interpreting the facts and in applying the norms. With regard to these we will make only a few remarks, as simply as possible, in keeping with the purpose of this study.

It can be difficult to distinguish the mere postponement of children from a true temporary exclusion of them. Someone who postpones children accepts them per se and as a matter of principle and wants to put off having them only for a while (e.g., for the first two or three years of marriage), and is not against accepting a child if one were to arrive despite the fact that the couple is normally using licit means to delay procreation until later. In doing this, they are not denying in principle the fact that marriage is ordered to procreation, neither as to the end nor as to the means. Someone who excludes offspring, on the contrary, even temporarily, refuses as a matter of principle the arrival of children during the predetermined time and does not recognize the other spouse's right to ask meanwhile for acts that are in themselves fertile. Very often this is also accompanied by the use of effective artificial contraception (regardless of its moral unacceptability) and sometimes not even ruling out the possibility of terminating an accidental pregnancy through abortion. It is not always easy to distinguish the two attitudes in practice, even though the logical and legal difference between them is an objective fact that can be expressed in the terms just summarized briefly.

Thus, it is not always easy to distinguish the postponement of procreation from the conditional exclusion thereof. Again, to put it schematically, someone who only postpones childbearing limits himself to a decision of the type: "I want children, but consider the present moment inopportune", and even here normally chooses morally acceptable means to achieve the purpose. On the other hand, someone who conditionally excludes childbearing decides, "Right now I do not want to have children; however, I reserve the right to change my mind when a certain thing happens that I deem to be the condition for being open to procreation." Possible examples are the attainment of a certain economic status, proof that the marriage is going well, or even the aban-

donment by the other spouse of a habit that is thought to be dangerous or expensive. Generally speaking, the difference between the two
attitudes seems clear enough: in postponement, the acceptance of children and the willingness to respect the structure of marriage and of the
conjugal act predominate, although with the desire to put off an actual conception; in conditional exclusion, in contrast, the predominant
element is the actual negation of the fact that marriage is ordered to
fecundity, made complete through means that are often immoral (and
often unilateral as well, showing contempt for the right of the other
spouse), along with the fact that the willingness to change one's own attitude is subordinated to an arbitrary, personal judgment. Note too that
conditional exclusion, though theoretically temporary (and sometimes
it may actually be so in fact), is always potentially perpetual. Indeed,
the subject, by excluding children conditionally, is implicitly willing to
make his own exclusion definitive and perpetual when the conditions
for becoming open to procreation—in his own unquestionable final
judgment—are not fulfilled.

To repeat: the position of someone who excludes children (absolutely, temporarily, conditionally) is different from that of the person who instead practices responsible parenthood.[1] The latter concept,
indeed, presupposes the acceptance of the structural ordering of marriage and of conjugal acts to procreation (without any exceptions, even
merely temporary or conditional ones) and the use of those methods of
regulating births that, in the light of our present scientific knowledge,
Church teaching declares to be respectful of the anthropological and
moral values involved. To put it even more simply, the proper attitude
includes above all acceptance of paternity or maternity, which are the
substance of the concept of "responsible parenthood". The adjective
"responsible" refers to the modality in which that basic notion of parenthood is put into action, which may indeed be regulated but in keeping with morality.

Obviously, the problematic cases mentioned here are not the only
ones that can come up in relation to the potential simulation of marriage through the exclusion of children (think of the problems related
to the new biotechnologies or of the debated question of whether the
new Code allows for another object of simulation against the good of

---

[1] Cf. Paul VI, *Humanae vitae* 7 and passim.—TRANS.

children, namely the intention to deny them a minimum of education).
It seems, however, that those indications can be an adequate basis for
the marriage counselor who seeks an initial pastoral orientation in the
matter. The advisor must have the prudence to refer the interested person to specialists, in a case that may present new or more complicated
problems such as the final ones just mentioned.

Guide for the counselor

In applying all that was said above, the pastor of souls whose advice is
sought and who is prudently seeking to investigate a marriage that is in
serious difficulty and its possible invalidity on account of the exclusion
of children will have to pay attention to the following points:

1. Whether the interested person has ever spoken generally about
familial issues, expressing himself in particular concerning procreation
and the presence of children in a family. This is information about
his mentality and upbringing that may serve as the foundation for the
investigation, representing a possible "remote" motive for simulation.

2. Whether the interested person has ever taken an explicit position
on children in his own marriage: when he spoke about it; in what terms
and in what context (e.g., in a serious conversation or else jokingly);
whether there are persons who can remember and confirm the expressions that he used.

3. Whether the same person who allegedly simulated is willing to
admit it before the tribunal, naming other possible witnesses to confirm
it. The lack of this willingness—especially in the case where there are
no other informed and willing witnesses—could present a serious difficulty for a possible cause. This is an element that should not be overlooked with regard to the practical advice that the counselor must give.

4. Whether the interested person expressed himself in terms of a
definitive rejection of children forever, or whether it was only for a
certain time or dependent on certain circumstances, so as to seek to
understand whether one is dealing with a true exclusion in principle
(albeit temporary or conditional) or with a simple postponement of

children. As mentioned, it is not easy to reconstruct *a posteriori* the actual will of the subject who supposedly simulated his consent. This, however, does not relieve the counselor (or the judge later on) of the obligation of seeking to understand the exact terms of this question.

5. What was the specific reason why children were excluded. The "cause" of the simulation, its motive, is indeed a very important element in establishing its plausibility. Although by itself alone the cause of the simulation is not the full proof of the fact, it is nevertheless true that it carries great probative weight. In jurisprudence it is often called *regina probationum* (the queen of proofs), precisely to note its probative importance, which cannot be overlooked.

6. Why the alleged simulator agreed to marry in the Church while excluding children. Was he practicing the faith? Was he aware of the fact that the rejection of children is something inadmissible by the Church and in itself a cause for the nullity of the marriage? The absence of Christian principles and the presence of a reason for contracting marriage that involves little Christian commitment (love for the other but in a superficial, emotional sense; the opportunity to lead a life less dependent on one's family of origin and to be able to engage with the spouse in more popular pastimes) are in fact generically compatible with simulation. Otherwise, one will find the contrary, that is, proof of a committed adherence to Christian life and to the Christian vision of marriage.

7. Whether any children were born of the parties' married life in common. A pregnancy can occur even despite the negative will of one of the interested persons (sometimes even of both), but ordinarily, the presence of one or more children is a contraindication with regard to simulation. In that case, one will have to examine how the alleged simulator reacted to the unplanned pregnancy. For example, did he propose an abortion, was he happy about the birth of children, did he look after them with interest and affection?

8. Whether there were potentially fertile relations between the spouses in the course of their married life. Was contraception practiced? By whose decision and with what means? Also, is there the possibility of proving contraceptive use, by means of witnesses who

knew the facts, or else through the deposition (or at least a written certification) of the physicians who supervised the use of contraceptive means that require a medical intervention (such as a prescription, or a procedure to insert an intrauterine device [IUD])?

9. Whether, in the course of the parties' life together, they sought elective abortions. This fact, which in any case loses nothing of its negative moral or canonical connotations, nevertheless has a rather strong relevance as circumstantial evidence, if it can be traced back to an original intention (in other words, one present at the moment when the wedding was celebrated) of the subject contrary to procreation. Clearly, one must investigate as well the feasibility of proving this, through witnesses, or by means of documentation, whenever the intervention was carried out in a health facility.

10. Whether, over the course of their married life, the parties returned to a discussion about children. Were there explicit requests for children on the part of one of them? How did the other respond? Were there discussions and conflicts over the matter? Above all, what influence did the possible conflicts over children have in the failure of their married life? Was said influence decisive; that is, was it a sufficiently strong indication of the intensity of the will not to have children, at least at the time of the separation? It will then be a matter of investigating whether that intense will can be considered as having existed at the time of the wedding as well.

11. Whether the person who allegedly excluded children has had children by other marriages that may have been contracted after the one with which the consultation is concerned. This circumstance is not a contraindication that would be invalidating in every case, but certainly it is a fact that will have to be explained reasonably to the tribunal, especially if the cause of the alleged simulation was of a general nature, that is, not connected to the spouse personally. Possible examples [of a general desire not to have children] would be selfishness, the desire for freedom, and the fear of transmitting a disease with which the simulator himself is afflicted—which reasons, it would seem, are likely to last indefinitely.

Examples

First example

The engagement of Laura and Paul lasted about three years. Paul was and always remained sincerely in love with Laura. She, though, was not so much in love. In fact, in the months preceding the wedding she had serious doubts about her feelings and, therefore, about the appropriateness of getting married. She spoke about it to her mother and also to her own pastor, who encouraged her, however, to continue with the wedding plans. She spoke about it to her fiancé, who was greatly embittered to learn of Laura's uncertainty.

Not knowing what to do, Laura decided on a trial marriage—she would get married to Paul while reserving to herself the right, if the "trial" failed, to leave him definitively and to resume her freedom. Therefore, about one month before the wedding, she had a gynecologist prescribe for her an oral contraceptive.

Their married life lasted only a few months, during which Laura's behavior showed her distrust of the marriage from the outset. She did not even finish moving her personal effects to the newlyweds' house and deprived Paul of all affection and conversation. Her use of the oral contraceptive was uninterrupted.

At the canonical trial, it was possible to prove Laura's prenuptial doubts (which Paul himself and the pastor who had counseled Laura admitted), as well as her decision to enter a "trial" marriage and her determination not to have children—at least not until there was a positive outcome of the trial marriage itself, since Laura had revealed her intentions to several reliable people even before marrying. Her use of the contraceptive was proved through written certification by the doctor who had prescribed it. This comprehensive proof resulted in a declaration of the nullity of the marriage.

The example is meant to emphasize the importance of a cause, a motive, for the simulation, even if it is of a subjective nature (in this case, the awareness of a lack of true marital love for a specific person), as well as the fact that the main reason, the exclusion of children, can in some cases be combined with other motives for matrimonial nullity, especially the exclusion of indissolubility, as happened precisely in the case of Laura, who had refused to make a lasting commitment to Paul because she did not feel secure about that union.

Second example

At the age of fourteen, Clare lost both her parents within the space of a few months, which left her an orphan together with her two much-younger brothers. In order to avoid the prospect of all three of them ending up in orphanages and perhaps being separated, Clare convinced an uncle who lived in the same region to assume the duties of guardian. Therefore, she was able to continue to live in her parents' house, together with her two brothers, under the guardianship and supervision of their uncle and his wife.

Clare herself took charge of her little brothers, not only caring for them personally but even going to work so as to contribute to their support. At around the age of eighteen she became acquainted with Alfred, a young man from the same region, who proved to be affectionate toward her, helpful, and well disposed toward Clare's younger brothers. Alfred was in love with Clare, who—although she did not feel much of an attraction to him and despite the fact that she had always had a sense of fear with regard to sexuality and childbearing—accepted his marriage proposal, since he was willing to welcome her brothers as well into the new family.

Clare, however, because of her aforementioned fear did not succeed in giving herself to her husband for several years, and their marriage remained unconsummated. After several years, however, Clare gave in to the advances of another man, with whom she had intimate relations. She repented and immediately confessed the affair to Alfred, who forgave her. Forcing herself, out of a sense of reparation for the sin of infidelity that she had committed, Clare also managed to have intimate relations with her husband too, although it caused her profound psychological and physical suffering. Finding herself pregnant, Clare had an abortion, both because of her fear of giving birth and because of her uncertainty about the father (given the chronological proximity of the relations that she had had with the other man and with her husband). Their married life then ended with their separation and divorce.

Several years later, Clare entered a civil marriage with someone else.

The problem with her younger brothers had been resolved, since meanwhile they had both attained majority age and financial independence. But her fears about having children remained. Clare became pregnant again and this time brought the pregnancy to term, although she needed extensive care from a psychologist and, at several points, from a psychiatrist as well.

In the canonical process the scarcity of direct evidence (i.e., evidence derived from witnesses who knew Clare's intentions about children at the moment when she married) was combined with the possibility of reconstructing with certainty a sure indirect proof, consisting of the facts relayed above: Clare's unhappy family history; her concern for her brothers, who were still small; her fear of childbearing; the way in which she finally was able to have relations with her husband; the abortion that she procured; and the way in which she lived and managed to bring her pregnancy to term in the civil marriage following her separation from Alfred. This set of facts corroborated the reliability of the parties in the case and of the few direct findings.

The example is meant again to stress the importance of the cause of the simulation (in this case, a borderline pathological fear of the prospect of childbirth) and to show the concurrence of the circumstantial evidence in attaining the moral certainty that the judge must have in order to declare the invalidity of a marriage. Only through a comprehensive and integrated evaluation of all the evidence can most cases be resolved, even the most difficult ones, assigning the correct weight to the statements themselves of the parties, as was briefly explained earlier in commenting on canons 1536 §2 and 1679.

Third example

Theodore was a young man from an uneducated family, but he was decent, generous, and hard-working. While taking public transportation to work, he became acquainted with Carol, with whom he fell in love. Carol, however, already had a three-year-old son, Louis, whom she had had by a relationship with a married man who had not acknowledged the child. Theodore endeared himself to Carol and also to Louis and proposed marriage, saying that he was also willing to acknowledge Louis, declaring him (albeit falsely) his own son.

Urged on by her own mother, Carol accepted Theodore's proposal.

Theodore acknowledged Louis within the context of the wedding ceremony. After the fact, however, Carol revealed her true sentiments toward Theodore. She began to lead a disorderly life (probably, though it was not proved with certainty, she was still seeing Louis' natural father). She left her husband's house after a few weeks of their living together. When Theodore denounced his wife's estrangement, she retaliated by baselessly denouncing him for having mistreated her, and she declared that she had procured the abortion of a pregnancy that had resulted from the few intimate relations she had granted to Theodore, although these were rudimentarily contraceptive.

Appearances notwithstanding, the case was extremely difficult to resolve. Carol, in fact, never appeared at the tribunal to cooperate truthfully by declaring her intentions concerning children on her wedding day. It was possible, however, to find several trustworthy witnesses who had spoken with her before the wedding and also after it, but at a nonsuspect time (i.e., at a time when there was still no thought of filing for nullity), to whom Carol had consistently expressed her own intention not to have children, for fear that Theodore might lose his affection for Louis. It also was possible to prove through witnesses her behavior immediately after Theodore acknowledged Louis and, again through witnesses, the abortion later admitted to by Carol, which it would otherwise have been impossible to prove, given that the facts of the case far predated the Italian law tolerating abortion (it had been a clandestine procedure). On the basis of the aforesaid evidence, the tribunal decreed the marriage of Theodore and Carol null.

This example is meant to illustrate that the absence of the truthful cooperation of the alleged simulator of consent may be a very serious obstacle to proving a case but not an insurmountable one. Sometimes it is possible to reconstruct that party's intention concerning the fruitfulness of marriage from other sources, or else through reliable testimonies and unequivocal circumstances.

Fourth example

[Reconstructing the party's intention regarding the fruitfulness of marriage] was not the case with Mary Ellen, a person who was nevertheless trustworthy and respectable. She claimed that her husband Richard had excluded children, but [she] was able to adduce only minimal evidence, which the tribunal could not deem conclusive.

Before their wedding, Richard was showing his new sports car to a mutual acquaintance. When the latter, who was also about to be married, discreetly expressed his serious plans to have a family, Richard bragged that he preferred cruising around in an automobile to family obligations. After more than two years of marriage, and during a serious nervous breakdown, Richard told several people that he wanted to let several years go by before having children.

The entire "direct" proof of Richard's alleged intention not to have children consisted solely of these two statements. Given the context in which the two admissions occurred, their probative force appeared rather meager to the judges. In the first case it was bravado, and in the second it was the words of a man who was psychologically disturbed, albeit transiently. Furthermore, Mary Ellen herself honestly admitted that, in their discussions before their wedding, Richard had never called into question plans for a normal family and that, after their wedding, at least some potentially fertile sexual relations had taken place between them, which is serious evidence against a true exclusion of children.

Finally, in his deposition Richard himself denied that he had excluded children from his marriage plans and introduced four witnesses who declared that they had heard him speak before the wedding about his willingness to have children. There was no reason to find these testimonies false, nor could other evidence and circumstances call into question the trustworthiness of Richard's denial.

This example is meant to emphasize that it is in fact a delicate matter to prove the simulation of marriage and that, before recommending that a cause be introduced, it is good to ascertain, directly or through referral to other experts, that there is a reasonable probability of success. Indeed the declaration of nullity depends on the possibility of ascertaining objective facts and not only (as surely was the case with Mary Ellen) on the reliability and the moral stature of the petitioner.

Fifth example

Luke was a son of farmers, but after earning a technical school diploma, he managed to find employment with a regional bank. He socialized with a rowdy bunch given to gambling and chasing women. During one of his escapades with his friends, he met Rose, the daughter of a building contractor, who fell in love with him. Seeing in the offing a possible marriage of convenience, Luke always acted gallantly toward the young woman, who was also afflicted with a physical defect. Whenever she intuited his ulterior motives and was frightened by them, Luke was always quick to cover her with kisses, oaths, and promises, until he convinced her to marry him.

After the wedding, Rose also saw Luke's true colors—always away from the house, given to gambling and womanizing—a fact that he did not conceal from his wife either, so as to humiliate her. Indeed, he had become cruel toward Rose because her parents—who were wise, prudent people—had helped the newlyweds by buying them a house and then had said that, since both of them had good, secure jobs, they would have to fend for themselves from then on. Thus, Luke's hopes of an endless series of gifts from his in-laws (which would have given him more money for gambling and for his dalliances) were dashed.

Rose, saddened and constantly cooped up alone at home, insistently asked Luke for a child, so that she could give to the much-desired baby the affection that her husband was obviously not interested in. Luke, however, always categorically refused that possibility, ridiculing and insulting Rose crudely because of her requests and her physical state and denying her in practice any conjugal life, which on rare occasions of intimacy was conducted in an unnatural manner when he imposed his will on her.

A positive outcome of the cause was possible, since Luke—who declared that he had come to his senses and repented thanks to the beneficent influence of another woman, whom he had met after separating from Rose—admitted his dishonest intentions with regard to Rose at the time of their marriage, that is, his deliberate exploitation of her with a view to expected material advantages, without any willingness to assume seriously with her the obligations of marriage, precisely, in this instance, an openness to procreation. Mutual acquaintances and friends of Luke who were called by him to testify gave evidence of his lifestyle and his intention not to have children, which he had already declared to his drinking buddies before his wedding.

The example is meant to underscore a particular problem: indeed, it might seem strange at first glance that a tribunal of the Church would put faith in individuals like Luke, that is, a person who already once deceived a woman so cruelly and mocked a sacrament. It is necessary, however, to stress that in such cases the tribunal proceeds very warily, precisely corroborating with objective evidence the statements of a person like Luke, and also analyzing in depth the credibility of the witnesses introduced by him. Moreover, there is no need to deny that, in cases like the present one, the tribunal, in giving its own declarative sentence of the nullity of the marriage, imposes on the one responsible for the simulation, in this case Luke, an administrative sanction, barring him from contracting further marriages. In this case, the ordinary of the place where the person tries to marry again canonically cannot proceed licitly without having conducted an in-depth examination concerning the interested party's effective change of intentions and the knowledge, on the part of the third person involved, of the preceding marital incident of the one who simulated consent. In this way the Church strives, with pastoral sensitivity, to foster a genuine conversion in the one who erred, but also to protect interested third parties from new deceptions as well as the Church's own juridical institutions from exploitation by individuals whose intentions are not upright. By making it more difficult for a proven simulator of consent to be admitted to a new marriage (through stricter requirements), the Church confronts the simulator's conscience with his own serious responsibilities in relation to the past and in view of the future. This is consistent with one of the specific purposes of the system of canon law, which is to set conditions so that individuals can attain the *salus animarum*, the salvation of their own souls.

VI

Exclusion of the Indissolubility of the Bond

Having considered the topic of the exclusion of the procreative purpose of marriage, we must turn our attention to a second form of simulation of consent, which unfortunately is also relatively common in Italy—exclusion of the indissolubility of the marital bond.

Elements of substantive law

Canon law considers marriage as an institution of natural law, in other words, as a juridical institution and a state of life inscribed by God in the nature of things and consistent with the very structure of the human person. Marriage is designed to allow the human person to develop correctly and in an orderly way his tendency toward interpersonal communion in mutual psychosexual fulfillment with a person of the opposite sex.

Indeed, this institution, marriage, fulfills supremely the demands of authentic love. Therefore, it is not self-enclosed but fertile; it is not divisible among several persons but is one; it is not limited in time and subject to changes in the feelings of its protagonists but is indissoluble.

It is important to stress two points immediately. First, the indissolubility of the marital bond does not appear—within this system—as a merely legal obligation, imposed externally by the will of the legislator. Rather, it corresponds to the deepest demands of authentic love, which can only be a gift of self that is total and, therefore, forever. This truth demonstrates the artificiality—and also the objective falsity—of the antithesis between the demands of love and the demands of the juridical institution of marriage, which unfortunately is rather widespread in the common culture of Western nations.

105

Second, it should be noted that, because of its origin in the natural law, indissolubility is a characteristic of every valid marriage, even one that is not sacramental. The Church indeed respects the will of God, and recognizes that perpetuity is inscribed within the natural institution of marriage; consequently, she maintains that this characteristic is proper to every true conjugal union.

Reformulating the foregoing statement in technical canonical terms, we must state that indissolubility is an "essential property" of marriage, as canon 1056 of the Code puts it—a property that is per se characteristic of every valid marital union. Hence it acquires in sacramental marriage a particular binding force for the contracting parties, precisely because of the symbolic significance that Christian marriage has in relation to Christ's union with the Church. In other words, the sacramentality of marriage reinforces but is not ultimately the basis of the obligation to respect its indissolubility.

But what does the expression "essential property" mean? It was coined to indicate that in speaking about indissolubility we are considering not the very essence of marriage—which as a contract is consent (can. 1057 § 1), and as a state of life is the "partnership" of the spouses' whole life (can. 1055 § 1). Rather we are considering precisely one of its "properties", that is, a characteristic of marriage as a juridical bond. In other words, marriage is by its very nature perpetual. But what is implied by the description of this property, this characteristic, as "essential"? It means that this property, although not the essence of marriage, is nevertheless as a matter of principle so pertinent to marriage that marriage cannot, again as a matter of principle, exist without it. In principle, marriage is indissoluble, and although affection and even the common life between the spouses can in fact diminish, the juridical relationship that binds them specifically as spouses cannot diminish.

As a result, acceptance of the indissoluble bond must be at least implicit in matrimonial consent, in other words, in the intention to marry. This acceptance is indeed nothing other than one aspect of the will to contract a true marriage. In contrast, whenever this property is negated or rejected as a matter of principle for one's own marriage and by a true act of the will, the matrimonial consent itself would as a result be defective, inasmuch as it would come to be directed toward an object that is not true marriage—marriage, that is, as understood in canon law (cf. can. 1101 § 2).

It is appropriate, however, at this point to make some clarifications and to examine this concept in greater depth.

We will not dwell here on an explanation of the concept of "positive act of the will", inasmuch as we already discussed it at length within the context of the general introduction concerning the phenomenon of simulation of matrimonial consent. We merely recall that it must be a true decision of the subject. This would not be the case, for example, with a simple anticipation ("I fear that my marriage will end badly and that we will first separate and then divorce") or an erroneous opinion about the subject of marriage ("In my opinion, it is right that a marriage of two spouses who seriously and permanently disagree should be dissolved, for example, by civil divorce"), inasmuch as these mental states pertain to the intellectual faculty of the person and are not necessarily operating on the level of the will.

The second example just mentioned (involving the erroneous opinion about the dissolubility of marriage in certain cases) prompts us to confront immediately a very delicate topic, related to what we might call the subjective aspect of simulation—the topic of the relevance of error in the matrimonial intention. By "error" we mean here an objectively erroneous idea, a mistake concerning the subject of marriage, obviously from the perspective of canon law. This might be, for instance, the idea of someone who maintained that it was appropriate and licit on occasion to dissolve the bond through recourse to civil authority or even through one's own autonomous decision that is not otherwise made in an official way.

The canon law of marriage on this point, based on the distinction between intellect and will and, above all, on the principle that consensus as an act of the will is the efficient cause of marriage, still takes the following stance regarding error—error is a state of the intellect, a false judgment that belongs to the sphere of knowledge and understanding. Therefore, as such, it does not necessarily influence the faculty of the will, and as long as it does not, it remains juridically irrelevant, since among other things it relates, in the present case, not to the essence but to one characteristic of the juridical institution. This is the chief provision of canon 1099, which defines the irrelevance of error relative to the properties of marriage (unity and indissolubility) and to its sacramental dignity. This is the case of error of law.

To give a concrete example: as a matter of principle Thomas might be convinced of the appropriateness of dissolving failed marriages. One could not by that very fact mechanically conclude, however, that he necessarily wants his own marriage with Kay to be dissoluble also, since he loves her and desires to have her as his wife for the rest of his life.

While still essentially reiterating this traditional position, canonical doctrine and jurisprudence do not forget, however, either the unity of the human person (the functions of his spiritual activity—for instance, the intellect and the will—can be distinguished but not rigidly separated) or the concrete psychological dynamism of personal decisions, whereby normally the person is led to decide in a way consistent with his own convictions, even if they are objectively erroneous. Therefore, the law itself, in canon 1099, foresees the possibility of a determination of the will caused by error, which therefore becomes operative, that is, it becomes the principle of the decision-making and action of the subject, who chooses and acts according to his own convictions.

It is clear that the reason for the possible nullity of marriage is the will, the subject's decision, and that the error serves as the ideological basis for the exercise of the will itself in a definite direction. It is just as true, however, that—according to a dictum that has become common nowadays in scholarship and jurisprudence—the more deeply rooted and obstinate the error is, the more likely also is its influence on the will and on the subject's decisions. And so, proof of this type of deep-seated error has become a common circumstantial element in the proof of simulation. This type of error is indeed a personal circumstance consistent with this hypothesis, in more technical language it is a "cause", a motive, of simulation.

To illustrate this even more clearly with a new example: a person who is radical in his education and opinions, a convinced proponent of divorce, who was even publicly active in favor of keeping the law on divorce during the 1974 referendum campaign in Italy, has a very strong "cause", a conceptual motive to reject indissoluble marriage. This cause, this ideological and cultural motive, will be much weaker, in contrast, in a noncommittal young man who passively goes along with the common mindset and maintains that divorce is now an everyday occurrence and declares himself in favor of it only so as not to appear old-fashioned. The conceptual depth of his erroneous conviction is much more superficial and, as such, less strongly oriented to guide the will in practice.

A will that is contrary to the indissolubility of the bond yet still "positive" in the technical sense, can—as is commonly taught—assume various forms. It can be explicit or implicit, absolute or conditional (i.e., possible). Let us clarify these concepts.

The will is explicit if it has as its direct object the rejection of the indissolubility of the bond: "I reject the perpetual tie with this person". It is implicit if this rejection is contained in a choice logically contrary to the acceptance of indissoluble marriage: "If my marriage with this person has a negative outcome, I will consider myself released from any obligation toward him, intending thereby to become completely free again to start a new loving relationship and family."

The will is absolute when—especially because of an ideological or cultural motivation such as the ones cited in the examples above—as a matter of principle it opposes the indissolubility of the marital bond: "I will never accept being tied down forever, which in my opinion is unthinkable and unacceptable in human affairs." The will is, on the other hand, possible or conditional when, although there are no reasons in principle contrary to the perpetual bond, there is, however, fear of a bad outcome of the marriage and therefore a desire to have a way out: "If things go badly, we will take our freedom back, we will unfasten the marital tie, and each one will be free to start a new life." This last-mentioned conditional form of exclusion of indissolubility is one of the most widespread. Indeed, as jurisprudence astutely emphasizes, a person who excludes the indissolubility of marriage does not per se desire the failure of his marriage but intends only to protect himself with regard to that possibility.

These last points lead us to consider briefly also the objective aspect of exclusion of the indissolubility of marriage.

The proper object of this exclusion is precisely the element of indissolubility, that is, the fact that the bond cannot be dissolved, neither by the two contracting parties (intrinsic indissolubility) nor by any human authority (extrinsic indissolubility). Indeed, it is well known that the two cases of the dissolution of marriage allowed by canon law as being referable to the action of an authority external to the spouses—the case of a nonconsummated marriage and the case of a nonsacramental marriage—are reserved to the Pope and justified by reason of his authority, not as head of the Church, Bishop of Rome, and successor of Peter, but as Vicar of Christ, an authority that is in fact more than human.

Therefore, the desire for a possible dissolution of the bond is the specific content of the exclusion of indissolubility. It is very important to focus on this, both from a substantive perspective, for the purpose of being able to discern what cases truly embody an invalidating exclusion, and also from a probative perspective. Indeed, although one cannot expect from everyone an exposition in legal terms of their own matrimonial intentions, it will be the responsibility of the judge (and possibly, even before that, of the counselor) to examine, through the words and concepts used by the parties and witnesses, what was actually willed by the one who is accused or who accuses himself of having simulated marriage by excluding its indissolubility.

To give a few examples: a party in a cause who said, "I was not thinking about the indissolubility of marriage", or "I did not believe in the indissolubility of marriage", or even "In case our marriage ever failed, we would separate", would express—barring further specifications—concepts that are too generic to prove any simulation. Indeed, someone who does not think about something cannot make a decision contrary to it. Someone who does not believe in indissolubility remains in the realm of mere error (unless there are further indications). And someone who thinks about separation intends per se the cessation of common life, without saying anything about the fate of the conjugal bond.

One must not stop at the surface of the words. Generic expressions may reveal that, in the specific case, it was a matter not of true exclusion of indissolubility but of intentions that only resembled it without being such. It will be the judge's task, without forcing the matter, to seek to understand what the subject really intended by helping him to make the necessary clarifications. Thus, even expressions that generally would lead one to think of a true exclusion of indissolubility, such as, "If it goes badly, I will break it off completely", "Each one will go his own way", "We will be free again as before", "I will look for another spouse", and the like, require prudent further investigation and a more precise formulation.

It therefore follows that the presumption of being able to break the bond is what constitutes the exclusion of indissolubility, but not the possible means that one thinks of using to bring about and to sanction the breakup. Hence, the fact that the interested party knew the legal possibilities for breaking the bond and planned them, for example, by speaking about a possible civil divorce, does not represent the substance of simulation but is only an indication or circumstantial evidence in favor of it actually having happened. The intention to dissolve the marital bond—in other words, not to commit oneself permanently at the wedding—is what brings about the exclusion of indissolubility, even if the subject did not plan a legal way to end the marriage. Thus, even the pact against indissolubility, that is, the previous agreement between the two contracting parties not to commit themselves permanently and to reserve for themselves the option to dissolve the bond between them, is for canon law only a circumstance that makes the case clearer and the proof easier and is not itself the substance of the fact of simulation.

We can now move on to some guidelines concerning the proof of exclusion of indissolubility.

As already mentioned in the introduction on simulation, in practice there is a traditional format for framing proofs, which revolves around verbal and nonverbal manifestations of the will. It is precisely the will that has to be reconstructed, insofar as it was or was not opposed—at the moment of the wedding—to the indissolubility of the marital commitment.

The direct reconstruction of the will results from the statements by the parties and by the witnesses referring to their verbal manifestations. Besides the general rules for the evaluation of the statements of the parties and of the witnesses (e.g., concerning their reliability, the time, and the source of their information), we should stress in this specific case the need, already mentioned, to have them explain as accurately as possible the concepts and the words that they used or heard, so as to enable the counselor to identify more precisely whether it is a true exclusion or only something resembling it without formally being such (an error, for example; a fearful anticipation; a wish or a boast; a series of random statements; etc.)

An indirect reconstruction of the will consists of the evidence and circumstances useful for the case. Among the elements of the indirect reconstruction the following can have a particular probative weight in matters of exclusion of indissolubility:

- The religious and matrimonial convictions of the subject who is said to have excluded indissolubility. The stronger the subject's convictions in religious and marital matters and the more they correspond to Catholic teaching, the more improbable becomes the rejection of an essential characteristic of Christian marriage, and vice versa. In fact, it is erroneous convictions about religion and marriage that can be a basic element, a remote "cause" or motive for simulation.

- The more proximate motives for the particular marriage. Unless the motives connected with the culture and ideological convictions are particularly well developed, then these more proximate motives will have to be investigated and discovered: for example, prenuptial doubts, uncertainties, and hesitations, or else quarrels and breakups during the engagement, that make it appear likely that the subject had tried to protect himself from marital failure that was foreseen and feared. In this sense, the family backgrounds of the parties (e.g., the marital histories of the parents, siblings, and friends) may be a proximate occasion for the development of an intention to simulate.

- Resistance to a religious celebration of marriage or the proposal of a civil ceremony. This can also have circumstantial significance, because indissolubility—being founded, initially on the natural law— is a characteristic of marriage that now, as a matter of fact, requires for its acceptance some religious motivation, which the Catholic rite objectively expresses as being present in the subject or at least to some extent allows us to presume. Also the choice of a civil union indicates, at least generically, openness to an institutionally dissoluble marital union.

- Finally, how the party reacted to the marital difficulties, especially when the alleged simulator became aware of the impossibility of overcoming the difficulties and of the uselessness of any attempt to salvage the marriage. The subject's attitude in such predicaments often sheds considerable light on his real will at the moment of the marriage ceremony, either confirming or denying what he said in his deposition or to the witnesses outside of the judicial forum.

Guide for the counselor

With these considerations in mind, a pastor of souls or an advisor of persons in marital difficulties who wants to investigate the possibility of an exclusion of the indissolubility of the bond, would have to inquire at least summarily about the following points:

1. The religious convictions of the person said to have excluded the perpetual commitment in marriage. As already mentioned, it is less probable that a practicing Catholic would have simulated a sacrament, whereas there is less logical difficulty with the fact that a person with fewer religious convictions might have excluded it.

2. The matrimonial convictions of the alleged simulator. For example, did he favor divorce? Had he ever commented on the marital situations of friends, relatives, or acquaintances, approving possible separations and divorces? Did he militantly support or sympathize with cultural and political movements that regard divorce as a right and a sign of civilization? Possible well-rooted convictions in the subject contrary to Catholic doctrine are a "remote" or background motive for simulation, and if rigorously and consistently held, can become the principal motive.

3. How the prenuptial relationship went. In particular, were there break-ups, difficulties, quarrels? Did the reasons for the difficulties still exist at the time of the wedding, or had they been overcome—at least in the judgment of the engaged couple?

4. Whether one or both of the parties, because of circumstances mentioned in point three, have doubts, fears, worries, or other reasons for uneasiness? Were they intense and unresolved at the moment of the wedding and possibly a cause of simulation? As jurisprudence teaches, these doubts or fears must be assessed subjectively, that is, in relation to the subject and to his specific characteristics, whether temperamental or having to do with his social and familial setting. Even though it seems excessive to "deduce" simulation from a consideration of the personality of interested persons, it is necessary to acknowledge that facts having to do with character, culture, and family can contribute invaluable circumstantial evidence to verify or disprove the alleged simulation.

5. Whether the alleged simulator is willing to admit in the judicial forum his own simulation and in what terms. Within the context of an advisory session, it will be necessary to seek to clarify as much as possible what the subject really intended concerning the perpetuity of his own marital commitment, before encouraging canonical causes that, after a more careful inquiry with the party directly interested, might then prove to be without any foundation whatsoever, either because he had never really decided to break the marital bond, or because he had decided to do so but only after the wedding, when faced with the actual failure of the union.

6. Whether there is any possibility of directly verifying the alleged simulator's intention to exclude the perpetuity of the marital bond, or whether the other spouse and other possible witnesses know about that intention and are willing to confirm it. As everyone knows, what counts is not the number of witnesses but rather their quality—a quality that depends on the time of their information, on its source, on the depth of their testimony, on the confirmation that it may receive from other witnesses from objective circumstances, and on the personal trustworthiness in general of the witness.

7. Whether—while hypothetically excluding the essential property of indissolubility—the subject celebrated the canonical marriage. Did he do so willingly or of necessity? Did he propose a civil union or even free cohabitation (which are possible signs of the intention to try to bind oneself less strictly than with the indissoluble bond of canonically valid marriage)?

8. Whether a canonical marriage was attempted while in theory excluding indissolubility because of love for the other party. The presence of love is indeed sometimes presented as a possible obstacle to the exclusion of indissolubility, with an argument of this sort: someone who loves a person wants to have that person with him always, and therefore it is not credible that he should exclude indissolubility. This reasoning, however, appears to be only partly true and cannot be the basis for a general presumption. Quite realistically, jurisprudence invites us to consider what type of love motivated the subject to seek marriage. Mere erotic and sentimental attraction, for example, which is intense but transient, is not a major obstacle that would render an ex-

clusion of indissolubility implausible. A much greater obstacle, on the other hand, would be love understood in a Christian way as self-giving, which is dedicated to the well-being of the other and of children, even in misfortune and with the waning of emotions. The counselor should investigate, therefore, what type of love there was in the case of the person seeking advice regarding a declaration of nullity.

9. Whether any children were born of the marital union. It is true that the parent-child relationship and the relationship between spouses are formally different realities, at least on the strictly juridical level, and that to dissolve one's marriage does not mean to dissolve the legal and emotional relations with one's children. It is equally true, however, that ordinarily having children also means strengthening in some way the bond with the fellow parent as well. The presence of several children, perhaps even spaced several years apart from each other, is therefore an element to be weighed carefully in its causes and explanations, since in itself it appears to be a sign that is generally contrary to the rejection of a future commitment to the point of not accepting its perpetuity.

10. How the subject who is said to have excluded the indissolubility of the marriage behaved when confronted with marital difficulties. A rapid disengagement and the choice of the easiest solution—separation and either de facto or civil dissolution of the bond—is an indication in favor of simulation, especially if the disengagement was unilateral and occurred in contrast to the goodwill of the other spouse, who would still have liked to try to fix the problems of their married life. On the other hand, even attempts by the spouses to overcome difficulties and to continue their common life are not in themselves an indication that is absolutely contrary to simulation. Indeed, as jurisprudence now commonly maintains, the exclusion of indissolubility occurs most often not out of a desire for its practical application but only as a precaution when there is fear that a marriage might fail, whereas per se the parties want it to be lifelong. It happens therefore not as a *casus desiderium* (desire for the breakup of the marriage) but as a *casus cautio* (precaution with regard to the feared breakup of the marriage).

Examples

First example

Ralph was a young man from a distinguished family, a well-educated gentleman with a sensitive character that was perhaps a bit weak. For many years—while he was a secondary school and university student —he socialized and even went on vacations with a classmate, Clare, who was also from a distinguished family and who was an extremely intelligent person with an iron will. The almost-daily association of these two young people, extending over a ten-year period, led almost automatically to their marriage, which they celebrated just a few weeks after they both graduated. Their married life lasted more than twenty years, and the interested parties had two children by agreement, to whom they gave every sign of being lovingly dedicated. Around twenty-four years after their wedding, by Ralph's unilateral decision (at the time he was seeing another woman), their married life together came to an end.

In order to explain and perhaps also to regularize his new situation, Ralph accused himself of having excluded from his own matrimonial consent the indissolubility of the bond, since even before the wedding he had noticed Clare's very strong and domineering character, and fearing an unhappy outcome of their union, he desired to have an "escape route" from it.

Ralph also called several witnesses, in particular two who confirmed that his intention had been such, as well as others who reported the habitually brusque way in which Clare, albeit involuntarily, treated Ralph even before their wedding, and who testified to the unease that it caused him. The evidence adduced by Ralph was considered insufficient, however, for the following reasons:

It seemed odd to the judges that the two witnesses who were informed about the exclusion of indissolubility on Ralph's part were persons with whom he had dealt rather infrequently, whereas nothing about such an intention was known to the many friends and acquaintances who gave depositions and with whom Ralph and Clare had had rather frequent contact. Without calling into doubt the good faith of Ralph and the witnesses, the judges explained these statements as random remarks that were made in particular contexts but did not prove a true and well-formed decision on Ralph's part. One of the witnesses was in fact having marital difficulties at the time and spoke about it with Ralph, which probably affected the way in which he expressed himself. Ralph himself no longer had any recollection of his own statements to the other witness, which was evidence that they expressed a feeling of momentary fear about his future marriage but not a true and proper decision not to commit himself permanently.

In the second place, Clare, who was vehemently opposed to a declaration of nullity, succeeded in forcefully reassessing the evidence of Ralph's prenuptial doubts and hesitation. The witnesses who reported her decisive ways and his resentment were also proved to have associated with the parties for brief periods when the wedding was still far off, whereas the friends with whom they usually studied and vacationed knew nothing about any uncertainty or unease on Ralph's part.

Finally, the fact that Ralph had continued their married life for so long, in spite of his statement that Clare's character had always been the same—that is, harsh and willful—even in the early days of the marriage; the fact that he had positively sought to have children, and never more so than in the very first years of their marriage; the fact that the end of their life together occurred not as a consequence of the reservations that Ralph purportedly had about his own consent (in other words, relative to Clare's character) but as a result of his relations with another woman—the judges considered these facts to be circumstances too inconsistent with an allegation of simulation for it to be deemed morally certain, notwithstanding Ralph's statements to the tribunal and the corroboration of the aforementioned witnesses.

The example is meant to recall the necessity, which is commonly emphasized by jurisprudence, of examining thoroughly the circumstances of a case. It is not enough that one element of proof seems to exist (in Ralph's case, the direct proof). It is also necessary to examine the effective weight of these probatory elements and their consistency with the overall course of the sequence of events. Clearly it will be possible to make a conclusive examination on these points only upon completing the instruction. Within the context of counseling, however, a careful hearing of the case will already allow any contradictory and problematic elements emerge early on. The counselor can then invite the parties to reflect more carefully and deeply on their situation and possibly avoid initiating proceedings that would serve only to cause additional pain, besides the sorrow resulting from the failure of a marriage of persons who are otherwise dignified and respectable.

Second example

Philip, a young factory worker, and Catherine, also a factory worker, became acquainted and dated for several years. Philip had a very pragmatic mindset that was focused above all on appreciating the most concrete and material aspects of life. Catherine, who had a good character and was sincerely in love, accepted Philip as he was and wanted to marry him.

Philip was more or less dragged into marriage. He was doubtful and not very enthusiastic, mainly because he had had to change his place of work and found himself in a factory larger than the first small rural plant, and now with other female colleagues to whom he was strongly attracted. He was especially attracted to one of the women, whom he began to spend time with regularly on the pretext of discussing labor union–related questions with her.

The pragmatic Philip did not fail to let others know about his lack of enthusiasm for marrying Catherine, both in his external attitudes and also in conversations in which he shamelessly declared that, if he had found some girl who had "turned his head", he would not have hesitated to leave Catherine and get married to the other. Reliable witnesses gave detailed reports to the tribunal of these expressions of Philip's.

During the course of their married life, Philip emphasized his disinterest in Catherine: never any sign of affection for her, little time spent at home, and many selfish demands with regard to their intimate relations. After only five months of marriage, without any serious reason and out of mere distaste for the minimal demands of married life, Philip unilaterally abandoned Catherine. On that occasion Philip manifested his contempt for his wife and for the matrimonial bond. Catherine in fact went into the hospital after experiencing the miscarriage of an early pregnancy, which Philip had not desired or expressed any interest in. On that occasion too he followed his instinct and desire for a freer, less committed life than the one that the submissive, affectionate Catherine already allowed him to lead.

The example emphasizes both the importance of considering the personality of the subject who allegedly simulated consent, since the chief cause for rejecting the conjugal bond may reside in his mentality (in this case, Philip's pragmatic selfishness), and also the importance attributed to the subject's behavior after the wedding, especially his attitude with regard to the seriousness of the marital bond. Obvious contempt for marriage a few months after the wedding, without the appearance of any serious reason for separating that could be ascribed to the other spouse, is evidence of the rejection of an indissoluble commitment in the marital bond.

Third example

Gerard was a young judge in a lower appellate court in the Republic of Italy, far from his native region. He was from a militantly secularist family and, before his appointment to the judiciary, had been politically active in the administration of a leftist party.

In the city where he worked he became acquainted with Laura, a very religious young woman. Gerard respected her religiosity but did not share it, since it did not correspond to his way of thinking and his upbringing.

The two joined in marriage at Laura's initiative; she wanted a religious wedding. Gerard agreed so as to please his fiancée but decided to accept only those aspects of the marriage that were in keeping with his cultural and civil convictions.

It should be noted, in particular, that the marriage of Gerard and Laura took place in 1970, when it was already certain that a law introducing the possibility of divorce in Italy would be approved, even for marriages whose civil effects were regulated by the concordat between Italy and the Holy See. Gerard knew the juridical and parliamentary terms of the problem and openly professed his support of divorce, not only as a legal institution that he generally considered to be positive because of its social effects, but also as a possibility and an option for himself. Gerard even declared this to colleagues with whom he discussed his forthcoming marriage.

Having expressed his conviction in words even before his wedding, Gerard had occasion to demonstrate its practical importance afterward. He became impatient with the married state, despite the fact that his wife tried to be agreeable in every way, for example, by acquiescing in a move to her husband's native region when Gerard decided to return there. In contrast, Gerard showed no consideration for his wife's aspirations, even opposing her desire to have children and, after only a few years of life together, starting a persistent effort to persuade her to accept the prospect of separation.

No sooner had the law gone into effect than Gerard resorted to civil divorce, after which he entered into a merely civil marriage with another woman.

Some years after the separation, Laura initiated a canonical process, and in his canonical deposition Gerard admitted the parameters that he had tried to set for his marriage. The judge believed him not only because of the direct testimony confirming them but also because they were consistent with Gerard's overall ideas in marital matters. His secularist view of life, his explicit support of divorce that was about to be introduced in Italy, and his knowledge of the juridical terms of the problem were considered evidence capable of demonstrating the presence in Gerard's mind of a deep-seated error in marital matters, such as would have prompted his will to adhere to only those aspects of the institution of marriage that he shared, therefore excluding, in particular, indissolubility.

The example is meant to illustrate the possible force, at least in some cases, of a deep-rooted and culturally reinforced mentality contrary to indissolubility, such that this mentality becomes an operative principle of the will in excluding from its own object anything that is inconsistent with one's own convictions. This error—for it to have an import indicative of a reason for excluding indissolubility—must be proved as morally certain. In Gerard's case—in light of his profession and the historical context—the error was real and deep-seated. It will be the task of the counselor in marriage cases of the lay faithful to discern when this error really is such, or on the contrary whether it is merely an expression of superficiality, boasting, or shallow conformity to the current mentality.

Fourth example

The last example means to illustrate once again the substantive and probative role of the cause of the simulation, showing that the cause can also combine the elements observed in the second and third examples: on the one hand, superficiality and selfishness, and on the other hand, motives of an ideological character.

Luke and Kathy were two young sixties radicals, adolescent rebels —in word, not in deed, of course—against "bourgeois" institutions and conventions. In reality, they lived off the wealth of their respective families while their own relationship was one of great liberty (from the moral perspective), in the sense not only that they had become accustomed to complete intimacy with one another but also that each recognized the other's "right" to have amorous and sexual "experiences" with third persons.

Their idea was to continue their relationship in that way, merely adding cohabitation to it, since they wanted to spend a certain period of time together abroad. They ruled out a civil union as well, which to their way of thinking was also contrary to "free love".

So as to be able to live in peace with their families, who were of a traditional mindset, and perhaps especially in order to benefit from their economic assistance, for the purpose of traveling abroad, Luke and Kathy made plans to be married in church, making no secret (not even to the pastor who was competent to authorize their wedding) of the fact that the religious ceremony was for them an empty formality and that they did not intend to renounce their mentality and their lifestyle.

Their intention was later proved not only by their brazen attitude toward the nuptial rite but also and most importantly by the way that they actually lived their married life, which was manifestly liberated from any bond and ended rather quickly when each went off with another partner. As a whole, the evidence gathered led the judges to recognize that the juridically relevant aspect rejected by Luke and Kathy in contracting marriage was specifically the aspect of a binding, lasting commitment. Perhaps other aspects of their consent could have been called into question as well, but—based on the proven facts and the remarks reported by the witnesses—the rejection of a definitive commitment to the spouse emerged from the sad incident as the more specifically relevant factor.

VII

Exclusion of Fidelity

Elements of substantive law

It is not as simple as it might appear at first glance to determine what the actual object is of this further possible form of simulation of consent. Traditionally, it was designated overall as *bonum fidei*, a term going right back to the reflections of Saint Augustine on marriage. But exactly what is to be understood by this expression?

Contemporary canonical scholarship has maintained for some time now that the concept of *bonum fidei* coincides with the concept of "unity of marriage", which is said to be an "essential property" of the very institution of marriage. The unity of marriage is treated in canon 1013 §2 of the 1917 Code and in canon 1056 of the present Code. This property of marriage implies that, for one and the same person, several matrimonial bonds cannot exist at the same time. The consequence of this interpretation that identified *bonum fidei* and unity of marriage is that a marriage was considered null if the unity of marriage was excluded, through an intention to institute a spousal relationship with a third person different from the spouse.

This interpretation was reinforced by a strict exegesis of canon 1081 §2 of the 1917 Code, which stated that the object of matrimonial consent consisted of the "perpetual and exclusive right over the body [*ius in corpus*], for acts that are in themselves suitable for the generation of children". As a result of this clear legislative definition, it was concluded that someone who promises to another person, other than the spouse, the right to these acts ordered to procreation violates the good of fidelity.

In this interpretation of the concept of *bonum fidei*, the intention to violate conjugal fidelity, by having sexual relations with other persons (whether or not the relations are ordered to procreation, for example, in the case of homosexual relations), had no juridical relevance with regard to the nullity of matrimonial consent, since it was not the concession to a third party of the right to sexual acts ordered to procreation but was rather a mere abuse with respect to that right which was also conceded to the spouse. To put it more succinctly, the positive will to violate fidelity was not a motive of matrimonial nullity.

This juridical interpretation began to be called into question in the early 1960s. Several rotal decisions pointed out that from a practical perspective—in the real world—someone who excludes the *bonum fidei* does not do so, at least not normally, in order to take on new obligations, in this instance, to make a commitment to a third party different from the spouse to engage with her (or him) in acts ordered to procreation. On the contrary, he does so in order to liberate himself from an obligation, the duty of being faithful to his spouse, with a view to indulging in a disordered exercise of his sexuality. Also called into question was the exegesis of paragraph 2 of canon 1081 of the 1917 Code, from which it was inferred that the possible object of the simulation against the *bonum fidei* was solely the granting to third parties of the right to acts that are in themselves suitable for the generation of children. This right, canonists began to remark, was defined by the norm as perpetual and exclusive. A violation of its exclusivity could therefore be relevant, whenever it could be interpreted not as a mere abuse in fact but rather as a denial in principle of the exclusive character of that right. Fidelity, therefore—that is, the obligation to abstain from sexual relations with persons other than the spouse—could be the object of a simulation of consent that renders the marriage null, if it is denied as a matter of principle or if, through its prearranged violation, the result is a denial of the exclusivity of the right (which belongs to the spouse alone) to acts ordered to procreation.

Rotal jurisprudence of the last two decades [approximately 1977–1997] has arrived at a position that can be considered usual in this connection: not only does someone who intends to grant to others besides the spouse the right to acts that are per se suited to procreation commit a simulation of matrimonial consent, but so does someone who excludes the exclusivity of this right, claiming the option to engage in sexual relations with other persons besides the spouse.

Solely by way of example we can cite in translation[1] the words of a decision of the Roman Rota. After recalling the conciliar teaching that

---

[1] From the original Latin via Italian.

the intimate union resulting from the mutual self-gift of the spouses and also the good of offspring demand the spouses' total fidelity,[2] the decision states, "Today the distinction between the exclusion of the *bonum fidei* and the exclusion of unity is clear: the first implies the denial of the exclusive right to conjugal acts relative to the spouse, while the other intends to grant it to other persons."[3]

This interpretation is defensible also in light of the Code of Canon Law currently in force. It is true that the object of consent is described differently now as opposed to the time of the 1917 Code, that is, as the gift of themselves that the bride and groom present to one another for the purpose of establishing the marital bond between them (cf. can. 1057 §2), but it is also true that the perpetual and exclusive right to acts that are in themselves suitable for the generation of children must be included in the essential object of the consent, as a technical-juridical formality that brings about the conjugal gift of self. To put it more simply: In what exactly is the conjugal (spousal) gift of self manifested? It is achieved through (or at least also through) the pledge to make oneself available to the spouse—and only to him—for those acts that are in themselves suited to the procreation of children. Someone who wants to pledge to make himself available perpetually and exclusively for these acts with a third person (thereby excluding the "unity" of the marriage), and who claims in principle the authority not to observe the duty resulting from the exclusivity of that right (thereby excluding conjugal "fidelity"), gives not true matrimonial consent but rather an intrinsically defective consent that therefore does not give rise to the matrimonial bond.

This jurisprudential development has objectively contributed to a clearer conceptual distinction between the unity of marriage and the duty of fidelity; however, it must be noted that several questions still remain open.

In the first place, and from the perspective of terminology, when speaking about the *bonum fidei* one must carefully distinguish which aspect one means to refer to: the unity of marriage or the duty to respect the commitment to spousal fidelity. The above-cited rotal decision seems to try to reduce the expression *bonum fidei* to fidelity, but an unambiguous usage in this connection has not yet been established.

---

[2] *Gaudium et spes*, 48.

[3] *Coram* Colagiovanni, February 2, 1988, *Decisiones seu sententiae* 80: 61.

In the second place, it is necessary to recall that the 1983 Code, in a manner altogether consistent with the preceding tradition, reserves per se the description of "essential property" of marriage to unity, as can clearly be inferred from canon 1056. The exclusion, by a positive act of will, of an essential property then produces the defect of the consent and the nullity of the bond (cf. can. 1101 §2). Can the duty of fidelity also be described as an essential property of marriage? This problem has not been examined in depth, also because it does not have much practical relevance. Jurisprudence appears essentially to consider unity and fidelity as two aspects of the concept of *bonum fidei.*

This problem is mentioned in order to point out an interesting reflection. Some have proposed considering the duty of conjugal fidelity, not as an "essential property" of marriage, but rather as an "essential element"—the exclusion of which would also produce the nullity of the bond according to the precept of canon 1101 §2—which is to be understood as a juridical obligation that can be related to the broader concept of "the good of the spouses" described in canon 1055 §1. This proposal is said to have two undeniable advantages: (1) it applies more clearly the conceptual distinction between unity of marriage, which is strictly speaking an essential property, and the duty of fidelity; (2) it contributes at least in part to specifying the content of the concept of the "good of the spouses", which has not yet been univocally clarified by jurisprudence and by canonical scholarship in its juridically essential and requisite aspects. On the other hand, there seem to be no obvious theoretical contraindications to considering the duty of conjugal fidelity as an "essential element" of marriage from the perspective of the juridical obligation. It is necessary to say, however, that this proposal is still a minority opinion and still has to be taken into serious consideration by jurisprudence and by canonical scholarship. For practical purposes, however, the systematic classification of the juridical duty of conjugal fidelity among the essential elements or properties of marriage produces no obstacles to the administration of justice.

A third problem—one of greater importance—remains to be dealt with. What exactly should be understood by "spousal fidelity"? And when does relevant violation of the exclusivity of the spouse's right occur? Understandably, the problem is of fundamental importance. Let us look at a few examples. Assuming the unity of the marriage (in other words, the subject does not intend to grant to others the right to acts in themselves suited to procreation, or in practice to institute several spousal bonds simultaneously), does someone exclude fidelity and nothing else if he claims the right to have heterosexual relations that are in themselves ordered to procreation? What about someone who wanted to have heterosexual relations while excluding their orientation to procreation? Or someone who claimed the right to have homosexual relations? It is easy to see how delicate the question is and how extremely relevant its practical consequences are.

Any attempt to formulate a solution must keep in mind the way in which the current legislation defines the object of matrimonial consent. Canon 1057 §2 of the Code defines it as the gift of self for the purpose of establishing the marriage. Surely this object includes within it, as an essential and defining element, the perpetual and exclusive right to acts that are in themselves ordered to procreation. However, since the legislator used a different way of expressing himself to indicate the object of consent, we must conclude that—while not intending to deny the definition previously in force—he wanted to present this object of the conjugal covenant in a more complete way, in reference to conciliar teaching. In this sense, authoritative jurisprudence and canonical scholarship have held that they could reformulate the contents of the object of matrimonial consent in terms of a "perpetual and exclusive right to the conjugal partnership of life". Part of this conjugal communion would be the sexual dimension, as availability for the gift of self by means of the perpetual and exclusive gift to the spouse of one's own genital sexuality, which naturally is to be exercised in keeping with nature and morality. A mental reservation allowing one to violate the exclusivity of that availability, by heterosexual relations even if they are not ordered to procreation, or else by homosexual relations, would be contrary to the object of the conjugal covenant and therefore would be a defect of consent—if intended, of course, with a positive act of the will. Can these instances therefore be classified as a violation of conjugal fidelity? This is, perhaps, more easily the case in the first scenario (the will to reserve for oneself the right to heterosexual relations, even though they may not be ordered to procreation), inasmuch as jurisprudence does not seem to distinguish what type of relations (whether or not they may be fertile) the party who allegedly excluded fidelity intended to have with one or more persons other than the spouse. The second case (the will to reserve for oneself the right to have homosexual relations) could be classified as a violation but less easily, inasmuch as it is not directly opposed to the gift of conjugal sexuality, which is by definition heterosexual. Such a scenario perhaps could more pertinently be classified as the exclusion of the "good of the spouses", a concept that would have to include the possibility of a minimal respect for the person of the spouse (to which the hypothesis of the mental reservation just considered would be contrary). Alternatively, it could be regarded as a case of psychological incapacity for marriage—either from the perspective of the act of consent (can. 1095, 2°) or with regard to the ability to fulfill the essential obligations of marriage (can. 1095, 3°)—since one would at least have to take into consideration the possibility that someone who claimed that he could continue to be a practicing homosexual after marrying might be suffering from a personality disorder or from a sexual disturbance so serious as to satisfy the canonical requirements for such forms of incapacity.

We must also recall, as another principle of substantive law, that—like any simulation of consent in canon law—a simulation that is possibly contrary to the unity-fidelity of marriage, in order truly to be such, must be committed with a positive act of will. What these words mean was already explained (in chapter 4), and therefore we do not need to dwell further on the subject here. It should just be recalled that the act of will simulating matrimonial consent may be either explicit or implicit. If explicit, it will be directly opposed to the principles of unity or fidelity in marriage (e.g., "I refuse in principle to accept a limit to my freedom in emotional and sexual matters, and I consider myself free to see one specific partner or several for this purpose"). If implicit, it will be directed toward an object that logically implies the rejection of the exclusive commitment to the spouse (e.g., "I am marrying Paula, but I do not want to give up my relationship with Catherine, and I also intend to continue it regardless of the wedding that I am about to celebrate with Paula").

Finally, as for the proof of an exclusion of the *bonum fidei* (in the two senses of the expression that have been identified), the traditional scheme is helpful: The principal object of the proof—in other words, the act of will contrary to the specific marital/spousal obligation—can be reconstructed either directly or indirectly. Direct reconstruction is through the words of the alleged simulator in the judicial forum, but most importantly, those he said outside of it and at a time as close as possible to the celebration of the wedding reported by well-informed, reliable witnesses. Indirect reconstruction is through the evidence and the circumstances that logically point to a true simulatory act of will on the part of the alleged simulator.

With respect to the evidential and circumstantial elements of proof, it seems appropriate to point out a few things that could prove to be very useful in the work of the pastoral counselor.

Fairly enough, canon law asserts that valid presumptions can be treated as evidence at trial only on the basis of certain and determinate facts connected with the matter of the dispute (cf. can. 1586). From this we must infer that—at trial—it will be necessary to verify in a precise manner what is asserted by the parties and witnesses. Concretely, to say that a man often betrayed his wife, without giving any other supporting information in terms of names, places, and the time of the alleged facts, so that the judge might duly verify the testimony, must be considered an irrelevant assertion as far as proof is concerned. So must reports of generic statements ("Everybody knew that he had other women") or baseless opinions without any factual justification ("If you ask me, that guy did not even think about being faithful to his wife"). The canonical consultant to couples in marital difficulties, knowing that the tribunal would have to ask the parties for these verifications, should examine, in the investigation before presenting a formal case, whether that would be possible, so as to avoid recommending a case devoid of proof.

We should also mention two types of situations, the probative value of which from the evidential perspective is often debated subtly and with various emphases: (1) multiple and occasional infidelities and (2) a stable relationship with a third person.

Very often, occasional infidelities, even if there are many of them, lead jurisprudence to make the presumption not of the exclusion of both unity and fidelity in the marriage but only of an abuse of the right granted to the spouse. Indeed, by distinguishing between the right and the exercise of that right, jurisprudence develops this line of reasoning: someone who occasionally fails to be faithful normally acknowledges the unity of his marriage and also the duty—as a matter of principle— of fidelity itself. It is only through weakness, bad upbringing, or the harmful influence of the culture or of companions, that he does not in fact respect those obligations, violating an obligation that he recognizes in itself and by which he knows that he is bound. This wise reflection is guided by human experience. It must not be forgotten, however, that this is a "simple" presumption developed by jurisprudence. In other words, it allows the direct proof of the contrary—that the person truly intended to deny the obligation of unity or fidelity, or of both, and not just to act abusively in violating them. In the second place, it is necessary to remember that—although the distinction between a right and its exercise is logical and traditional in jurisprudence and therefore should be preserved—it is difficult to imagine a right that is granted but constantly deprived of its use in practice. To put it more simply, there can be such massive abuses (quantitatively) of the duty, especially of fidelity, as to be evidence of a denial of the juridical obligation itself in that regard.

The evidential value to be attributed to a stable relationship existing at the moment of consent is debated in jurisprudence. This would be the case of someone who said, "I am marrying Paula, but I want to continue and in fact am continuing my intimate relationship with Catherine." Some judges take this as decisive evidence, almost as full proof of an implicitly simulatory intention contrary to fidelity, if not altogether against unity. Others regard it as ambiguous evidence, to be considered very prudently. What can be said in this connection? Such a scenario is reminiscent—at least from the perspective of scholarship— of the interpretation that reduced the *bonum fidei* to the single essential property of the unity of marriage, inasmuch as it puts the spouse and the lover on the same level—as if this were realistic—from the perspective of granting acts that are in themselves ordered to procreation. Therefore, it is necessary to abide by the interpretation that reserves judgment on a case-by-case basis. It is not possible to declare with certainty that someone who has a mistress at the time of the marriage, and wants to keep her, is simulating against the *bonum fidei*. Although this fact appears to be relevant to a circumstantial proof of a simulation that is opposed at least to fidelity (in other words, a fact that makes one strongly suspect this exclusion), it normally needs other supporting evidence. Certainly, in such a case, the corroborating evidence does not have to be as strong as in a case in which there were no specific facts—such as an ongoing relationship on the side before and after the wedding—that could be linked to the party who claimed to have excluded fidelity.

Guide for the counselor

The pastor of souls or the advisor who places himself at the service of couples in difficulty with a view to a possible case of matrimonial nullity, whenever he finds himself in need of examining in greater depth a possibility of nullity connected with the *bonum fidei*, could pursue the following lines of investigation:

1. What was the party's lifestyle? Was he an individual who readily indulged in promiscuity and amorous flings? This is a personal circumstance of a general character that can nevertheless provide illuminating context.

2. What were his ideas on the subject of marriage? Did he accept the unity of marriage and the consequent obligation of fidelity? What may have been his reasons for unacceptable unchristian ideas on the subject? Is it possible to prove that he held such erroneous ideas (e.g., through persons who heard him express them)?

3. Was the subject faithful during the engagement? If not, what sort of relations did he establish? (Occasional flings? Stable relationships?) Is it possible to prove these facts? For example, is there an admission by the party and by the other persons involved; are there witnesses with detailed knowledge about the facts (names, dates, places); are there letters or other useful documents?

4. What intentions did the party have, as the wedding day approached, with regard to these flings and, more importantly, relationships? Particularly in the latter case, it is important to find out what arrangements the party may have made with the lover: Did he intend to break off the relationship once he was married, or on the contrary to continue it despite the wedding? Obviously, it will be necessary to seek proof of this as well, through witnesses, reliable documents, and facts having evidential value that either do or do not confirm what is asserted in the canonical trial.

5. Why did the interested person contract marriage, specifically Christian marriage? In other words, what was the reason for celebrating the wedding? According to a rule of jurisprudential practice, the weaker this reason (weak in the religious and moral sense: for example,

due to self-interest or influence by third parties), the more likely the rejection of a marital obligation may appear, and vice versa.

6. Had the interested party formulated in words, before the wedding and specifically in reference to his own marriage, whether he felt that he was bound uniquely and exclusively to the person of the future spouse, as far as the exercise of sexuality was concerned? If not, were there persons who heard him make serious statements on this subject with conviction (and not just flippantly or boastfully)?

7. Had the subject fulfilled the duty of fidelity while married? Did he violate it with a person he had already been seeing before the wedding and according to plan, or by starting a new relationship, or else with casual contacts? How long after the wedding did these incidents take place, and with what frequency? All of these circumstances must be proved with certainty (in keeping with can. 1586) and hence on the basis of reliable sources, with names, facts, and dates verified. It is clear that these are circumstances that can have different probative weight in relation to an alleged simulation of consent, in proportion to the extent and content of the reconstruction of the simulation. To take an easy example, the evidential value of a relationship pursued with the same person uninterruptedly regardless of the celebration of marriage will be different from the value of a relationship begun only several years after the wedding, maybe when the marriage was already going through rough times.

8. How did the party justify his infidelities if they were challenged by the spouse or by others? Did he arrogantly assert his own "right", or acknowledge the offense that he had committed and promise to and actually make amends? These two subjective attitudes lead to two different explanations concerning the will of the subject with regard to the obligation of fidelity in itself.

9. What attitudes did the party have toward the spouse? Did he accept children, and how did he care for them? Did he contribute to family life, economically and by his own presence? While it is possible to imagine in the abstract about spouses who are "perfect" in every way yet unfaithful, it is reasonable to think that someone who fails in such a serious matter will betray his lack of love for his spouse and their family in other areas. It will also be relevant to find out when this loss of affection occurred.

Examples

First example

George was a brilliant college graduate who held a position of responsibility in public administration. After a long engagement he married Violet, his classmate throughout his years at university. He had two children with her and lived with her for almost twenty years, during which Violet was always close to her husband in his brilliant career, standing beside him on many public occasions. Then their life together came to an end when George fell in love and went to live with Patricia, whom he met years after his marriage to Violet. In order to obtain a declaration of the nullity of his marriage and to get married to Patricia, George declared before the tribunal that he had betrayed Violet several times, both in the course of their engagement and during their married life, by having ongoing relationships with other women —in particular, with a woman named Clementine, who at that time was very young. George went so far as to claim that on the day before his wedding he had brought Clementine to a famous and artistically important church, far from their city, and gave her a wedding ring, and promised to consider her the true love of his life and that he would free himself as soon as possible from Violet, who was soon to be his wife. George reportedly also obtained an apartment for Clementine in another city where he often traveled on business, where he supposedly continued to see her for years.

The incident seemed to all appearances quite clear, replete with plausible details that might lead one to think of an exclusion of the unity of marriage, since George had promised (according to his version of the story) to consider Clementine as his true wife on the same footing as Violet herself, if not in a privileged position. George said that he had pledged to have relations with Clementine suited in themselves for procreation and to consider her the true love of his life, continuing in fact his relation with her immediately after his wedding with Violet.

The tribunal, however, rejected George's petition because on balance he produced no real proof of his thesis.

In no way did he demonstrate the presence of an anomalous cause that made him marry Violet against his will. He produced no evidence of the other women with whom he allegedly betrayed his fiancée and later his wife. As for Clementine, although she appeared before the tribunal to second George's account about the gift of the wedding ring and the promise, in her deposition there were serious contradictions with George's. Moreover, concerning the importance of George's relationship with Clementine, the instruction substantially reassessed the statements by the petitioner. Not only was no concrete supporting evidence for the relationship given (vague witnesses; no proof of Clementine's presence in the city where the two supposedly met for years), but George's actual behavior contradicted the promises that he had made to Clementine. Not only did he have two children with his wife while doing nothing for twenty years to free himself from her, as he had promised his lover, but he also sought to hide from Clementine the fact that he had children, deceiving her again with vague promises. Many people, moreover, some of whom were above all suspicion, such as exemplary priests, were able to testify from firsthand knowledge to George's love for his wife and family.

Especially for the reasons set forth above, the tribunal did not lend credence to George's story, which in many respects lacked supporting evidence and was contradicted by objective facts. As for the relationship with Clementine, while hypothetically admitting the truth of the fact, the tribunal deemed it no more than an abuse of the conjugal right that was also granted to Violet. Even granting all of George's allegations, Clementine was not the love of his life but a naïve and romantic young woman who was deceived and exploited as a "kept woman" for his own convenience—still assuming that this fact itself was true.

This example shows that, even though the counselor does not have to conduct a complete instruction of the case, he must not allow himself to be influenced by what appear to be textbook cases but rather should remind the person who consults him both of his duty to present his story truthfully and also of the fact that the tribunal will seriously look into his statements. Having said that, the counselor will be able to give his opinion while reminding the interested party that this opinion stands only to the extent to which the facts presented are true. If the statements of fact are not true, an opinion that recommends a canonical cause will probably be disproved by the tribunal's efforts to verify the facts themselves.

Second example

Richard and Letitia were clerical workers who had been engaged for several years. Richard, a strong-willed, hardworking, clear-thinking fellow, was sincerely fond of Letitia, a somewhat superficial young woman with little resolve or initiative.

After an engagement lasting several years, and after they had saved some money and found a house, the two were married. All went well during the honeymoon and in the first days after they returned. Less than a month had passed since the wedding when Richard found by chance a notebook that Letitia had carelessly left around the house. On it, written in the form of a diary, were described Letitia's feelings for her own boss at work and also, in great detail, the relations of a sexual character that Letitia had begun to have with him several months previously, in motels, in the office, and in random places. Richard was upset and rightly confronted Letitia with the need to make a choice. She, however, assumed a very ambiguous attitude, with generic promises of amendment, while still meeting with her boss. Richard, not seeing any good will or engagement on her part to observe a fundamental commitment of marriage, left Letitia for good.

The cause was very difficult from the perspective of proof. There were few testimonies concerning Letitia's relationship with her superior (the two of them worked alone in a little branch office) and no direct testimony about her intentions, especially during the prenuptial period, concerning the commitment of fidelity. Letitia acknowledged, however, the diary found by her husband and confirmed its contents. From that document it became clear that, as the wedding approached, Letitia did not intend to break off her relationship with her boss, toward whom she felt an irresistible physical attraction. She feared that that relationship would end sooner or later, but for her part she intended to encourage it as long as possible. In fact, she wrote to and telephoned her lover even during her honeymoon and resumed intimate relations with him as soon as she returned from the trip. Despite her vague promises to amend her ways and her professions of love for Richard, Letitia, once she was found out, did not make decisive choices to respect her spouse's exclusive right to the gift of herself from the perspective of genital sexuality, showing by her deeds that she had not really intended to assume that obligation, which she considered less important than her emotional and sexual needs.

The example highlights the fact that sometimes, despite the scarcity of direct testimonial proof, there are documentary evidence (the diary, which was certainly authentic as to the author and the time) and circumstances (the adulterous relationship was suspended only during the honeymoon and only because of the distance between Letitia and her lover; Letitia's de facto unwillingness to leave her lover) that can lead to a morally certain reconstruction of the marital intention of one of the parties in rejecting one of the obligations of marriage—in this case, fidelity as an exclusive gift made of the exercise of one's own genital sexuality to the spouse.

Third example

Katia was a good-natured, simple, somewhat naïve young woman. She met, became engaged with, and married Rembert, a restless young man who liked very much to have fun and hang out with his friends. Rembert did not make Katia happy. He was often away from home with his friends and not very attentive to his wife or sensitive to her needs, for example, the fact that she wanted children, if only to make up for the lack of affection caused by her husband's behavior. Their marriage failed after a few years. Katia remarried civilly and, wishing to regularize her new union, introduced a cause of matrimonial nullity based on the exclusion of fidelity on Rembert's part.

Unfortunately, the tribunal had to give a negative response to Katia's petition. Indeed, on the one hand, the direct proof was largely inadequate. Rembert's friends did not confirm that they had heard him make statements about fidelity in marriage but instead rambled on, offering only their rather inaccurate personal opinions without any foundation. On the other hand, the indirect proof (i.e., indications and circumstances) was generic because the witnesses offered nothing but generalizations ("He liked the girls"; "He was always surrounded by girls") and no precise facts. It was contradictory because, whenever there seemed to be precise facts, the differences in the depositions were such as to make it impossible to tell what had actually happened. One witness, named Millie, declared in particular that she had had a relationship with Rembert even before his wedding. However, according to the witness herself, it was broken off in a way that did very little to prove an exclusion of fidelity. Indeed, according to Millie, her relationship with Rembert had already ended shortly before he married Katia, and it was resumed only about a year after the aforesaid marriage but following a chance encounter and continuing for a very short time. Not only did the facts set forth by Millie prove little in themselves with regard to simulation, but for his part, Rembert himself made the reconstruction even more confused by insisting that he had met Millie only after his wedding with Katia. None of the witnesses was able to settle the question with any certainty or make it possible to determine whether Millie or Rembert was telling the truth.

The example is meant to recall that, before suggesting a cause, it is necessary for the counselor to have some guarantee that it is possible to prove at least minimally the intention to simulate on the part of the subject who is accused of excluding fidelity. In particular, it is necessary that there be a minimal guarantee that the facts on the basis of which the judges will have to make presumptions can be reconstructed to the point where they can be considered certain and determinate. In this case, and from the judiciary perspective, the incident with Millie was anything but certain; the other "many girls" that the witnesses spoke about were anything but determinate. In other words, great prudence is required in order to spare young women of proven virtue, like Katia, disappointments that might have been avoided.

Fourth example

Laura was a fine young woman. She worked as a schoolteacher, was highly respected, and also did volunteer work. As a volunteer, she met Paul, with whom she fell in love. They became engaged and then married, without any misgivings on Laura's part, although it seemed to her that in the final weeks before the wedding Paul had been not as enthusiastic and had been less convinced. Over the course of several months, Paul gradually assumed an attitude of deep detachment from Laura (the silent treatment, rude remarks, continual unexplained absences from home), until he unilaterally left her.

Once the separation occurred, Laura had to find out from mutual friends that during the final months of their engagement Paul had once again encountered a certain Jessie, with whom he had had a child several years before. Back then the relationship between Paul and Jessie had ended, but it had started again in the final months of Paul's engagement with Laura. It had continued despite the wedding, and when Paul left Laura a few months later, Jessie was already expecting another child by him. The child was acknowledged by both parents, and Paul also acknowledged the first child whom he had had years before with Jessie but whom she alone had acknowledged at the time.

During the canonical trial Paul and Jessie acknowledged their relationship, which they had resumed in the final months before his marriage with Laura, and admitted that they had decided to continue it notwithstanding the planned wedding. This was corroborated by several friends of Paul, who had come to know of the fact and had sought to dissuade Paul from that plan, although they did not have the heart to inform his fiancée. Paul himself, who emerged from the incident as a person of weak character, overpowered by Jessie's personality, had not had the courage to declare his real intentions by calling off the wedding once all the preparations had been made. Certainly, however, he had decided to continue his relationship with Jessie, and in fact, he became increasingly involved with her, so much so that a few months after the wedding she was already pregnant by him. Paul's paternity of that child and his acknowledgment of the first child were also certified by documentation. The above-mentioned friends confirmed both the facts and Paul's prenuptial intentions with regard to Jessie, which were implicitly injurious to his obligation to consider Laura as the sole recipient of the gift of himself by reserving properly conjugal acts to his spouse alone.

The example is meant to caution the counselor that the case, which is clear enough in itself, could have been quite difficult to prove if Paul, Jessie, and Paul's friends had not agreed to collaborate truthfully in reconstructing the facts. Laura, indeed, learned everything only after the separation had occurred, from third parties who had ties of friendship with Paul. The counselor, therefore, in giving his first evaluation as to the feasibility of a canonical cause, will have to be careful, not only about the cause's theoretical foundation, but also about its actual demonstrability before the tribunal. This is because the tribunal can decide only on the basis of proven facts.

VIII

Total Simulation of Consent

Having considered several cases of partial simulation of matrimonial consent, we must now turn our attention to the scenario that canonical scholarship and jurisprudence (but not the Code, per se) call "total simulation".

Elements of substantive law

It was said earlier that total simulation must be distinguished from so-called partial simulation, which we have already dealt with, at least in some of the more frequently occurring scenarios. But what exactly is the reason for this distinction? Answering this question can be a useful and practical way of clarifying the principles of substantive law relative to the matter to be discussed.

Partial simulation is the kind in which there is a matrimonial intention but one that is intrinsically contradictory. Or, as other authors less felicitously put it, in partial simulation there is, besides a matrimonial intention, another intention that annuls it, since it is in principle contrary to one of the essential elements or properties of marriage. Such would be, for example, the intention of someone who wanted to contract marriage while positively rejecting the fact that the institution of marriage is ordered to procreation or to its indissolubility or to its unity and the juridical obligation of conjugal fidelity—precisely the cases that we have already dealt with. Such a twofold intention should be considered intrinsically defective. It asserts that it wants marriage but positively opposes an essential element or property of marriage, without which, as a matter of principle, marriage itself cannot exist.

Total simulation, in contrast, is characterized by the fact that the simulatory intention (in other words, the subject's real intention, which is different from the one solemnly declared) is directed toward the very essence of marriage, that is, the partnership of the spouses' whole life and the comprehensive assumption of the duties of the (juridical) situation of spouse with regard to the other party.

To put it perhaps more simply, whereas in the case of partial simulation the subject does want a marriage but a truncated marriage lacking one of the aspects that are considered indispensable by canon law, in total simulation the subject positively intends to reject marriage itself. Appearances notwithstanding, he wants not to marry and not to assume the conjugal obligations and rights in their entirety.

Although some authors—relying especially on the common juridical effect of such simulatory phenomena, namely, the nullity of marriage —propose doing away with the distinction between partial and total simulation, prevailing canonical scholarship and jurisprudence maintain it, especially because of a psychological difference that allegedly can be discerned in the active subject of the simulation.

Indeed, whereas someone who simulates "partially" can have the intention to enter a true marriage and the persuasion that he is doing so (assuming that the subject does not know or consider that his intention is intrinsically contradictory because it excludes an element or a property of the normative structure of marriage), someone who simulates "totally" necessarily has an awareness that he is not contracting a true marriage, inasmuch as his will is by definition contrary to the very essence of the juridical institution and to the totality of its legal and moral obligations.

Canon law, both in the 1917 Code (can. 1086 §2) and in the 1983 Code (can. 1101 §2), calls total simulation the exclusion of the *matrimonium ipsum*, of the marriage itself, indicating precisely that such a simulatory intention must strike at the very essence of the institution, both at the moment when marriage comes about [i.e., when matrimonial consent is formally but insincerely expressed] and in the projection of the moment on the state of life that ought to result from it. Thus, someone who is unwilling to make any marriage contract or marital "covenant" (cf. can. 1055 §1), and consequently to establish with the other party any "partnership of their whole life" (cf. can. 1055 §1 and 1057 §2), simulates consent "totally".

Canon law explicitly declares that—as with any instance of simulation—the will that simulates consent totally must be "positive". In other words, it must be a true contrary intention, the product of a genuine decision. Hence, this cannot be merely a matter of a lack of will, or of a will that is without zeal or conviction. To clarify this, jurisprudence and canonical scholarship declare that someone who simulates consent totally "wants not to marry", in other words, positively intends that no change of his own state of life and no obligation of a conjugal nature should result from the celebration that he goes through with. In contrast, someone does not simulate totally if he simply "would rather not marry", or does so reluctantly, with little conviction, influenced somehow by convenience or by third parties. As the classical authors summarize it: a *nolle* [an unwillingness] of the subject in relation to the marriage is not enough. What is needed is a *velle non* [i.e., a decision not to marry] in order for there to be true total simulation.

This distinction is of great importance in order to grasp total simulation correctly as a concept and to have sure parameters for discernment in concrete cases, without falling into the ambiguities and errors that are so easy when one must judge such intimate and personal facts as the real contractual intention of a subject. There is no need to insist further on this extremely important aspect, however, inasmuch as we already discussed it rather fully within the context of chapter 4.

Therefore, total simulation is the exclusion of the marriage itself, of the *matrimonium ipsum,* as canon law puts it literally. But when does such an exclusion happen? How is it conceivable that a person would want to place the act of celebrating a wedding while at the same time denying that as a result he should become the other person's spouse, with the associated rights and duties?

Jurisprudence has highlighted several concrete scenarios of total simulation, cases in which such a possibility is conceivable and not illogical, although it certainly pertains to the pathology of matrimonial consent. Consequently in addressing them, one cannot gloss over an impression of a certain abnormality and divergence from what normally "ought to be".

In keeping with the purpose of this volume—which is to provide a basic, practical resource for the pastor of souls—in presenting several of these scenarios of possible total simulation we will dwell on the clearer cases, setting aside those that are still mere scholarly speculations and do not yet have interpretative criteria with some degree of certainty and acceptance in practice.

In order to formulate conceptually such a serious act as an absolute simulation of consent, it will be necessary to find a motivation that, at least subjectively, is equally serious, so as to present a logical explanation for the simulation. (This has to do with the *causa simulandi*, which is of great importance also as a probative element.) Otherwise—that is, in the absence of a motivation of this sort—it will be difficult to imagine so serious an act as the outward giving of matrimonial consent accompanied by the positive internal intention not to give any consent in reality.

Hence, total simulation of matrimonial consent is found in the following cases:

a. When there is a positive rejection of the other person as one's own spouse. This scenario, based on aversion toward the other party, can for example occur as a reaction to an imposition of marriage. Whereas it can happen that someone who is coerced just goes through with the wedding passively (which may possibly be classified as the defect of consent described in can. 1103), it can also happen that someone, having been forced to marry and feeling incapable of confronting the threat or the force that compels him to do so, decides meanwhile to make sure that his internal consent is lacking by refusing to accept the obligations that result from an act that he regards as being imposed.

b. When there is an intention not to give any consent, with a firm resolution not to contract marriage but rather to make a merely external gesture, to "playact". This scenario can occur in practical cases similar to the preceding one (being forced to marry), or in the case of a stubborn rejection of ecclesial institutions by someone who recognizes no other obligation to remain in a marriage (or not) than the one derived from his own will, and attributing to the married state only those obligations that he arbitrarily and subjectively intends to give to it, as may happen specifically in the case of persons who are ideologically opposed to the mores of society and of the Church, such as hippies, sixties radicals, and committed anarchists.

c. When there is a firm intention to reject the minimal elements of the conjugal partnership understood by canon law to be essential to marriage—in other words, when someone refuses to create a permanent partnership of life ordered to the well-being of the spouses and of the children (cf. cann. 1055 §1 and 1096). In that case there would be a radical discrepancy between what is willed by the subject and the typical ecclesial function of the marital covenant as understood by the Code (technically speaking, the juridical "cause" of the conjugal covenant). This can occur in extreme cases, when for example someone marries so as to receive from the spouse material support in everyday life (which is one of the aspects of the conjugal communion) while refusing to commit himself to those sorts of conduct from which the other spouse could also receive moral and material support and a minimal psychological, emotional, and sexual integration that is appropriate to married life. These are indeed extreme cases (as is only logical in such a serious and anomalous juridical act as the total simulation of consent), which can approximate other forms of simulation: for example, against the "well-being of the spouses" (in case of the denial of any willingness to give mutual assistance), or against the "good of children" (in case of the denial of any willingness to establish communion on the psychosexual level).

d. When a subject exploits the wedding ceremony for a purpose totally extrinsic to the establishment of the conjugal bond and its rights and duties, which he positively intends not to assume. For example, this type of simulation would occur if someone were to marry solely to benefit from the other's wealth, or if the wedding ceremony were understood only as the legal act that allowed expatriation from one particular country and resident status and maybe even citizenship in another country where the party wants to live. It must be carefully emphasized that total simulation occurs only when the following conditions obtain: the intended purpose is extrinsic to the typical aspects of marriage; the purpose is intended exclusively with respect to the establishment of the conjugal bond, and it involves the positive decision not to assume marital obligations and not to acknowledge the relative rights of the other party. This is of essential importance, in order to avoid undue confusion with what may be simple subjective reasons that urge someone to get married yet without rising to an instance of total simulation.

Let us look at a few examples, in the interests of simplicity and clarity. A woman from a country devastated by war or famine would simulate marriage totally if she married an Italian civil engineer or soldier for the sole purpose of being able to expatriate and to reside in Italy, without really wanting him as her husband and while refusing to assume in fact any marital obligations and intending to cease the charade once the goal was attained. The same woman would not simulate if she had fallen in love with said civil engineer or soldier and married him, intending to become his wife while being motivated additionally by the prospect of abandoning her unfortunate native land.

Similarly, a man does not simulate marriage if he marries—albeit not so gladly—in order to make amends for a pregnancy that he caused in a young woman, or to become more independent from his own family of origin, in which there may be conflicts. Despite the fact that these purposes (ensuring the legitimate birth of one's offspring; establishing a family of one's own, independent from one's family of origin) are not altogether extrinsic to marriage, they often figure solely as motives that prompt someone to enter into marriage, albeit rather unwillingly or hastily, but without a positive intention to establish no bond or to assume no conjugal responsibility toward the other spouse. The failure to flesh out the distinction between a subjective motive that simply prompts someone to contract marriage and, in contrast, the intention to subordinate totally the wedding ceremony to a purpose extrinsic to marriage while at the same time refusing to assume any conjugal obligation, can lead to harmful confusions and to unjust judicial practice, inasmuch as it is based on an erroneous and superficial application of the law.

e. Some canonists and tribunal judges maintain that total simulation of consent occurs also in the case of the positive exclusion of the sacramental dignity of marriage. The reason for this is logical, based as it is on the Catholic doctrine of the identity and inseparability, for baptized Christians, of a valid marital covenant and a sacrament (see can. 1055 §2). As a result of this aforesaid identity-inseparability, someone who positively rejects the sacrament is considered to be rejecting implicitly the covenant as well. We will not dwell here on this scenario of simulation or on examples thereof, inasmuch as the journal *Quaderni di diritto ecclesiale* has already dealt with it clearly.[1]

---

[1] See *QDE* 4 (1991): 79–96.

Great care must be taken in the case of a marriage that a party claims to have gone through with only *pro forma*, for example, to comply with the desire of the other party or of the families, or else to go along with social conventions, particularly in the case of persons who, although baptized, have fallen away from the practice of their faith and from liturgical and sacramental life. In such cases great care is necessary inasmuch as jurisprudence maintains that the intention to place a formal act does not always and necessarily contain a positive rejection of the substance of the obligations associated with that act. Indeed, the performance of a *pro forma* act could contain only the erroneous conviction of the uselessness of the act itself (e.g., the celebration in a church, before a sacred minister) and not a positive intention to reject the consequences of getting married. To put it in simpler terms: Timothy could be convinced of the uselessness of the church wedding, which for him is just a mere formality, yet at the same time truly intend to be the husband of Kay, with the rights and duties of the married state.

Not reckoned among the commonly accepted scenarios of total simulation of matrimonial consent are (1) the cumulative exclusion of the so-called three goods of marriage: offspring, unity, and indissolubility, which must instead be considered as objects of a possible partial simulation; or (2) the exclusion of some integral but nonessential element of marriage itself, such as actually and stably living under the same roof. Thus, the simple lack of conjugal love is not in itself simulatory matter. This lack can truly be the motivating cause of a simulation (e.g., "I am marrying such-and-such a person, even though I do not love him, solely to benefit from his wealth, without really intending to become his spouse and without taking upon myself the related duties") but not the juridic fact of simulation in itself, which is rather the act of the will.

As for the proof of a possible total simulation of matrimonial consent, we should recall briefly what was already said concerning both the general principles relative to the phenomenon of simulation and some of its specific forms.

This proof, which has as its specific object an act of the will, sets out to reconstruct that same act *directly* by finding witnesses who heard—during a serious, in-depth conversation at a nonsuspect time—verbal expressions of the actual will of the alleged simulator. On the other hand, it sets out to reconstruct that act *indirectly* through inferences that are logically allowed by the evidence and by the circumstances of the case.

It is worth repeating that (1) in order for facts having evidential and circumstantial value to be relevant, they must be presented as certain, determinate, and consistent with the object of the cause (cf. can. 1586), and (2) among those facts, particular relevance must be assigned to the *causa simulandi*, that is, the motive that supposedly prompted so serious an act as the simulation of consent. As previously noted, in the absence of a valid motive, any simulation, and above all total simulation of consent, becomes inconceivable and extremely difficult to prove.

Guide for the counselor

The pastor of souls who suspects that there was a total simulation of consent in a marriage case presented to him, should inquire about the following points:

1. What were the religious, political, and social ideas and convictions of the person who is suspected of having simulated marriage? Indeed, an anti-Catholic and anti-institutional mentality can be a motive—although often a remote cause—for refusing to allow oneself to be bound by a formal covenant according to an institutional form of marriage.

2. Did the subject suspected of simulation reveal, by his behavior, that he had some ulterior motive in contracting marriage, or some selfish or less noble reason? It will be useful to investigate whether he showed worry or anxiety about some particular secondary aspect that is extrinsic to marriage (for example: the wealth of the future spouse, the legal effects of marriage in his country with regard to residence, citizenship, etc.)

3. What was the main reason why the person married? The counselor should pay attention to the possible concurrence of different motives, since even motives that are less candid or desirable (such as providing an unborn child with a legitimate family) do not necessarily

involve the intention to reject marriage in toto along with all of its duties.

4. Is the person suspected of simulation willing to explain, even before the tribunal, what his real intention was in contracting marriage? Furthermore, and most importantly, did he manifest that intention at a time that could indicate a possible cause (as close as possible chronologically to the wedding) to persons who can be found and are credible and willing to give testimony?

5. How did the subject actually honor his marital commitments over the course of his life together with his spouse? Indeed, even though total simulation must be understood as something more complex than the "arithmetical" sum of the individual exclusions of the essential rights and duties of marriage, examining whether the person observed these duties and exercised these rights can nevertheless have considerable importance as evidence for the purposes of proof. Thus, for example, it will be useful to know how long the couple's married life together lasted and who was responsible for ending it; whether there were intimate relations, when and with what frequency; whether or not fidelity was observed and, in the case of nonobservance, how so. Massive violations of essential rights deriving from marriage, although they do not in themselves constitute the matter of simulation, are evidence of some importance. Determining with certainty the presence of a person's intention not to *fulfill* his marital obligations, not unreasonably makes one suspect the possibility of the presence of an intention not to *commit* oneself to them either.

6. How did the subject act with a view to keeping the advantage that he had obtained, or else how did he react once the advantage diminished or failed to correspond to the simulator's expectations? To elaborate here again on examples already cited, certainly there is circumstantial relevance in knowing how the woman who wanted to flee war or famine behaved toward her husband and with regard to her marriage once she had obtained Italian citizenship and an adequate income; or in finding out how the man who married without love, merely to benefit from the wife's fortune, acted upon discovering that there was no fortune or that it had meanwhile been spent.

Examples

As usual, we give several examples of the concepts just explained for instructional and illustrative purposes.

First example

Philip was a skillful fellow from a humble background who through hard work established for himself a solid, enviable economic position as a building contractor. As a young man, while still just starting his career, he agreed to marry Connie after she became pregnant. Connie, however miscarried before the wedding. She said that the miscarriage was natural, whereas Philip thought that it was all rather mysterious (to the point where he doubted the very existence of the pregnancy).

After many years of life together they separated because of Connie's infidelities. Philip convinced himself that he had simulated the marriage totally, since he had gone through with it both reluctantly, because of the stormy engagement, and somewhat bewildered by the unclear incident of Connie's pregnancy, which had been the proximate cause of the marriage.

Philip dealt honestly with the tribunal. Connie was very reticent, especially about her own infidelity. Despite Philip's sincerity, the tribunal nevertheless had to reject his petition.

Indeed, Philip was unable to adduce any direct proof of his simulation. In other words, there was no witness who had heard him declare that he intended not to contract a true marital bond, being no longer convinced by and no longer trusting his fiancée, Connie. Moreover, Philip made a sincere deposition that contradicted the possibility of the simulation for which he was arguing. To give just one example, he had said a merely formal "I do" during the wedding ceremony, "to which", he continued, "I have always been faithful in fulfilling the obligations that I vowed to assume at the altar." Philip's statement makes it clear that he, in reality, understood and accepted the obligations resulting from the celebration of marriage.

The facts, then, which are often more eloquent than words, show that he honored his marital obligations for about twenty years, since he had two children by Connie, worked hard for the well-being of his family, and remained faithful to his wife even when confronted by her infidelity. He was even opposed to separation, again wanting to act in the children's best interests. All these circumstances are clearly contrary to the claim of the mere "formality" or utter emptiness of the commitments (theoretically positively rejected) made by Philip at the time of the wedding.

Finally, as to the examination of the motive of the alleged simulation, the only thing proved was that the engagement had been stormy, that the couple had quarreled even on the day before their wedding, and that Philip, on the way to church for the ceremony, had told a friend that he no longer wanted to get married but quickly calmed down and in fact went to the wedding at the friendly encouragement of the latter.

The example highlights how subjective conviction—even when it is in good faith, as in Philip's case—does not always correspond to the reality of the ground of nullity that is invoked. Before creating a harmful illusion, the counselor, through a rapid review of the complete set of facts of a specific marriage, may be able to help the interested person evaluate his own situation more realistically.

Second example

Bernard and Mary Grace married because of a pregnancy, and the baby was born after their wedding. Both were still quite young and had to comply with the authoritative wishes of their respective parents. Bernard did so very reluctantly, though, since he did not want to marry and would have preferred just to live with Mary Grace.

The two had no other children after their wedding, and their married life together lasted only a few years and was marked by Bernard's disinterest in his family. Some time after their separation and divorce, Bernard, who had returned to the practice of the faith, wanted to clarify his situation with Mary Grace and claimed that his marriage with her was invalid.

Besides his statement to the tribunal that he had submitted to his parents' decision while internally rejecting the married state and its obligations, which he regarded as an imposition, Bernard introduced several witnesses, but their testimonies were rather generic, noting only his reluctance to go through with the wedding ceremony and therefore not constituting a true direct proof of simulation.

Bernard adduced facts, however—facts that were proved with certainty—which sufficiently and unambiguously corroborated his claim before the tribunal. In the first place, he explicitly adhered to Marxism at the time of his wedding, which was manifested by his formal enrollment in the Communist Party and in the Italian Federation of Labor Unions (CGIL), as well as by his militant political activism. In the second place, Bernard was an atheist at the time of the wedding, which was confirmed by several witnesses, among them the priest who later brought him back to the faith. In the third place, his repeated actions seriously contradicted his conjugal duties. (Besides his minimal interest in his family, it was proved that he used drugs from time to time, was involved in erotic liaisons with men and women, and attempted to involve his wife as well in group sexual experiences.)

These facts about Bernard's cultural and personal world, together with the proof of the strong pressure that had been exerted on him to marry—pressure that he had obviously resented and had not promptly and passively yielded to—made his statement to the tribunal credible, even though it was not confirmed by the statements of witnesses directly pertaining to his act of will.

The example is meant to highlight the importance of the presence of a plausible cause, of a motive for the simulation, which in Bernard's case was twofold as to its kind and level: a remote cause that was based on his religious and cultural mindset at the time, and a proximate cause that consisted in his reaction to a marriage that the nineteen-year-old Bernard perceived as an intolerable imposition.

Moreover, his serious failure to observe his marital duties, and his attempt to involve his wife in the same misconduct, led the judges to conclude that he truly did not consider her to be his wife and failed to respect her and her rights as a person and as a wife.

Third example

Jack and Kate broke up after several years of married life together, without having any children. Jack, a young physician, had received quite a few favors from Kate's parents, small-town business people, who had assisted him as he began his medical practice, allowing him to use free office space for his consulting room and finding clients for him in the area. Jack and Kate were supported economically by Kate's parents, allowing them to lead a very comfortable life right away, with vacations, a boat, and occasional trips.

Kate, with Jack's approval, petitioned for a declaration of matrimonial nullity, claiming that Jack had totally simulated marriage. The tribunal, after a careful instruction, ruled that none of the scenarios of total simulation alleged by Kate had been proved.

In the first place, it was not proved that Jack had completely subordinated his matrimonial consent to the purpose of attaining a goal extrinsic to marriage itself, at the same time rejecting altogether the reality of marriage and its obligations. What did emerge were the advantages gained by Jack from the help of Kate's parents, who were pleased by what they viewed as the prestigious marriage of their daughter to a physician. But there was no certainty that Jack had married for these advantages alone, thereby rejecting Kate as his own wife. On the contrary, it was proved that Jack, after only a few years of exemplary married life, began to display attitudes that alienated the sympathies of Kate's parents, thereby reducing the material advantages that had resulted from their initial enthusiastic fondness for their son-in-law. In this hypothetical scenario of simulation, Jack, who was still just starting his career, reasonably ought to have continued to feign affection.

Moreover, there was no proof that Jack intended to exclude a partnership of life with Kate. Rather, there was evidence that he was in love with her and wanted to live with her. It is true that he passively agreed to the religious wedding, since he himself did not practice the faith, but he did so without seriously proposing some other way of bringing about their union and without manifesting any radical opposition to the sacrament. If anything, he merely showed disinterest in the ceremonial dimension of the wedding but without any true, noticeable decision opposing the substance of that formality.

Concerning the goods of marriage (even though the sum of possible acts excluding them individually does not constitute total simulation of marriage), here too nothing clear emerged with regard to Jack's position. It was not certain that he did not want children. In fact, sometimes he had even spoken about the subject in a way that was not negative at all. Only toward the end of their life together was Jack unfaithful, but only occasionally, and he declared to the tribunal that he had not envisioned that possibility at the moment of his wedding. As for the indissolubility of marriage, Jack merely said that he had had a secular understanding of marriage, without, however, allowing himself, through discussions with relatives or friends, to realize the radical character of his concept of marriage insofar as it differed from the canonical concept.

This example is meant to suggest a prudent approach to cases being examined, so as not to allow oneself to be taken in by some rather external aspect without realistically evaluating its actual weight. The material advantages that Jack obtained from his marriage cannot merely be presumed but, as in such cases, must be proved to have been the sole cause of his consent. Here, then, the logic of his behavior needed to be coherent with the claim of total simulation. However, the fact that he adopted an attitude that swiftly alienated the sympathies of those who were the source of the very material advantages that he was supposedly pursuing exclusively rather militates against a claim of total simulation.

Fourth example

Paula and Nicholas knew each other from the high school they attended, in different grades, in the late sixties and early seventies. Both belonged to leftist protest movements, not just superficially, but with sincere conviction. They even organized gatherings and leaflet campaigns and participated in the political life of their native city.

Having completed their university studies in different departments, Paula and Nicholas began to consider making the relationship they had been in for years more permanent. They wanted to cohabitate but voluntarily chose a religious wedding so as not to have to argue the matter with their respective families. For them, however, it was quite clear that the religious ceremony involved no additional obligation beyond those determined by their own free will. At most, Nicholas was inclined to acknowledge the regulation of the marital relationship as something determined by the state.

Several friends knew about their convictions, based on the principle of self-determination by the individual will alone, as applied to the substance of marriage. With this attitude Paula and Nicholas approached their wedding.

Paula, however, had noticed for some time that her affection for Nicholas was diminishing. Indeed, in the final months of their prenuptial relationship, she had begun to feel a certain attraction for a colleague whom she had met at her new job. After a few months of marriage, Paula noticed that her attraction for her colleague was increasing, and therefore unilaterally and without any debate she informed Nicholas that she was getting out of their marriage. Almost immediately she went to live with the colleague and within a few years had four children with him.

To several acquaintances Paula admitted that she was unhappy about the sorrow she had caused Nicholas but declared that she felt perfectly justified in acting as she had done, since it was consistent with the marital ideas professed by both of them before their wedding.

Since the canonical trial proved through witnesses all the facts summarized above, the tribunal concluded that, in this case, Paula, in marrying without any religious convictions whatsoever, and already emotionally cool toward Nicholas and beginning to take an interest in her colleague, had had a plausible motive to apply positively her erroneous marital convictions, to the bond that she was contracting with Nicholas. In essence, she refused to establish with him a unique partnership of their whole life that was ordered to the well-being of the spouses, resulting in perpetual fidelity. Rather, Paula maintained and decided that the rules of her life together with Nicholas were subject to her own will, not conceding that her decisions would be affected by the rules of the institution of canonical marriage, even though, for altogether spurious and contingent motives, she had decided to be married in church.

This example underscores a question of a systematic nature, which is perhaps not without interest for pastoral counselors who deal with possible cases of matrimonial nullity. In the case of Paula and Nicholas, besides total simulation, it was agreed that the tribunal should examine another ground of nullity as well: the exclusion of indissolubility on Paula's part.

The tribunal, however, having found that Paula's rejection of marriage was more thoroughgoing and comprehensive and was not relative to just one property of the marriage, ruled that total simulation had occurred. That being the case, they dropped the other ground of nullity, inasmuch as it was logically included in the first. Indeed, it makes no sense to think that someone who excludes marriage itself could at the same time want marriage while excluding one of its properties.

From this somewhat technical consideration, there emerges, as a didactic recommendation for the work of the consultant, the practical suggestion not to overlook the logical connection between the various possible grounds of nullity. The canonical consultant should dedicate his efforts to investigating one of them, but only once other grounds have been ruled out that, in the canonical system, have logical precedence. Given a thorough examination of the matter, the consultant may arrive at a well-founded conviction for the existence of a specific ground of nullity that will persuade him to lay aside further inquiry into other subordinate grounds. However, further inquiry into these other grounds may still be pursued after qualified specialists are able to make a more in-depth assessment of the case.

IX

The Impediment of Impotence

In a book for the use of pastors who counsel couples that are having serious marital problems and doubt the very validity of their marriage, some mention must be made of the impediment of impotence. This ground of matrimonial nullity, although it occurs infrequently, nevertheless must be considered carefully, not only because of the historical tradition that accompanies it in the field of canonical studies, but even more importantly, in order to avoid misunderstandings during pastoral counseling. Such misunderstandings, although probably made in good faith, could objectively cause problems that make an in-depth examination of a specific marital situation practically impossible, or else create false hope as to the success of a canonical case.

It is in fact obvious that speaking about impotence inappropriately —in other words, in a manner that does not correspond to the real canonical discipline—can produce negative reactions in someone who feels that he is being unfairly and superficially singled out as incapable in such a delicate area as sexuality. It may also lead to faulty judgment about the validity of one's own marriage—a judgment that would not find acceptance in a tribunal that intended to judge according to the common interpretation of canon law.

Therefore, it is necessary to point out simply, but with a certain degree of precision, the elements of teaching and jurisprudential practice concerning the impediment of impotence.

Elements of substantive law

The concept of matrimonial impediment

The word "impediment" was just used a little earlier. It is being employed for the first time in these practical reflections on the subject of the canon law of marriage. Indeed, until now we have dealt with some of the vices (e.g., error about a personal quality deceitfully induced, constraint) or defects (e.g., the various forms of simulation) of matrimonial consent as an act of the will (cf. can. 1057 §2), considered in its intrinsic sufficiency.

This act of the will, however, as canon law expressly prescribes (cf. can. 1057 §1), must be made by a legally competent person, that is, one who is able and authorized by canon law to place that specific act. To put it more simply: the man and the woman who intend to exchange matrimonial consent with each other must be subjects recognized by canon law as free from any fact or negative circumstance that the law itself sets forth as an obstacle to the establishment of a valid conjugal bond.

The state of incapacity established by the law—specifically in reference to the matter of marriage—takes the name of "impediment".

From the technical perspective, an impediment can be defined—considering canon 1073 and canon 10 conjointly—as an incapacitating law. In other words, an impediment is an ordinance, a norm of positive law, that establishes or declares a person to be unable to perform a particular juridic act—in this case, marriage—and that consequently brings about the invalidity of the marriage if it is celebrated anyway (canonically, we say "attempted") while the impediment itself existed.

A careful reading of canon 1073 will allow the reader to note a particular expression: the impediment dealt with by the law is described as "diriment". This term highlights the fact that the impediments established by canon law not only prohibit the celebration of a marriage, but also—since they render the person incapable—impede the valid creation of the marriage bond. *Dirimunt consensum* means they frustrate or render nonproductive and ineffective the consent that is given.

Indeed, the 1917 Code foresaw a second category of prohibitory impediments. They prohibited the celebration of a particular sort of marriage. If the marriage was contracted anyway, it was valid but illicit. The 1983 Code did not in fact do away with all prohibitory impediments to marriage (e.g., can. 1124), but—whether for the sake of ecumenical sensitivity or so as to make the normative prescriptions themselves sound more pastoral—it simply stopped calling them impediments.

Technically speaking, impediments are incapacitating laws. Therefore—according to what is plainly stated in canon 18—they are subject to strict interpretation, that is, an interpretation that rigorously understands the norm in its proper juridical sense, without any possibility of extending it to similar cases. This is quite logical. Since impediments are in fact norms that limit the free exercise of rights, it is clear that their actual application should be as certain as possible and also strictly limited to those cases that, because of their greater importance, the norm intends to sanction with nullity.

Diriment impediments render or declare a person incapable of marriage. This bipartite way of expressing the idea draws attention to the source, that is, to the essential origin of the impediments. Indeed, although from a normative perspective every diriment impediment is an incapacitating law, not all impediments have the same origin. In other words, not all impediments find their reason for existence in requirements of the common good of equal weight. These reasons and these requirements of the common good, on the contrary, have different binding value.

Thus, to put it in the classic language of canonists, there are impediments that directly express the natural divine law, that is, the order that the Creator inscribed in things, which then—perceived by a human being through reason—becomes the source of a moral and legal obligation. Thus, for example, impotence [in the technical sense of the inability to perform the marital act] is a situation that conflicts with the very nature of the conjugal institution, which by its nature requires the possibility of a sexual union between the spouses.

There are impediments that express positive divine law, in other words, those juridical obligations that result not only from the law that God inscribed in the reality of things (as in the case of the natural law) but can actually be found in revelation itself. It is thus that we can understand the impediment of a "prior bond" (see can. 1085 §1), in which the impossibility of the simultaneous existence of two valid conjugal unions should be traced back, in the Catholic interpretation, to the words of Jesus in the Gospels of Matthew (19:1–12) and Mark (10:1–12), in other words, to facts that can be found in revelation and can be referred directly to the Lord's teachings.

Clearly, these two types of impediments can only be "declared" by the canon law system. Indeed, the legislator cannot on his own initiative set down the essential elements of natural law impediments, but must merely recognize and proclaim them. Much less could the legislator eliminate from the positive law personal incapacity to contract marriage, except by betraying his own duty to respect the peculiar nature of the canonical system itself, that is, a systematic way of organizing the ecclesial community that starts from the word of God and from the Christian vision of the human being.

Other impediments, in contrast, must be recognized as being of "ecclesiastical law", derived as they are from an appropriate choice made by the human legislator. This is not to say that they are based on a merely arbitrary exercise of the authority that places them, without any ecclesial and moral reason at their foundation. Nevertheless, they are certainly more susceptible to the discretion that the ecclesial authority has either to establish them (and therefore possibly also to abrogate them), or else to adapt their form to the concrete historical and spiritual demands of the community. A few examples may make this clearer.

To establish an age under which a person is physically and psychologically considered to be unfit for marriage (see can. 1083 §1) is a reasonable measure that above all protects the contracting parties themselves. Determining this age, however, may be the object of discretionary evaluation on the part of the legislator. The 1917 Code had raised the age limit with respect to earlier legislation. The current limit —notwithstanding contrary opinions—confirmed the limit set by the 1917 Code, above all because canon law is applicable worldwide, even in countries where marriage is entered into at a rather young age.

In another example, a profound moral requirement demands that a criminal action should not be "rewarded" with marriage. Thus, someone who seriously restricts the conditions for making a free choice on the part of an individual of the female sex (the impediment of abduction in can. 1089; see also can. 1397), or goes so far as to take the life of his own or someone else's spouse with a view to marrying a particular person, whether or not that person is an accomplice to the crime (the impediment of crime in can. 1090 §1; cf. also can. 1397), becomes bound by an impediment, a juridical incapacity, with the person desired as his new spouse.

So too, particular choices of a way of life—such as having received the sacrament of orders (can. 1087) or taking a vow of chastity (specifically a public and perpetual vow professed in a religious institute, can. 1088)—make the subject by a positive act incapable of marriage.

In conclusion, the impediments of ecclesiastical law certainly obey logical pastoral requirements of the ecclesiastical community, such as those that can easily be inferred from the examples just cited. These requirements, however, are not absolutely and manifestly opposed to God's will for marriage as it is made known through rational and theological reflection on the institution of marriage, or else through the actual words of the Lord as recorded in the New Testament. Therefore, impediments of ecclesiastical law can be the object of a dispensation—in other words, an exemption from the obligation that results from the law in a particular case, which is granted by the competent authority in a particular case for a just cause (cf. can. 85)—whereas impediments of natural and divine positive law cannot be dispensed.

Having briefly explained the concept of matrimonial impediments, we can turn to an analysis of the substantive law relative to the specific impediment that we intend to deal with in this discussion.

Copulative impotence

It must be stated clearly right away that, in tackling this discussion, we will not enter very analytically into detailed descriptions of the medical questions connected with the topic. These can easily be examined in depth by consulting treatises of matrimonial canon law and textbooks of legal medicine and are of interest mainly to specialists (physicians, judges, advocates). We will present, instead, the concepts necessary for an initial orientation on the part of the pastor of souls who is dealing with a marriage case in which he suspects the presence of copulative impotence.

The norm pertaining to the impediment that we are dealing with is contained in the first paragraph of canon 1084 of the current Code. It states that copulative impotence (*impotentia coeundi*) that is antecedent and perpetual invalidates marriage by its very nature whether that impotence is on the part of the man or of the woman, and whether that impotence is absolute or merely relative.

In seeking to understand the concrete meaning of this norm, we must first find a definition of impotence. In this connection it must be emphasized that the current Code—which does not innovate but only states more explicitly what was the corresponding norm in the 1917 Code (can. 1068 §1)—takes into consideration, as an impediment that invalidates marriage, only "copulative" impotence. In other words, canon law considers incapable of marriage those individuals who are not able to engage in "the conjugal act". In order to define impotence, it is therefore necessary to clarify what is to be understood by this term.

Especially in recent years, this term has been the subject of a series of reflections by some scholars of canon law who have sought to change the traditional notion of impotence. These reflections, however, have not led to the establishment of a prevailing scholarship that clearly modifies the traditional one. Moreover, they have not brought about a change in the concept of the conjugal act that must be deduced from the law itself and from the jurisprudence of the Rota. Consequently, for our mainly practical, pastoral purposes, it suffices to describe the traditional concept of the conjugal act.

The law currently in force gives us a very clear guideline on this topic. The first paragraph of canon 1061, in describing the concept of the consummation of marriage, states that a marriage is consummated when the spouses have performed between themselves in a human fashion a conjugal act that is suitable in itself for the procreation of offspring.

The conjugal act is therefore the act of physical union between the spouses from which can follow the conception of a child. The ability to perform such an act is, among other things, no doubt part of the essential object of matrimonial consent. The spouses, indeed, have no right to the procreation of offspring, since childlessness can occur also due to circumstances independent of their will. They have a right only to the acts from which conception can result.

As was said in the summary of the contents of canon 1061, in order to consummate marriage, these acts must be performed "in a human fashion". Scholars debate what this means. Surely, in light of the work of revising the Code and also of an authoritative guideline from the then Congregation for the Sacraments[1]—which was the dicastery of the Holy See delegated to evaluate requests for dispensation from an allegedly nonconsummated marriage before submitting it to the Supreme Pontiff—it must be stated that it is enough that such acts not be the result of violent action.

---

[1] Cf. *Litterae circulares*, December 20, 1986.

But what are the objective elements that make up the conjugal act? These objective elements—to describe them more precisely—consist of those actions that characterize the natural sexual act: the penetration of the woman's vagina by the male genital member, with subsequent ejaculation in the same.

The sexual "potency" required for marriage, therefore, requires of the male spouse a male member capable of an erection sufficient—in quality and duration—to permit an at-least-initial penetration into the woman's vagina and to allow ejaculation within it. For the female spouse, on the other hand, it requires the presence of a vagina capable of receiving the male member until the moment of ejaculation.

Before listing—if only summarily—some particular aspects related to the notion of male and female impotence, it is necessary to remark that this impotence, for the purposes of the canonical matrimonial impediment, is relevant if it directly impedes one of the essential aspects of the copulative act: erection, penetration, and ejaculation on the part of the man; penetrability and tolerance of the male member until ejaculation on the part of the woman.

This notion of impotence—specifically *coeundi*, that is, an inability to engage in marital intercourse—does not therefore include the consequences of the act of intercourse once it has been performed correctly or the possibility of attaining the end to which it is ordered, in other words, the actual procreation of offspring. Along this line of reasoning, the classical canonists distinguished between the *actio hominis*, that is, the spouses' ability to unite with one another carnally in a natural manner, and the *actio naturae*, or the natural development of the consequences of that act. They attributed juridical relevance only to the former.

Nowadays too—even though the abilities of science to influence the *actio naturae* itself have grown considerably—canon law limits its own consideration of impotence (the impediment of impotence) to the ability of the spouses to perform a natural sexual act in a human manner, in the sense specified above.

From what has been said it follows that simple sterility—the actual infertility of marital intercourse that is performed correctly, that is, naturally—is irrelevant with respect to canonical matrimonial capacity, as Church tradition constantly testifies and as the current norm still clearly reiterates. In fact sterility, as canon 1084 §3 says, neither forbids nor invalidates a marriage. The norm just cited does allude to a possible indirect invalidating relevance of sterility, through a reference to canon 1098, which foresees the invalidating effect of error deceitfully induced [i.e., fraud] concerning a personal quality of one of the spouses that of its very nature can seriously disrupt the partnership of conjugal life. Sterility could be such a quality. Obviously, however, in such a canonical scenario the relevance of sterility for the purpose of proving the invalidity of a marriage is not direct (in other words, sterility as such) but rather indirect, as a personal quality that per se is apt to disrupt the partnership of life seriously and that was the object of deceitfully induced error [fraud] injurious to one of the spouses.

Returning to an analysis of the concept of impotence *coeundi*, we must consider several distinctions relative to that concept, some of which the law itself makes, while others are suggested by practical reality. As already mentioned, canon law specifies that copulative impotence has incapacitating relevance both when it pertains to the subject of the male sex and when it concerns the subject of the female sex.

Before saying a few words about two particular questions relative to impotence, whether male or female, it is good to recall that at the origin of copulative impotence one may find an organic cause, one that affects the physical constitution of the copulative organs (their possible absence, malformation, relative disproportion); or a functional cause, one that affects their functioning, which is defective because of a nervous or psychological disturbance. If the psychological disturbance acts directly and specifically on the sexual processes, such psychological impotence is called "primary". If, on the other hand, it is only one of many symptoms of a psychiatric pathology that affects the person more completely, the psychological impotence is called "secondary".

Male impotence, in light of what has been said thus far, occurs when a cause—whether organic or dysfunctional—impedes the various phases of the sexual act on the part of the man. That is, essentially, when it prohibits at least an initial penetration into the vagina and ejaculation therein. With regard to the latter it seems appropriate to recall that— putting an end to an old scholarly controversy that had resulted in discordant practice among the dicasteries of the Holy See itself—a decree of the Congregation for the Doctrine of the Faith determined, with a pronouncement that is considered to be a direct expression of the natural law, that sexual potency on the part of the male requires the ability to ejaculate in the vagina but not that the ejaculate be "produced by the testicles", thus including male gametes.[2] By virtue of this decree, therefore, those individuals who have no testicles (congenitally or as a result of their removal), or in whom the tubes that are supposed to carry the semen produced by the testicles to the urethra are obstructed (here again, whether congenitally or after a vasectomy), but are still capable of ejaculating a liquid (albeit infertile) in the vagina, must be considered sexually potent.

Female impotence occurs when the woman, because of the absence of a vagina, impenetrability, or ailments that make it unable to allow the male member to stay in the vagina until ejaculation, is not capable of engaging in marital intercourse. A delicate problem relative to female impotence must be mentioned so that pastors may be suitably informed. It results from a controversial teaching about the very concept of vagina, which according to some authors necessarily comprises a twofold opening: to the external genitals and to the uterus. One consequence of this definition would be that a woman born without internal reproductive organs, or who had undergone a total or partial hysterectomy (removal of the uterus but not of the cervix), or else who—because of the retroversion of the uterus itself—had a similarly occluded vagina, would be considered impotent. This position, however, in light of the analogy with the decision by the Congregation for the Doctrine of the Faith on the matter of male impotence, cannot be considered certain. In this matter there is at least a doubt of law that a woman in such conditions should be considered impotent. Therefore, by virtue of canon 14 and canon 1084 §2, the marriage of such a woman could neither be impeded nor declared invalid by reason of copulative impotence.

Canon law further distinguishes between absolute and relative impotence. By absolute impotence is meant the kind that renders the individual incapable of performing the conjugal act with any individual of the opposite sex. For example, a man who, because of a nervous defect influencing the functioning of his blood vessels, has no sort of erection at all would be impotent in this way. So would a woman who, because of a congenital malformation, had no vagina.

Relative impotence, by contrast, is a situation in which the conjugal

---

[2] May 13, 1977; *AAS* 69 (1977): 426.

act is impossible between two particular individuals of the opposite sex. This may occur, for example, in the case of a particular situation of a psychological nature that prevents one of them from achieving physical union specifically with his own spouse.

The current Code does not reproduce a further distinction that the previous legislation considered. This distinction, indeed, did not have to do with copulative impotence in itself but rather with the knowledge that the parties contracting the marriage had about it. Thus, in the 1917 Code, canon 1068 §1 declared that (copulative) impotence invalidates marriage whether or not the other party knows about it. The silence of the current legislation about this characteristic of impotence that invalidates marriage cannot lead us to conclude, however, that the legislator wanted to modify the juridical effects of this distinction, both because the argument *e silentio* is of dubious methodological relevance, and because the lack of a distinction on the part of the law ordinarily does not allow distinctions on the part of the interpreter. Moreover, the invalidating effect of copulative impotence is founded not on subjective considerations (what the contracting parties knew or wanted) but rather on objective facts. It belongs to the nature of things (cf. the words *ipso naturae iure* in the 1917 Code, can. 1068 §1) and therefore to the nature of marriage (cf. the words *ex ipsa eius* [*matrimonii*] *natura* of the 1983 Code, can. 1084 §1)—expressions that the codifying commission[3] considered equivalent[4]—that marriage involves the possibility of the conjugal act between the contracting parties. In order for this possibility to exist, it is necessary, that from a rigorously objective perspective and according to an indispensable requirement, the contracting parties themselves be, in themselves and relative to one another, capable of performing that act.

As is evident from the legislative text, copulative impotence has the effect of invalidating marriage only if it is antecedent and perpetual. What is the concrete significance of these characteristics?

The characteristic of antecedence means that the impotence must already be present at the moment of the marriage ceremony. This char-

---

[3] On March 18, 1963, Pope St. John XXIII created the *Pontifical Commission for the Revision of the Code of Canon Law*—now become the Pontifical Commission for Interpretation of Legislative Texts.

[4] Cf. *Communicationes* 9 (1977): 361.

acteristic is therefore not very specific from the theoretical perspective, since it applies per se to every ground of matrimonial nullity, which must exist at the moment when the nuptial covenant is celebrated. On the other hand, it can involve particular difficulties from the practical perspective, that is, with regard to proof, especially when dealing with cases of functional impotence (of psychological origin) and relative impotence (strictly in reference to the spouse). In the absence of prenuptial factual evidence, jurisprudence resorts to the presumption of the antecedence of any impotence that is manifested as of the first attempt at the conjugal act and the cause of which can be traced back to before the wedding. The delicate nature of such proof should not escape the reader.

The characteristic of the perpetuity of impotence establishes that the only kind of impotence relevant to the validity of marriage is permanent—and not transient—impotence. Such perpetuity must, however, be understood in its proper sense, which is juridical and not clinical. Clinical curability is only one of the possible criteria for determining the juridical perpetuity of impotence. Indeed, whenever a situation of copulative impotence might be clinically treatable but by immoral means, or by means that are disproportionate to the subject's actual circumstances, or else through interventions that would endanger his life and health, then the impotence would be considered juridically perpetual. In this case too one can imagine the difficulties of proving the perpetuity of impotence, especially in reference to a case of functional impotence of psychological origin. Without adopting the extreme position which maintains that the perpetuity of psychologically induced functional impotence cannot be proved, we should surely agree that it is particularly difficult to prove. It requires a very careful investigation both into the concrete circumstances of the case and into the psychological dynamic that can be reconstructed as being the basis for the dysfunction.

The perpetuity of impotence is justified by the fact that the right and obligation to acts that are in themselves suited to procreation, although it always binds the spouses, does not nevertheless bind them *pro semper*, that is, at every moment of their married life. This fact cannot be circumvented by reducing temporary impotence of psychological origin to the form of incapacity described in canon 1095, 3°. Indeed, such an expedient, besides leading to a conclusion at variance with the traditional discipline of the Church in the area of sexual potency for marriage, would lead to (1) the inconsistency of regarding temporary impotence of psychological origin (covered by can. 1095, 3°) as invalidating, but not impotence of another sort that may also be temporary; and (2) the implicit modification of the very concept of the obligation to acts that are in themselves suited to procreation, which would come to be considered implicitly as obliging *semper et pro semper*, that is, at every moment. Such a position is an objective exaggeration of the dimension of the exercise of sexuality in marriage, corresponding perhaps to contemporary culture but not to Christian anthropology and to the ecclesial concept of marriage itself.

Guide for the counselor

In investigating whether a marriage case can be classified as one of copulative impotence, the counselor must exercise special discretion, keeping in mind—in addition to what was said at the beginning of this chapter—the merely preliminary character of his own investigation as well as the respect that must always be shown for the personal privacy of the faithful (cf. can. 220).

Thus, when someone seeks a consultation and spontaneously mentions serious sexual difficulties in his marriage, the counselor must discreetly and respectfully investigate the following:

1. Whether the marriage was consummated, possibly explaining to the interested person the canonical concept of consummation, as summarily explained above. Indeed, it is clear that the nonconsummation of marriage can be an important element of proof of copulative impotence, whereas its consummation precludes the possibility of supposing a true case of impotence.

2. If the nonconsummation of the marriage is asserted, it will be necessary to inquire prudently about the reason for it, clarifying its cause and origin (in generic, descriptive terms). Obviously, one can suspect a case of impotence only if its cause is plainly not subject to the free will of the spouses. It must instead be attributed to a physical or functional obstacle outside of their control and voluntary influence.

3. Whether the party or the parties confided in anyone about the difficulty they encountered. Indeed, even though in such a delicate mat-

ter it is commonly accepted practice that particular probative weight should be attributed to the depositions of the parties, even if they are the only ones—given the requirements of the law (cf. cann. 1536 §2 and 1679)—the testimony of credible persons about confidences that they received at a procedurally nonsuspect time can be remarkably useful.

4. When the impossibility of having sexual relations presented, for example, whether there were attempts at sexual intercourse before the wedding with negative results that continued after the wedding itself. It is clear that such a fact—although morally reproachable—can be useful for the purposes of certifying the antecedence of the impotence.

5. The sexual health of the subject who is supposedly impotent, both before and after the wedding. Whether he ever had genital troubles, whether he had a normal puberty, whether he underwent examination by a specialist, or therapy, surgical interventions, or hospitalizations.

6. Especially when a psychologically based form of impotence is suspected, at least an initial picture of the development of the subject's psychological health.

7. How the sexual difficulties were dealt with once they manifested themselves—by repeated attempts at conjugal acts; by advice from friends; by recourse to physicians; by the attempt at possible remedies. It goes without saying that the failure to attempt appropriate remedies is—apart from exceptional cases (e.g., the absence of copulative organs)—a contraindication to proof of perpetual impotence.

8. For the purposes of an objective reconstruction of what is described in points 5 through 7, whether the possibly impotent subject is willing to waive the professional confidentiality of the treating physicians and to authorize the health-care institutions to release files of any hospitalizations or treatments received.

9. His willingness to submit to a possible examination by an expert —if this is not patently futile, of course (cf. can. 1680). Indeed, especially in cases of psychologically based functional impotence, the expert, by ascertaining the cause of the disturbance, could provide valuable information also with regard to its antecedence (by determining the time of its origin) and perpetuity (by providing information of a prognostic character).

Examples

First example

Genevieve, an energetic woman with a university degree, became acquainted with Emil, a small-business owner several years younger than she. They had a morally correct engagement, in which the difference in their characters emerged strongly: Genevieve was strong and dominant, while Emil was insecure and submissive toward her.

After they were married, at the moment of its consummation, Emil had some erectile difficulty and failed at their first attempt. Genevieve attacked him verbally, badly humiliating him. From then on, their infrequent attempts at sexual union all had the same result.

Almost nothing was done to deal with the problem from the medical and psychological perspective, while outwardly—that is, in dealing with relatives, friends, and acquaintances—the couple took care not to show any of the difficulties in their sex life. After around ten years of life together, without any improvement on the level of psychosexual integration, relations between the spouses deteriorated in a more general way, and eventually they separated.

Genevieve claimed that the marriage was invalid because of copulative impotence on Emil's part. He participated in the case, cooperating as necessary with the tribunal. The following elements of proof emerged:

In the first place, the nonconsummation of the marriage was considered proved. This was verified by Genevieve's physical integrity by concordant statements by the parties, supported by testimonies concerning their reliability, and by testimonial evidence from persons in whom the parties had confided about their sexual difficulties or about the end of their life in common.

It emerged nevertheless that, during their common life, nothing really serious had been done to investigate the causes and curability of Emil's difficulties in performing the marital act—only a few visits, which had discovered nothing negative on his part. These visits were not followed up with appropriate examinations or treatments or therapeutic advice.

The tribunal ordered an expert opinion about Emil, who submitted to an examination by another physician, who diagnosed a form of impotence but through a procedure and reasoning that the tribunal considered unconvincing. The expert, in fact, limited himself to an external examination of Emil, not finding any malformation or anatomical defect. He deliberately avoided conducting other examinations involving medical instruments, maintaining that they were too disturbing for the subject. He deduced impotence from the simple fact that, for several years, conjugal union had never been accomplished. As mentioned, this expert opinion did not convince the tribunal, both because of the inadequacy of the method of examination and because of the forced logic of the conclusion. It was held that this did not prove true impotence, since among other things, it furnished no information about its possible cause or curability.

These findings—together with the fact that in the course of their married life nothing serious had been done in terms of therapy and that there was at least the possibility that Emil's reactions in the area of sex were influenced by Genevieve's humiliating attitude about the difficulties during their first attempt at intimate relations—led the tribunal to conclude that Emil's impotence was not proved and that neither were the legal characteristics of antecedence and perpetuity.

The example is meant generically to recall the difficulty of proof in cases of impotence and to remind the counselor that, even in the presence of sexual difficulties having a certain relevance, it is necessary to be extremely careful about invoking this legal scenario—especially when said difficulties have not been seriously investigated from the diagnostic and therapeutic perspective. In such a case, the counselor should seek to refer the interested parties—as much as possible—to more in-depth examinations. Only when these have been carried out with negative results would it become morally and juridically justifiable to recommend separation and the idea of a case of matrimonial invalidity.

Second example

Laura, a young woman from a small provincial city, was acquainted with Paul, who was around ten years older than she. During their engagement, which was of average duration, Paul showed great courtesy and gallantry toward Laura and was very respectful of her moral decision to save intimate relations until after the wedding.

After the ceremony, however, serious erectile difficulties on Paul's part became evident. In fact he was completely unable to sustain an erection necessary for the completion of the conjugal act. After a long time, at the insistence of Laura, who was desperate upon seeing her own hopes for her marriage and family frustrated, Paul reluctantly underwent several medical examinations. They included tests involving medical technology (the Doppler exam) and found seriously compromised blood vessels in the penis (both arterial and venous), which in turn compromised the possibility of an erection. The specialist dealing with the case, however, was unable to pursue the analysis by investigating the causes of the vascular disturbance and describing a treatment because Paul—after the initial examinations—refused to submit to further testing and possible treatments.

After the spouses separated and Laura introduced a canonical cause because of her husband's impotence, the instruction found what was already summarized above. The nonconsummation of the marriage was proved by the concordant statements of the parties and by several witnesses who had learned of it from them at a nonsuspect time. The physician who had examined Paul—several years after the wedding, however—was questioned. In light of the still merely initial state of the examinations that had been performed, he reserved judgment as to the causes of Paul's impotence and as to the curability of his condition. This specialist considered Paul surely incapable of sexual relations when he visited him (around eight years after the wedding) but felt that he could say nothing certain about the time of origin of the disturbance, about its cause, or about whether or not it could be treated. Paul, moreover—despite the promise he had made in his deposition— did not want to be examined by the expert appointed by the tribunal, who could have completed the tests begun by the treating physician.

Foreseeing the inadequacy of the proof about impotence and its legal characteristics, Laura's advocate availed himself of a possibility provided by canon law (cf. can. 1681 and art. 7 of the *Litterae circulares* of December 20, 1986, by the then Congregation for the Sacraments): the option of asking that the cause of nullity be suspended and "transformed" into a request to the Holy Father for a dispensation from the matrimonial bond by reason of the proved nonconsummation of the marriage. After carrying out the legal requirements, the tribunal accepted this request. It completed the instruction according to the requirements for a petition for dispensation and sent the acts to the Congregation for the Sacraments. This dicastery, having subjected the case to a study by a panel of three of its experts, considered Laura's petition well founded and presented it to the Holy Father, the only one competent to grant this dispensation (cf. can. 1698 §2), with a favorable outcome.

This example intends to highlight how less-than-full cooperation on the part of the person who is allegedly impotent can be a serious obstacle to the proof. In this case, in light of Paul's lack of success at intimate union with Laura from their first attempts, and since a serious vascular compromise had been ascertained, it might have been possible to consider proved both his impotence and the antecedence of the disturbance. The lack of an opportunity to investigate further the cause of it (anatomical? neurological? also psychological?) and the resulting impossibility of determining its prognostic and therapeutic aspects (which is one element, though not the only one, of the judgment about the perpetuity of impotence) were significant difficulties from the perspective of proof. Hence, it is advisable for the counselor to stress very clearly, in speaking with the interested party or parties to a possible canonical cause, the necessity of collaborating fully and truthfully with the tribunal, even if it is personally burdensome, for instance, by submitting to medical tests and expert examinations. The tribunal, indeed, can pronounce in favor of nullity only after having reached positive moral certainty about the case.

Furthermore, the example means to remind the advisor of the existence of the procedure of papal dispensation from the bond of a valid but nonconsummated marriage, a procedure that can be initiated directly or that can replace—under the conditions listed in the canons being cited—a case of matrimonial nullity that has already been begun. But we will return further on in a later chapter to this particular canonical procedure for dealing with marriage cases.

Third example

Monica was engaged to Arthur for around three years. She felt affection and admiration for him but not physical attraction; on the contrary, she experienced an aversion. Underestimating its importance, she married him anyway. Intimate union was impossible, however. When Arthur approached her to complete the conjugal act, Monica experienced great pains, reactions of refusal, and involuntary contractions of the genital organs.

She placed herself under the care of specialists and even underwent surgical procedures that ought to have facilitated coitus. All this notwithstanding, her reactions did not change. In their attempts to consummate their marriage—which were numerous, given her good will, yet unproductive—Monica became pregnant twice through the absorption of the semen emitted by her husband on her external genitals. The two pregnancies and births, however, did not change her reactions to Arthur and to intimate relations with him.

Given Monica's complete cooperation with the case, it was possible to hear the testimony of the physicians who had treated and helped her over the course of her married life. They all were inclined to a diagnosis of vaginismus of psychological origin, in other words, not due to any genital difficulties, given that the necessary treatments that had been carried out *in loco* had had no effect. It was also possible to ascertain that, on the occasion of her first pregnancy and first delivery, her hymen was found to be still intact.

Because of Monica's willingness, it was also possible to obtain several expert opinions on the basis of long conversations with Monica about her case history. These confirmed the diagnosis of primary vaginismus and dated it from the prenuptial period. They supported the judgment of its perpetuity, given the lack of success of the various treatments that had been tried. It was possible to investigate adequately the psychological cause of Monica's impotence—which surely existed, at least relative to Arthur.

The example means to emphasize once again the importance of the truthful collaboration of the person whose sexual capacity is to be investigated. In Monica's case it was possible to rule out—in light of the reconstruction of her clinical history and of the expert opinions —the possibility that she was manifesting only a certain difficulty in having sexual relations, which may result from disgust or coital pains (dyspareunia). It was also possible to conclude that she had a condition of true copulative incapacity because of vaginismus, which a classical manual of legal medicine defines as "a morbid sensitivity of the vulva and the vaginal canal, which at the least stimulus contract spasmodically, rendering the genital tract impenetrable. The muscles of the perineum, the hips, and the back are involved in the contraction. . . . Attempts to overcome this condition provoke even more energetic contractions. . . . The local hypersensitivity is usually accompanied by an anxiety neurosis, and hence the mere thought of the sufferings that coitus (or even simple touches) would cause her sometimes provoke convulsive crises in the woman. There have even been cases in which these unfortunate women, downright terrified by the idea, have been driven to desperate acts of violence against themselves or against the husband."[5]

Fourth example

Alexandra and Carl became acquainted through their work, since the young man occasionally visited the office where the young woman was employed. They began an emotional relationship in which, according to a custom that is unfortunately all too common today, they also went on to have intimate relations. Moreover, feeling modern and liberated, the two allowed themselves to become involved in experiences of group sex as well. In truth, it was Carl who proposed it, but Alexandra let herself be persuaded to participate.

This happened several times without causing any problem for Carl. Alexandra, however, began to develop a form of disgust for those practices, a feeling that turned also into a sort of deep resentment of Carl. Alexandra was no longer willing to participate in the orgies, and hoping to rebuild her relationship with her fiancé on a new and better foundation, she asked and he agreed that they would stop all sexual activity, even between the two of them alone, and would celebrate a church wedding. After the ceremony, however, Alexandra's feeling of aversion toward Carl did not leave her but rather grew more and more. As a result the young woman was no longer capable of letting her husband approach her to have sexual relations, even when they were performed in a natural manner. Alexandra would have liked to, inasmuch as she had hoped that marriage would be precisely the thing to fix things and her feelings toward Carl, but she was never able to.

---

[5] For the citation and for further information about this example, see the ruling *coram* Bruno April 3, 1987, in Apostolic Tribunal of the Roman Rota, *Decisiones seu sententiae* 79: 211–27.

When Carl approached her, she felt that she was "losing it", and an insuperable sense of revulsion drove her to rebuff him very forcefully. Then when Carl—foolishly thinking that he might arouse Alexandra's interest in sex—suggested that they contact their old friends again so as to have more "exciting" experiences, everything collapsed. Alexandra could no longer even look at Carl and hastily separated from him.

As may be imagined, the case is anything but simple, since the two parties of this case—including Alexandra—cannot be considered incapable per se of having sexual relations. They had them with each other and with other persons before they married. It was nevertheless possible to prove the following two circumstances. First, by means of witnesses to whom the couple had confided their sexual difficulties after they were married, including their primary physician, it was proved that after the wedding Alexandra in particular had no longer been able to let Carl approach her to have sexual relations, as a result of the young woman's very strong emotional reactions. Second, through a series of in-depth psychological consultations to which Alexandra submitted, it was proved that the trauma that she had undergone because of the disordered experiences during her engagement had activated an insuperable mechanism of rejection toward Carl, especially from the sexual point of view. In practice, Alexandra—who considered Carl responsible for having involved her in those squalid experiences—had become incapable of tolerating intimate union with him. Given the seriousness of the young woman's psychological reaction, it was impossible to foresee whether and under what conditions even prolonged psychiatric therapy would be able to cure her. In canonical terms—at least the judges thought so—the young woman had become, already during the engagement period (and hence antecedently), incapable of coitus with Carl (and hence relatively impotent) in a perpetual manner (as circumstantially proved by the unfavorable prognosis).

Without going into the moral considerations that could also be discussed, this example tries to illustrate more clearly in practice the concept of relative impotence of psychological origin and also to give some sense of the complexity (in human terms, even prior to probative and more generally canonical concerns) that such cases can present.

Fifth example

Catherine and Jude emigrated to Italy from a foreign country. Finding that they had in common not only their place of origin but also their line of work, they thought of getting married. Both, however, were aware that Jude had a serious neurological illness, one of the most frequent consequences of which is copulative impotence. In Italy Jude had undergone brain surgery, which brought his illness to the attention of the health-care professionals who recorded it in the clinical files of his hospitalizations.

Partly in order to overcome their homesickness, and partly in the hope that Jude's health might improve, the two married anyway, of course concealing from the pastor Jude's medical conditions. Their life together lasted several years, during which it was never possible for Catherine and Jude to unite as husband and wife, since his serious neurological illness caused Jude to be physiologically unable to achieve marital union. At first Catherine was very patient with Jude, but with the passage of years she began to feel increasingly frustrated as a woman without a normal married life and without any prospect of motherhood. Although she had to admit that she had known about Jude's conditions from the start, she became vehemently intolerant of his physical situation.

At Catherine's insistence, and because he was still truly in love with her and afraid of losing her, Jude resolved to try to overcome his situation of copulative incapacity through a surgical intervention. Actually, within the course of several years, he underwent two operations, the technical details of which we will spare the reader. Suffice it to say that the purpose of both was to provide Jude with a penile prosthesis. The first procedure took place in a public hospital and consisted of the implantation of a rigid prosthesis. The second, however, took place in a private clinic (which therefore involved considerable expense) and consisted of the implantation of a prosthesis that was inflatable by means of a complex hydraulic mechanism.

Despite these interventions and despite the fact that they were also successful (from a strictly surgical perspective), the situation between Jude and Catherine did not change. In fact—perhaps also out of shame and embarrassment at wearing prostheses of this sort—Jude never successfully achieved a marital act with Catherine. The disappointment of their repeated failures eventually spoiled the relations between the two definitively, leading them to separate.

In the cause of matrimonial nullity, initiated by Catherine but with full cooperation on Jude's part, it was possible, precisely because of his willingness, to reconstruct a complete case history of his condition. The tribunal was able to obtain the clinical files of his illness (which went back to the years before the wedding), in which the symptom of copulative impotence was already documented, as well as the files of the two surgeries to implant a prosthesis, with all the certifications and prior diagnoses. It was also possible to question the specialists who operated on Jude and who witnessed, in his postoperative check-ups —which continued for some time—the complete failure of the treatments and his ongoing state of impotence.

This example is meant to offer more than one consideration. First of all, to recall that—as the 1917 Code explicitly stated—copulative impotence renders the person objectively incapable of marriage, regardless of the knowledge and acceptance that the other spouse may have of the situation. In fact, it makes unavailable to the subject an element that is part of the essential object of the marital covenant, that is, the gift of oneself through the willingness to engage in those acts that are proper to spouses and that are in themselves suited for procreation. The person who does not have the ability to give himself in this way cannot contract marriage.

In the second place, the example recalls that the "perpetuity" of impotence that is relevant to the validity of marriage is not a clinical concept but rather a juridical one. The clinical impossibility of resolving the problem at the basis of copulative impotence is only an indicator of its juridical perpetuity, which could, however, still exist even if the situation, in theory, were clinically alterable (for example, because of the immorality or the dangerousness of the treatment). In Jude's case —aside from the fact that the surgical treatments applied did not work —it is doubtful that the operations of the sort that he underwent (even the first one, which was paid for by the national health-care program) could be considered procedures to which a husband was obliged to submit, given their objective complexity and the psychological repercussions that they have on the subject. Even the omission of these surgeries would not diminish, at least in the opinion of this author, the juridical perpetuity of the state of impotence.

From a procedural perspective, the example of Jude and Catherine allows us to illustrate a particular application of canon 1680. This norm provides that in cases of matrimonial incapacity for psychological reasons (a later chapter will clarify the sense in which the "mental illness" mentioned by this canon is to be understood) or because of impotence the judge must consult with an expert, unless this is manifestly futile. The case of the two parties in this example is one of the cases in which the futility of an expert opinion may be considered obvious. The fact that the complete clinical documentation of Jude's medical history was made available to the tribunal, as well as the opportunity to interview the two clinicians who had treated him for years, implanted the prostheses, and monitored the outcomes of the interventions, put the judges in a position to make an adequate and therefore certain reconstruction of the case.

X

Inability to Consent

(*Canon 1095, 1° and 2°*)

In our reflections to help pastors and other counselors of couples with intractable marital problems, we must now begin to deal with one of the most current and delicate topics, the psychological incapacity to marry. The study of this problem has witnessed in recent decades an extremely important convergence of efforts: hundreds of rotal decisions pertaining to this subject have been issued, and even larger numbers of studies have been published—books, articles, reports on research in academic institutions. In some countries in fact the cause of marital nullity due to psychological incapacity has become almost the exclusive parameter for assessing the validity of a marriage, and as a result the consideration of any other possible ground of marital nullity has practically disappeared.

In order to provide advisors with an orientation that is faithful to the directions of the legislator and to rotal decisions that have the institutional function of fostering unity of canonical jurisprudence,[1] the topic will be treated according to the method and the style used thus far. Avoiding erudition and extreme positions, this chapter presents instead what appears to be the confirmed doctrine and jurisprudential practices.

Elements of substantive law

Marriage is, with regard to its origin, a "covenant" (cf. can. 1055 §1), which canon law also describes with the equivalent term "contract" (cf. can. 1055 §2). By this expression canon law does not mean to

---

[1] Cf. the apostolic constitution *Pastor bonus* on the Roman Curia, art. 126.

179

situate an act of such lifelong importance on the same level as any other contractual business (e.g., real estate) but rather to call attention to the fact that the marital covenant is brought about through the concurrence of the wills of the contracting parties on the same object.

Thus, with the utmost clarity, canon law affirms that marriage is brought into being, is produced, by the consent of the parties (cf. can. 1057 §1), consent that is effective if it is expressed in legitimate form and by persons who are legally qualified to give it (or, to put it negatively, not disqualified by a marital impediment). In another, more classical expression, consent is the "efficient cause" of marriage. According to the incisive Latin formula, *matrimonium facit partium consensus,* the consent of the parties is what brings marriage into being.

The same law also defines what consent is. It is none other than the act of will of each of the parties, which is directed toward that special self-donation that is accomplished by assuming marital rights and duties (cf. can. 1057 §2). The grant to the other party (from the moment when consent is given) of the rights belonging to the marital state, and the assumption (again from the moment when consent is given) of the duties belonging to the marital state with regard to the other party, to possible children, and to society, bring about this donation of self that is specific to marriage and lend a legally practicable and ethically sustainable meaning to this same donation.

It seems clear then that consent, from the subjective point of view, must be considered an act of the will. This faculty, which belongs only to persons, presupposes intellect and actualizes freedom. The latter, indeed, can be actualized only in conjunction with an act that is human, in other words, that recognizably belongs to the person and can be imputed to him because it has been placed on the basis of (1) an adequate understanding of its significance and (2) a likewise adequate freedom in performing it.

Of course, we do not want to forget that man's freedom is a "historical" freedom and therefore not absolute in the sense of unconditional. Nevertheless, the Christian view of the human person, which is also within this historicized context of freedom, has always recognized and affirmed an essential possibility of freedom for the person. Freedom is dependent on the intellect and the will, in other words, on the capacity for moral responsibility. Thus, for matrimonial consent to be a properly human act, and therefore (as a psychological act) intrinsically sufficient in itself, it will have to be based on the essential availability and functionality—in the subject who gives consent—of the faculties of intellect and will duly coordinated in that complex operation which is the human decision.

The first two clauses of canon 1095 deal with this subjective aspect of consent, and therefore we must consider them briefly.

First of all it must be stated in advance that, although from a formal perspective canon 1095 as a whole is a novelty in positive canon law, it is commonly thought to express a principle that can be derived directly from the natural law, a norm springing directly from the very reality of things. In other words, canon 1095, from a substantive perspective, does nothing but make explicit the twofold principle whereby matrimonial consent must be sufficient in itself, both as an act of will that is intentionally directed toward its object (cf. can. 1095, 1° and 2°) and as an act of will that is directed toward an object that is truly possible for the contracting party (cf. can. 1095, 3°). In this latter case the consent, although complete in itself as an act of will, would fall short of its object and would therefore be at least ineffective juridically. We will discuss this latter scenario, however, in a later chapter of this book. In the current chapter we will limit ourselves to the former, that is, to consensual incapacity in the proper sense.

The scenarios of matrimonial incapacity in canon 1095, 1° and 2°, for the most part are new norms only in the formal sense, since they are substantially a simple reiteration of a principle of natural law, which ipso facto is always in force. The 1917 Code did not formally state the possible cases of psychological incapacity to marry. The substantive norms to be followed, in a case where possible incapacity was to be proved, were deduced from the definition of consent that the 1917 Code formulated, or from general principles pertaining to the validity of juridical acts, or else, by analogy, from the norms regulating the determination of penal imputability, which the 1917 Code had particularly elaborated and reorganized systematically to great effect.

In an effort to apply these norms, the jurisprudence and the scholarship of recent decades have carefully researched and reflected on this subject and have formalized concepts (e.g., that of "discretion of judgment") and presumptions (e.g., regarding lucid intervals between acute phases of a mental illness) that we will return to later. This research effort was fostered by the development of several scientific disciplines, such as psychology and psychiatry, and also by developing cultural sensitivity to the subjective aspects of personal experience.

Thus, in the postconciliar revision of canon law, it was neither possible nor desirable to ignore the advances in knowledge that were available (specifically, in those disciplines complementary to canon law) or the aforesaid doctrinal and jurisprudential reflections of a more profoundly juridical character.

In this way—concerning the subjective aspect of consent as an act of will—the legislator came to point out two scenarios of possible psychological incapacity to marry: lack of sufficient use of reason (cf. can. 1095, 1°) and grave lack of discretion of judgment (cf. can. 1095, 2°). What exactly do these expressions mean?

It is not at all easy to define them, at least from the formal perspective, especially when it comes to making a clear-cut distinction between the two scenarios. Proof of this is the fact that there is not yet a unanimous scholarly consensus on the subject, but rather there are explanations that differ considerably, both with respect to their content and with respect to their persuasive force. Thus, for example, some claim that canon 1095, 1°, refers to a principle of a general character that is valid for all juridic transactions. This explanation, besides the drawback of having to presume that the legislator intended to make an obvious, redundant statement, seems to pay little attention to the fact that the norm refers to use of "sufficient" reason. But, we must ask, sufficient in relation to what? Obviously in relation to marriage— and, more precisely, to the essential rights and duties that must be the object of the consent. It would, in other words, be a psychological act proportionate to the seriousness and the contents of the decision to marry. But then we must ask again: What is the distinction with respect to the concept of "discretion of judgment", which essentially consists —as we will see—in the adequacy of the subject's critical assessment with regard to the obligations of marriage?

In investigating this difference, we should reject explanations that simply refer to the type of pathology or of altered mental status induced in the subject (e.g., psychoses that cause the lack mentioned in n. 1; less serious disturbances—such as certain neuroses—that cause the lack mentioned in n. 2), inasmuch as they simply sidestep the juridical, formal aspect of the question.

More convincing are the explanations that refer to the distinction between the capacity for abstract understanding (1°) and the capacity for critical understanding (2°) of marital rights and duties, or that consider as part of the concept of discretion of judgment (2°) the intervention of the subject's volitional faculty as well and its coordination with the intellect (which, in contrast, n. 1 of the canon does not take into consideration). Other explanations take sufficient use of reason to be a necessary but not a sufficient element of the broader concept of discretion of judgment, which would be the most suitable unit of measurement, so to speak, for evaluating the subjective aptitude for consent as a psychological act.

Indeed, in jurisprudence, it appears that the concept of discretion of judgment is the one ordinarily utilized to assess the intrinsic adequacy of matrimonial consent. Therefore, in order to be clear, it is then necessary to ask: How are we to understand the expression "discretion of judgment"?

Presently it is possible to count on a sufficiently uniform understanding of this expression both in the scholarly and jurisprudential settings. "Discretion of judgment" means essentially two things.

In the first place, it means that it must be possible for the act of consent to be based not only on an abstract, notional understanding of marital rights and duties but also on a critical assessment of these rights and duties, in other words, on practical assessment of them, in relation to their obligatory content (which is not exhausted at the moment of the nuptial covenant but unfolds in one's future married life). Certainly, it cannot be required that marital rights and duties be evaluated in all their ramifications and appreciated in all their possible permutations in the most varied contingencies of life, but neither can one be content with an evaluation that—with regard to a critical appreciation of the obligations that one intends to assume—falls short of the minimal requirements. Moreover, while it must not be forgotten that marriage is a "natural" right of the human person and of the baptized individual (cf. can. 1058), neither can we disregard the fact, as some authors effectively put it, that it is a "contract" different from and more demanding than other important legal acts, such as the purchase of a property or an automobile, because of the moral and vocational consequences involved in it.

In the second place, "discretion of judgment" requires internal freedom, that is, self-determination in connection with the choice of marital rights and duties. The question here is not whether others are exerting external compulsion (which, under proper conditions, could be relevant along the lines of can. 1103) but rather whether the motivation within the subject is so "abnormal" or "pathological" (in common parlance, not necessarily in the clinical sense) as to deprive him substantially of freedom, for example, by causing him to decide on an obviously irrational marital choice.

In conclusion, in order to place an act of matrimonial consent that is sufficient in itself—that is, a true human act, juridically imputable to the person who places it—the subject must be endowed with a sufficient use of reason that allows him to grasp in the abstract his marital rights and duties. In addition, he must have sufficient critical capacity to evaluate practically, even if only minimally, those same rights and duties. Finally, he must have a substantial capacity for self-determination with regard to the rights and duties of marriage.

At this point the attentive reader cannot help but ask: When is the use of reason not "sufficient"? When is critical assessment beneath the minimum required? Or else, When is the capacity for self-determination inadequate? Or, When is the possible lack of discretion of judgment "grave"?

These questions must be answered in two phases: first of all, from a more formal perspective, then from a more practical point of view. As we will see, however, the two levels of response are profoundly integrated, since the first of them is the essential condition for understanding the second.

This needs to be explained. What do we mean by the more formal level of response? We mean that it is necessary to find general criteria suited to determine whether it is possible to evaluate the degree of the person's psychological capacity in connection with marital rights and duties. This operation—an extremely delicate one—will have to be performed on a juridical level, with methodological rigor, by highlighting general criteria (which in this sense are "formal") consistent with the principles of the legal system itself. These criteria can then be employed in an evaluation on the more practical level, where the judge comes into contact with the material facts of the case and with the scientific disciplines other than law. In other words, in order for the interpretation of the facts to be correct and in order for the interdisciplinary dialogue to be useful, the judge will have to have some sure guidelines, some objective criteria, so as to guard as much as possible against the possibility of error, ambiguity, and arbitrariness.

To put it even more simply, in order to be able to conclude that a certain behavior is a symptom that indicates a state of incapacity, or in order to accept the interpretation of the facts given by a certain physician or expert, it will be necessary to have criteria for judging and evaluating that—without contradicting the principles of matrimonial canon law—effectively help to arrive at a decision that can be sustained from every point of view: that of interdisciplinary method, that of legal logic (not only formal but also with respect to the fundamental principles of the legal order), and that of a substantial respect for the facts and for the truth.

What then might these formal criteria be, the juridical principles for correctly measuring the contracting parties' psychological capacity to assume marital obligations? Placing a stamp of approval on decades of doctrinal and jurisprudential inquiry, Pope John Paul II made a substantial contribution to this subject, which offers objective help in disentangling this difficult question. This contribution results particularly from two authoritative interventions by the Pontiff: his 1987 and 1988 allocutions to the Roman Rota. We say "particularly" inasmuch as remarks on the same subject appear in both earlier and later allocutions than those of 1987 and 1988, which confront this question more analytically.

In this context, it seems opportune to dwell only on clarifying the juridical value of these interventions,[2] as well as the basic criteria that they offer for our question.

One could maintain that although these allocutions are "authentic" interpretations of the norm set down by canon 1095, they cannot be considered an interpretation given *per modum legis* [by way of a law] in the sense of canon 16 §2, since the formal requirements are lacking. Those who support this theory think that the papal allocutions are manifestations of the *mens* of the legislator to clarify a norm that is formally clear but problematic in its concrete application. Following canon 17—the *mens* of the legislator is not normally considered to be the interpretation itself (as this theory holds) but rather only a criterion for interpretation that refers to the mentality and to the style of government of the legislator himself.

Aside from the question of exactly what status can be attributed to

---

[2] The scholarly journal that has promoted this book of ours has already dealt with these formal criteria. Cf. L. Ghizzoni, "Il matrimonio fra psicologia e diritto canonico", *QDE* 1 (1988): 118–25.

them, these two allocutions must be understood as authoritative directions that cannot be ignored in the application of canon 1095. In them the Pope offers several canonical principles in a matter of particular importance that involves doctrinal questions (e.g., with respect to the Catholic doctrine on the indissolubility of marriage), as well as the good of the community (e.g., certainly regarding the state of life of the faithful). Therefore the submission of intellect and will that must be given to the ordinary Magisterium (cf. can. 752) should also be given to these principles.

We should not underestimate the nature of the audience to whom the allocutions are addressed. Indeed, we must recognize that the Roman Rota has a special function of fostering the unity of canonical jurisprudence (*Pastor bonus*, art. 126)—through an *auctoritas rerum similiter iudicatarum*, which should be considered an authoritative example for local tribunals. It is therefore reasonable to argue that an address given by the Holy Father to the Roman Rota is implicitly addressed to all the judges and tribunals of the Church. Moreover, the general value of papal allocutions has been previously and readily recognized in similar allocutions for settling delicate juridical questions (e.g., the 1942 allocution of Pius XII on the concept of moral certainty, or the one by Paul VI in 1976 on the juridical value of conjugal love). The fact that an admonition contained in these papal addresses may seem particularly urgent for some parts of the Church does not detract from their doctrinal or disciplinary value for the rest of the Christian community.

As for their content, the 1987 and 1988 allocutions contain several principles that are extremely important in defining the juridical criteria for assessing canonical matrimonial incapacity. In the first place—as is clearly stressed—the Pope carefully invites canonists to distinguish between difficulty and genuine incapacity. Indeed, "only *incapacity* and not *difficulty* in giving consent and in realizing a true community of life and love invalidates a marriage."[3]

But what is the difference between difficulty and incapacity? On this subject the Pope offers another criterion that—although precisely of a general and formal character—points to the actual content of this distinction: "The hypothesis of real incapacity is to be considered only when an anomaly of a serious nature is present, which, however it may

---

[3] Allocution of 1987, no. 7, *AAS* 79 (1987): 1457. [Emphasis in original.]

be defined, must substantially vitiate the capacity of the individual to understand and/or to will."[4] This incapacity prevents either giving consent or carrying out the obligations assumed.

In other words, only a substantial impairment of the faculties innate to the human person—intellect and will—can produce the incapacity to exercise a person's natural right to marriage. To deprive someone of the exercise of this right under conditions that do not include that substantial limitation of the person's natural faculties should be considered abusive and not in keeping with the reality of the facts.

In order to understand correctly this criterion offered by the Pope, we must repeat and underscore the intrinsic *ratio* for it. It is certainly not of a practical character—as some in the media commented—since under that hypothesis the *ratio* would have to be found in the need to "restrict" the applicability of psychological incapacity as a ground of nullity so as to correct extensive interpretations that had surfaced in some regions of the world. Instead, this *ratio* should be understood more correctly and profoundly at the level of the Christian view of the human person, called to realize his own vocational ideals even in the midst of difficulties and opposition of various sorts, even those of a psychological and unconscious nature, which do not necessarily affect the subject's freedom substantially. It seems clear—and the two addresses of the Pope to the Rota for the years 1987 and 1988 plainly bring this to light—that the criterion for determining psychological incapacity to marry is deduced from the Christian anthropological vision and serves to safeguard the freedom and dignity of the person, in contrast to deterministic approaches that, in the final analysis, undermine or eliminate responsibility from the moral perspective.[5]

Thus we can talk about incapacity in the proper sense (for all of can. 1095—inasmuch as the allocutions make no distinctions and the matter itself does not logically require any distinctions) only in the case of a serious form of "anomaly". Both before and after the 1987 and 1988 papal allocutions, the rotal jurisprudence has shown in a substantially constant way that such an anomaly must be found in a "pathological" condition of the subject (although not in the strictly clinical sense, as the examples that we will analyze below will show), since mere

---

[4] Ibid.

[5] Cf. allocution of 1988, no. 5, *AAS* 80 (1988): 1181.

unpreparedness, bad habits, given character traits, imprudence or a lack of diligence in making decisions, lack of education, or the bad example of others is not enough to make a person incapable of deciding or of acting differently.

Once this has been made clear, we can move on to the second phase of our response as to when the use of reason is not "sufficient" or when the lack of discretion of judgment is "grave". However, it must not be forgotten that the formal criterion for determining psychological incapacity is also valid for the incapacity to assume the essential obligations of marriage (can. 1095, 3°). In practice, as a result of our findings thus far, when a form of pathology is such as to impair substantially the person's natural faculties of intellect and/or will, the use of reason is not sufficient and the discretion of judgment is grave.

But what are these pathological forms? Over years of careful study, jurisprudence has identified many of them, but we can mention only a few while also recalling several principles of application that emerge from an attentive consideration of the jurisprudential record.

Some of the major pathological syndromes in the field of psychiatry, such as psychoses (e.g., schizophrenic or manic depressive), may correspond to the criteria for consensual incapacity if they have reached the clinically manifest stage, in other words, the point of full-blown mental illness. In this case, we must note one of the few general presumptions (or perhaps the only one) that jurisprudence has formulated with regard to the proof of incapacity. Given episodes of full-blown psychosis, especially schizophrenia, prior to consent and given similar episodes afterward, incapacity should be presumed, even if the consent was given in a state of apparent recovery—in other words, in a lucid interval. Indeed, in light of current scientific knowledge, such a lucid interval is not a recovery of mental health but rather the remission of the more disruptive symptoms of the illness, perhaps kept under control by pharmacological treatments. The contrary presumption is valid, on the other hand, in all other cases, even for the initial or prodromal stage of one and the same psychotic illness. The subject should be considered capable unless there is positive proof of the fact that the illness had already produced intrapsychic dissociation in the subject, even without the appearance of those subsequent disruptive symptoms that can be observed even by the average layperson.

Even minor pathologies can influence consensual capacity, especially with regard to a lack of discretion of judgment. These include, for example, certain forms of neuroses, provided, however, that the disturbance is grave and relative to those elements that, being the object of matrimonial consent, must also be the object of the necessary critical assessment. In this category are, for example, neuroses that involve serious difficulties in one's sex life. In the same way, serious neuroses that manifest themselves in the form of obsessive ideas or of serious types of anxiety can cause limitations of the internal freedom on which discretion of judgment is founded.

Even in the case of personality disorders one must presume the subject's capacity to consent. Incapacity remains the exception. The possibility of incapacity must be correlated with the clinical gravity of the disturbance and with its connection with any one of the conjugal rights and duties. Thus, for example, a borderline psychotic personality, characterized by unpredictable behavior, irrational decisions, and possible lapses into temporary psychotic episodes involving a loss of contact with reality, can influence the subject's critical evaluation and his capacity for self-determination.

Consensual capacity can also be compromised by states that can be described as pathological only in the improper sense. These result from exogenous factors such as intoxication with drugs or alcoholic substances, both acute and chronic, or abnormal states of suggestibility, such as some truly exceptional cases of hypnosis or media-induced suggestion.

As for acute intoxication resulting from the use of alcohol or drugs, it seems obvious that the possibility of forming a judgment about the subject's capacity will depend on the reconstruction of events relative to the type and the quantity of substance taken, the time at which it was taken in relation to the wedding, and the effects on the subject's behavior during the actual celebration.

As for chronic states of intoxication, in contrast, it will be necessary to assess their seriousness in connection with the best accredited scientific parameters (there are, for example, standardized tests to screen for the various phases of chronic alcoholism, correlated with its effects on the intellect and the will). It will also be necessary to evaluate the subject's actual behavior in relation to marital obligations. The possible nonobservance of these obligations should be considered a gauge of the subject's critical assessment of them. In particular, the use of drugs must be weighed on a case-by-case basis, inasmuch as the presumption rigidly proposed by some judicial decisions, whereby a drug addict must always be considered incapable, seems untenable. What emerges instead is this guideline: habitual dependence on hard drugs is an important indicator in favor of incapacity. Finally, it must not be forgotten that at the root of alcoholism and drug addiction can often be found personality disorders, the investigation of which cannot be overlooked in assessing the subject's consensual capacities.

Something must be said on the topic of immaturity, which in recent decades has been extensively developed, as evidenced, for example, by the very large number of sentences that have had to confront this problem, and also by the scholarly research that has attempted to clarify the question theoretically. Indeed, this question is in itself rather complex and exceedingly difficult, because of a structural vagueness of the very concept of immaturity. On one hand, this term can designate the essential ineptitude of a subject for a particular task (in this case, the exchange of matrimonial consent and/or the assumption of the related obligations). On the other hand, and perhaps more often, it indicates only the subject's incomplete and suboptimal control (or, better, his not yet complete and optimal control) of all his psychological, emotional, and moral capabilities. In other words, "immaturity" refers not to his radical ineptitude but rather to his merely imperfect preparedness. Furthermore, the term "immaturity" seems to designate different realities in different disciplines. In the psychological field, for example, assuming (as not all experts do) that the concept of immaturity has any scientific validity, it indicates any defect that keeps the subject at a distance from the ideal point of arrival at maturity. In the juridical field, in contrast (or at least in common usage in matrimonial canon law), the term "immaturity" means the subject's radical incapacity to give consent or to live the married life, such that immaturity is discussed precisely as a specific factor at the basis of a possible incapacity to marry. Finally, the difficulty in dealing with the topic of immaturity derives from the fact that an important distinction is not always clear or clearly applied: the distinction between psychological immaturity (which would mainly concern the logical-critical capacities of the subject) and affective immaturity (which would mainly concern the emotions and therefore the sphere of motivation in decision making and of consistency in acting).

The prevailing rotal jurisprudence admits immaturity as a reason of matrimonial incapacity strictly by way of exception but not as a rule, establishing the principle—which is juridically precise albeit still rather formal—that only the sort of immaturity included in the legal categories of grave lack of discretion or the inability to assume the essential obligations of marriage is relevant to the subject's capacity to contract marriage. In other words, not every form of personal immaturity, whether psychological or affective, produces the subject's incapacity for marriage but only the type that, by way of exception, reaches a particularly serious degree.

The problem then becomes once again that of defining when a particular anomalous psychological situation—in this case, generically described as immaturity—is so grave as to be the possible source of incapacity, either to consent or to assume and carry out the essential obligations. This definition cannot be based exclusively on the detection of immature symptoms present in the subject's choices and behaviors in a way that is uncoordinated with a more in-depth and detailed investigation of his life. And this is because, as the Holy Father also recalls, "In fact it is not difficult to see within the contracting parties infantile and irreconcilable aspects, which in such a situation become inevitably the *proof* of their abnormality. It may, in fact, be a case of people who are substantially normal but who have difficulties which could be overcome."[6]

The criterion of "gravity" will be the criterion of grasping—in a comprehensive view of the facts of the case—the formal, structural reasons (i.e., those relative to the level of the functionality of the person's natural faculties) that alone can account for the diminution of the subject's free determination of specific decisions and behaviors. In other words, the criteria for determining on what exceptional occasions a form of immaturity produced matrimonial incapacity are no different—nor could they be—from those that must be satisfied for any other form of psychological incapacity to marry.

As proof of this we must cite not only the low percentage of rotal decisions that have recognized immaturity as the cause of an incapacity to marry but also the fact that, in such exceptional decisions, the generic "diagnosis" of immaturity not infrequently seems to be

---

[6] Address of 1988 to the Roman Rota, *AAS* 80 (1988): 1183. [Emphasis in original.]

narrowed down, over the course of the case, into more specific diagnostic terms, especially in the area of personality disorders or of serious neuroses relating to the object of consent. This goes to prove, precisely, the fact that the gravity that must be established is correlated with the sure presence of an outright anomaly essentially harmful to the subject's natural faculties.

To conclude the discussion about substantive law, we must make some mention of the topic of proving a possible involuntary defect of consent along the lines of canon 1095, 1° and 2°. Indeed, the reader has certainly already asked himself several times: But how is it possible to prove everything that the law, authoritative doctrine, and jurisprudence require?

Essentially, the proof of incapacity can be structured around a three-fold assessment: (1) the reconstruction of the constituent acts and behavior of the subject, in particular those most closely related—in time or importance—to the decision to marry; (2) the reconstruction of the subject's possible clinical history; and (3) the in-depth study by an expert of the subject's psychological condition. Obviously, this three-fold assessment should be adapted to the concrete demands of the case, which may result in the prevalence of one of the three types of assessment mentioned. It is clear, for example, that in the case of a psychotic illness with pre- and post-nuptial hospitalization, the documentary reconstruction of the subject's clinical history will have decisive weight, whereas in a case of alleged acute alcoholic intoxication, it would make little sense to have an expert investigation, especially years after the fact. With respect to the three types of assessment pointed out, we can say the following by way of summary.

As for the facts to be reconstructed concerning the subject's behavior, it will be advisable to recall that they—being within the scope of the judge's work and responsibility—must be reconstructed with particular accuracy. Indeed, as canon law clearly prescribes, it is possible to make presumptions and logical deductions only on the basis of certain and determinate facts (cf. can. 1586). This reconstruction is of great importance also for the purpose of providing trustworthy material to the expert for his professional interpretation. In fact, the value of this interpretation will obviously be diminished if it turns out to have been based on facts—considered ''symptoms'' of a relevant anomaly—for which no actual proof is shown. Thus, for example, it will not be enough that someone is willing to declare as a witness that so-and-so, who is allegedly incapable, appeared "strange" to him. This assertion, indeed, remains a mere opinion devoid of probative value until the person who makes it explains what criteria and, above all, what facts his opinion is based on.

It seems clear also that these facts will be of greater importance the closer in time they are situated to the matrimonial consent and the more they pertain to one of the marital obligations. Indeed, it would be strange to think for example that we could consider someone incapable of assessing these obligations with sufficient use of reason, or that he had seriously lacked discretion of judgment concerning them, if it turned out that for his part he had observed said obligations, maybe even for a very long time.

Since incapacity to marry, and consensual incapacity as well, must be based on an anomaly that substantially impairs the natural faculties of intellect and will, it will be necessary to reconstruct the clinical history of the subject—in other words, the course of possible contacts with doctors and clinical institutions, of treatments and institutionalizations. The absence of such a clinical history (except in rather exceptional cases of acute intoxication with psychotropic substances or even more exceptional episodes of autosuggestion) will not normally go to prove incapacity. This is not to say that the lack of a clinical history is an invalidating obstacle to a proof of incapacity. There are indeed some personality disturbances, for example, that experts describe as "ego-syntonic"—in other words, they are not disturbing to the subject but are disturbing only to others. For this reason the subject might be convinced that he is perfectly well and has no need of medical treatment and therefore would not seek it unless compelled by others. What this means, rather, is that the lack of a clinical history is generally—absent evidence to the contrary—an unfavorable indication in trying to prove a consensual defect. It is only an indication, since the judgment about the possible defect of consent is a judgment of a juridical sort that does not exhaust the analysis of its factual basis by reconstructing the clinical record. The clinical record is just one of the elements that the judge must take into consideration.

Finally, the third hinge on which the proof of possible consensual incapacity turns is the assessment by an expert, which the Code of Canon Law calls for, referring specifically to matrimonial cases (cf. cann. 1574 and 1680). In this connection it is important to recall briefly that in procedural law the expert is only a consultant of the judge and that the judge himself remains free in evaluating the expert opinion. Of course, he is free not in an arbitrary way contrary to reason or justice. The judge, instead, must make a critical reading of the expert findings (whether ex officio or requested by a party, or even extrajudicial), stating reasons for his own acceptance or rejection of the expert's conclusions (cf. can. 1579 §2). This critical reading cannot be based on arguments belonging to the expert's discipline (if the judge had already mastered it personally, he would not have needed the expert) but rather must be based on arguments that jurisprudence had already previously developed. Among these are the agreement of the expert's conclusions and arguments with the facts of the case (cf. can. 1579 §1); the intrinsic logic of the expert report; the methodology used; and the expert's contact with the individual being evaluated.

In the allocutions mentioned earlier, the Pope explained another extremely important criterion for evaluating an expert report—verifying its anthropological presuppositions, that is, the consistency of its view of man with the one formulated by Christian anthropology that, by logical necessity, is presupposed by canon law. Indeed, it is clear that an expert who in his interpretation of the facts starts from a view of the human being that is markedly different from the Christian view (e.g., a deterministic view that denies freedom almost a priori, or a view that implicitly restricts the exercise of the right to marriage only to individuals who were particularly gifted or likely to have an optimal outcome) would offer the judge a response that would be of limited applicability and hence with regard to the evaluation.

Finally, we should recall something that counselors of couples with serious marital problems should also take into account in order to encourage the responsible cooperation of all the interested parties and so as not to create facile illusions: it is difficult to complete in a useful fashion the reconstruction of an individual's clinical history and an expert examination without the sincere and truthful cooperation on the part of the person whose own capacity to give matrimonial consent is in question. Nowadays in fact it is rather difficult—because of an appropriate respect for personal matters and for professional confidentiality—to find physicians willing to testify, or else managers of health-care institutions ready to issue certificates or clinical records without the required authorizations. Even at the level of expert testimony, then, although expert testimony based on documents alone is no doubt possible, it nevertheless may not be very persuasive if the lack of contact with the interested party is not made up for by reliable clinical information already present in the documentation.

Guide for the counselor

A counselor of a couple who is considering the possibility of an involuntary defect of consent for lack of sufficient use of reason or for a lack of discretion of judgment would have to investigate the following points:

1. How the engagement went and, above all, what the reasons were for any possible difficulties or breakups. Were they due to oddities, eccentricities, or anomalous behaviors of the allegedly incapable party, and if so, which ones?

2. Whether the person who is alleged to be incapable had difficulties in any important area of life: relations with family and with other persons; study or work; fulfilling his own social obligations (e.g., military service or abiding by the laws and rules of civil life).

3. Whether the person who is supposedly incapable of consent had a clinical history of psychological difficulties. Was he treated by doctors? (If so, can they be found, and are they ready to testify?) What diagnoses were formulated, and what treatments were prescribed? Were these treatments still ongoing at the time of consent? Were there prenuptial institutionalizations: When, where, for how much time, and with what documentation?

4. How the subject spoke before the wedding about his impending marriage and about marital obligations. In particular, did he exhibit eccentric or markedly immature opinions about this topic? Was there a confrontation with other persons about these opinions, and what capacity for reasoning and self-criticism did the subject display in this regard?

5. Whether the subject was convinced that he should get married or whether instead there was some anomalous reason that drove him to

marry: for example, a pregnancy, serious scruples, or the suggestions of other persons. It will be very important to seek to reconstruct as accurately as possible the subjective weight of such external factors. Although in and of themselves they cannot constitute a substantial defect of internal freedom, it is nevertheless true that they can have considerable influence on persons who are particularly suggestible, unsteady, and predisposed.

6. Whether the subject had expensive habits that influenced his psychological state, such as the use of drugs or alcohol. What substances were taken, and in what quantity? Were there related medical interventions, and if so, with what outcome?

7. How the subject behaved during the marriage preparations and on the day of the wedding itself. Were there actions that were inappropriate in those circumstances, awkward statements, loud arguments?

8. How the subject fulfilled his marital duties. Indeed, although we must not forget that the incapacity to fulfill the obligations that one has assumed is a separate heading of nullity because of a defect of the object of consent (cf. can. 1095, 3°), it is nevertheless difficult to imagine that someone who was incapable of assessing the obligations of marriage and of resolving to assume them would then have observed them perfectly, maybe even for a long time. One would have to expect, more reasonably, some failure in the carrying out of these delegations as well.

9. What the subject's clinical history, if any, was after the wedding. Indeed, although it is true that the assessment of consensual capacity is strictly connected with the moment of consent, the study of the clinical development of the person who is allegedly incapable can shed considerable light on his actual condition at that precise moment.

10. Whether the person whose incapacity is in question is willing, in the event that a canonical cause is initiated, to subject himself to expert examination, or at least to release from professional confidentiality the doctors or institutions that may have treated him.

Examples

In conclusion, several examples are offered so as to illustrate better, with the didactic purpose typical of this book, the complex material set forth in this chapter.

First example

Julia was a young woman from a nonbelieving family, and she herself was not baptized. At the age of eighteen she began to live independently of her family, which moreover had never really taken care of her. Not having a regular job, Julia began to cohabit with a certain Troy. This was a very disorderly living arrangement from the moral perspective (there is no reason to go into detail here), which ended because Julia was a victim of domestic violence.

While socializing in "artistic" circles, Julia, who was interested in art, met a certain Pasquale, who had just been released from a treatment center for drug addiction. His rehab had been only partially successful. Pasquale in fact continued to smoke marijuana and to abuse alcohol. He was not working and had moved into a farmhouse—really a shack —owned by his parents.

Julia started to live with Pasquale. The premarital cohabitation lasted about three years. Actually, it was a disastrous experience. Pasquale had no interest in Julia as a companion, not even sexually, and he mistreated her physically. More than once she left the cabin, but she always returned. Moreover, their financial situation was extremely precarious. At Julia's initiative, the two started a very modest business of producing artisanal crafts. Pasquale, however, worked only occasionally, indulging as noted in marijuana and alcohol and neglecting also the administrative tasks related to their little business.

During those three years of premarital cohabitation Julia was approached by a local priest. Wishing to improve her knowledge of the Christian faith, Julia started to study and to consult regularly with this priest, until eventually she requested and received baptism. After receiving this sacrament, she—being an honest person and rigid to the point of scrupulosity—began to think, "I am a Christian; I am cohabiting without marriage. I must get out of this immoral situation, and therefore I have to get married." Notwithstanding the advice of the priest who had introduced her to the faith, Julia did not realize that the reasonable solution was to break off the disastrous cohabitation and obstinately insisted on marrying, although Pasquale was essentially indifferent about the matter. Their married life, however, was the exact replica of the cohabitation that had preceded it. Probably the marriage was not even consummated, and their life together as man and wife lasted only a few months, ending because Julia fled from Pasquale's increasingly violent excesses.

When a canonical cause was initiated, in addition to the facts summarized above, Julia herself submitted to examination by experts. It was possible to certify that behind her honesty and rigidity, which she certainly manifested in good faith, lay in reality a serious personality disturbance, a borderline psychosis that left her on the verge of losing contact with reality. Her personality disorder, along with the events of her marriage and the way in which she had decided on it, convinced the tribunal that Julia had seriously lacked discretion of judgment, if not from the perspective of assessing one of the rights and duties of marriage, then certainly from the perspective of her internal freedom, since her pathological personality had caused her to make an apparently moral choice that was in reality profoundly irrational and not free.

The example needs no particular comments, except to say that consensual incapacity can coexist with the complete good faith of the subject and that consistency between the facts and the expert reconstruction is one of the best criteria for verifying that a case of incapacity is well founded.

Second example

Mark was an instructor at a drug rehabilitation center. He had once been a heroin addict but had completed a program at the center with seemingly positive results. Therefore, toward the end of his rehabilitation program, he had been appointed instructor of the other residents of the community. His job was to set an example for them of how one could swear off drugs and to supervise their behavior. Being almost at the end of his rehabilitation program and having apparently achieved positive results, Mark was allowed to have greater freedom—specifically, he could leave the center to run errands and to do small jobs.

Mark met Jeannie, a volunteer and a supporter of the rehabilitation community. They struck up a relationship and had brief encounters at the center and during some of Mark's absences from it. They had intimate relations, and Jeannie became pregnant. So they decided to get married. Mark was dismissed from the community and told Jeannie that it was because he, in getting his girlfriend pregnant, had given a bad example to all the other residents, betraying the confidence that had been shown in him as an instructor. He also told Jeannie that he had been treated very poorly by those in charge of the center and wanted to have nothing more to do with them. He did not invite them to the wedding and dissuaded Jeannie from having anything more to do with them.

Mark found a modest, entry-level job making home deliveries, and their marriage was celebrated posthaste and unpretentiously. Jeannie, who had lost both her parents, already had at her disposal the house that they had left to her. During their brief prenuptial cohabitation there (between his departure from the center and the wedding) and in the initial days of their married life together, Jeannie noticed nothing strange about Mark. Exactly two weeks after the wedding, Jeannie used Mark's business vehicle to go shopping. On a curve, the glove compartment popped open, revealing drug paraphernalia. Jeannie immediately confronted Mark with her discovery. He tried unconvincingly to deny it but then—after the young woman's friends and relatives intervened—admitted that he had started using heroin again in his final months of residence in the rehabilitation community, taking advantage of his moments of freedom and taking up again with old companions. He also admitted that the reason why the community had sent him away was not so much Jeannie's pregnancy as the suspicion that he had gone back to using drugs, which Mark had been unwilling to face and explain, knowing that he would not be able to deny it for long. Finally, he admitted that in the few months before the wedding, while already living outside of the community, he had gone back to frequent intravenous heroin use, obtaining funds by pocketing some of the payments for the deliveries that he made and spending the money given to the young couple by relatives as wedding gifts. The balance of their joint account confirmed that he had withdrawn money. Friends too confirmed that Mark had asked to borrow money from them for implausible reasons.

Jeannie dealt resolutely with Mark. She said that they could resume their married life together only after he had been cured. Mark agreed to enter a new rehabilitation center. After just one day, however, he voluntarily left, fled the country, and for a long time was impossible to find.

When Jeannie initiated a canonical cause, the outcome was not positive as far as incapacity was concerned. Indeed, it was not possible to reconstruct exactly the level of drug use to which Mark had returned at the time of the wedding, and because of his noncooperation (his participation in the trial amounted to a short deposition in which he admitted the facts, and then he again went abroad, leaving dubious addresses), it was not possible to conduct an expert investigation of his personality. The facts about his drug use from the first rehabilitation center—where he was enrolled when he met Jeannie—went back many years. Those from the center where he stayed for only one day were too meager to be decisive. At the first center, moreover, no psychological testing had been done on Mark that could have made up for the lack of expert testimony. Furthermore, although Mark had admitted that he had started taking drugs again some time before, at the time of the wedding he was not yet manifesting particularly strange behaviors or those that are typical of the worst phases of drug addiction. When he had left the rehabilitation center and was staying in Jeannie's house before the wedding, she herself had noticed nothing until they were married and she made her dramatic discovery.

For the aforesaid reasons, it proved very difficult to determine with moral certainty Mark's lack of discretion of judgment, since it was not possible to ascertain the level of drug use that he himself admitted and that witnesses confirmed, or to study his personality.

The case, on the other hand, did have a positive outcome on the ground of deceit, since in the present case we find the elements required by canon 1098, which are also found in the example reported in chapter 3 on error of fact concerning the same individuals, Mark and Jeannie.

This example—from a didactic perspective concerning psychological incapacity to marry—is meant to illustrate summarily how, in the absence of valid medical documentation and given the impossibility of expert assessments, some cases that may appear simple to the layman can be remarkably difficult to prove, although at the same time it may still be possible to prove the existence of another cause of matrimonial nullity.

Third example

The engagement of Cynthia and Pete did not go well. Pete was very jealous and said strange things to his fiancée. He accused her of paying attention to other young men and would not be persuaded by Cynthia's reassurances. At one point she tried to break off the engagement, but Pete started calling on her again and Cynthia went back to dating him. Their relationship led also to intimate relations, and Cynthia became pregnant. In the little provincial town, the logical solution, it seemed to both of them and to their families, was marriage.

As the wedding day approached, Pete's behavior did not improve. On the contrary, his jealousy of Cynthia became increasingly intense. A few days before the ceremony, upon returning to the house of Cynthia's parents after a dinner for relatives from both families, Pete, noticing his fiancée's muddy boots (it was winter and the weather was nasty), made a scene, jealously accusing her of having met a lover, whereas until that moment they had been together, in the presence of their relatives. Although worried, Cynthia was not so alarmed as to abandon their wedding plans, which had been announced, as had her pregnancy.

A few weeks before this incident, Pete had been admitted to a hospital in that region for various complaints. At that time he was assigned to the medical ward, but his file (which was later obtained as part of the documentation of the case) noted the beginnings of delirium on the part of the subject. He saw other people "giving him the evil eye"; he suspected that they were laughing at him and trying to play pranks on him.

After the wedding Pete's situation worsened very rapidly. He began to mistreat his wife, even physically, despite the fact that she was still pregnant, and he made absurd accusations. For instance, he said that she had concealed her true identity from him and was secretly playing opposite him as an actor in a televised reality show. In his social life and at work too, Pete's behavior indicated that he was headed for a breakdown. An employee in a small food service business, he reported to law enforcement authorities that poisonous substances were being administered to him to harm him and "to fry his brain", as he himself put it. The employer had to sue him for slander in order to defend the reputation of the small business. The judge ruled that there was no reason to proceed because of Pete's mental illness at the time of the incident.

The incidents of domestic violence, the extravagant statements to the police, the strange behavior at work, and also the medical treatments that Cynthia had to undergo because of her husband continued. Cynthia, who meanwhile had given birth to the baby, separated from Pete, so as to protect the little one from his outbursts. Even after the separation, Pete continued to harass Cynthia with his jealousy and irrational resentment. He even began to wall up the door to her apartment with bricks and mortar and was taken away for involuntary hospitalization based on reports from neighbors.

Other hospitalizations followed, with increasingly clear diagnoses pointing to paranoid psychosis. During the course of the canonical trial too, Pete manifested the deplorable state to which his illness had reduced him. He appeared a few times but on days and at hours of his own choosing, repeating his unlikely accusations with regard to Cynthia, embellished with increasingly unrealistic details. Cynthia was no longer an actress but rather the secret head of a criminal band that had carried him off in a helicopter and taken him to a mysterious locality where they hatched international plots with several officers who had survived from the Third Reich.

Compensating for Pete's unavailability for expert examination, on the excuse that he had duties as a surgeon in the United States (a practice that he claimed to have engaged in from the age of five), was the abundance of clinical records that the tribunal was able to obtain: practically speaking, all the files relating to Pete's hospitalizations, from the first one prior to the marriage to the many that followed the initial period of their marriage. In addition, the complaints that Pete had filed and his written ravings, which he also handed over to the tribunal, were useful material for the expert, who diagnosed a paranoid psychosis that was already full-blown at the time of the wedding, although it had not yet manifested itself in all its most disruptive symptoms.

On the basis of the expert diagnosis and of the facts that emerged in the instruction, the tribunal acknowledged Pete's lack of discretion and his inability to assess critically the rights and obligations of marriage, for example, the obligation to respect his wife's physical and moral well-being.

This example is intended to emphasize the importance of acquiring clinical documentation in cases of consensual incapacity, documentation that, if abundant, clear, and unambiguous, as in the case of Pete, can be the decisive element of proof and can even make up for the impossibility of firsthand examination by an expert.

Fourth example

William had had a rather unfortunate life, especially at the time of the delicate passage from childhood to adolescence. His parents, who were of modest means yet loved one another, died within a few years of each other, leaving William alone with a younger brother. William was placed in an orphanage for a short time and later was taken in by a maternal uncle, who was married and had a family. The uncle and his family were truly fond of William, who acknowledged that he always got along well with them.

Assisted also, at various times, by the charity of several priests in the area, William earned a college degree and found a job, distinguishing himself by his good work. He attended the local parish, where he experienced together with other youths the upheavals (ecclesiastical as well) of the seventies. On the threshold of young manhood, William met Miriam, who was a few years younger, with whom he entered into an engagement that lasted around four years. Despite some contrary opinions—for example, that of the aunt who was his guardian, who thought that the characters of the engaged couple were too dissimilar —William and Miriam solemnly celebrated their wedding. Their married life lasted around six years, with its good moments and also with difficulties that led the two young people to separate, although they hesitated and had second thoughts, given their good faith and the basic religious upbringing of both.

When he began to live with another woman afterward, William disputed the validity of his marriage, claiming a lack of discretion of judgment on his part due to alleged immaturity resulting from his unhappy family experience, assuming that he had gotten married while in a situation of conflict and prey to various uncertainties. He even relied on a pretrial expert report that supported his thesis.

The instructional phase of the canonical trial put William's claim in a much different light. In the first place, the facts that he adduced as proof appeared overemphasized and reinterpreted a posteriori. Contrary to the claim that he was a somewhat irritable and moody character, it emerged that William was a fine young man, at home and at work, and that years ago he had adapted well in the home of his uncle and aunt. There was no confirmation of the claim that there had been particular conflicts during his engagement, especially, as William maintained, with Miriam's parents. She herself, also involved in the case, denied it, and no one else confirmed it. Nor did anyone corroborate the prenuptial doubts that William claimed in court to have had. Not only could no confirmation of this be brought forward, but even the persons who at the time were closest to the young man emphasized his confidence and joy as he approached marriage. Nor did any evidence emerge with regard to the six years of married life that would support the claim of a deficient critical assessment on William's part of his marital obligations. No serious violation of his marital obligations emerged as proved. On the contrary, William had to admit that once, when confronted with the willingness of a female acquaintance to start an extramarital relationship, he had been able to resist and to keep the commitments that he had made with Miriam. Their marriage failed instead because of subsequent divergent interests and because of Miriam's weariness in following William in his preferred recreational activities, such as attending the away games of his favorite soccer team.

In the second place, the technical evidence proved to be counterproductive for William's claim. The pretrial expert report that accompanied the petition lost much of its value inasmuch as it was based essentially on a one-sided account by William, which was refuted by the testimony of witnesses during instruction. The author of the expert report, however, did not go beyond a diagnosis of immaturity in a slight or intermediate degree, with narcissistic personality traits.

During the canonical trial two official expert reports were then made, both of them about the actions and the person of William. The first, thoroughgoing and consistent with what was proved by the evidence, avoided psychoanalytic extrapolations based on an uncritical acceptance of the petitioner's current story and pointed out mildly neurotic personality traits in him. In keeping with the principles of Christian anthropology (e.g., not mistaking the operation of the unconscious in the psychological life of a human being for a necessarily pathological phenomenon), it declared that these traits had had only slight influence on the subject's critical capacities in general.

William, at his advocate's suggestion, designated his own expert, who produced a report criticizing the first official expert report. It did so, however, in a logically inconsistent way. It admitted the essential preservation of William's critical capacities and shifted the evaluation of the case to the perspective of canon 1095, 3°. This, however, was done rather vaguely with regard to the criteria that it cited, arguing, for example, that the marital relationship did not "work". This expert report was also inconsistent in its conclusion, since it did not venture to assert William's psychological incapacity (for any of the reasons mentioned in can. 1095) but only recommended the admission of another official expert report, for the sake of William's peace of mind.

This new official expert report was prepared, and—at the conclusion of an exhaustive examination both of the acts and also of William personally—it confirmed the results of the first official expert report. William's personality traits, which are to be carefully distinguished from disturbances of a psychological sort, by no means ever impaired his intellect and will, neither in making decisions nor in putting them into effect. His childhood experiences may also have had some effect on him but not in a substantial way that would deprive him of the ability to evaluate his own choices and to honor his commitments.

This example is intended to warn the counselor against letting himself be swayed by particularly sad cases (such as those relating to William's childhood) and against stereotypes that often do not fit (the orphan who remains immature; the only son who cannot become independent of his parents; the boy who lived in an institution and rebels for the rest of his life; etc.) Instead the advisor should evaluate the actual course of events, seeking with reference to the facts some initial exemplification or verification [of the petitioner's thesis]. The same caution should be used with psychological opinions that are based on one-sided accounts or are unclear in their clinical and (possibly) medicolegal outlook. Urging someone to initiate a cause on the basis of reports that have not been verified or of unilateral, vague psychological opinions often leads to disappointments during trial.

XI

Incapacity to Assume the
Essential Obligations of Marriage

(*Canon 1095, 3°*)

In the preceding chapter we dealt with the topic of psychological (in)capacity for canonical marriage, by commenting on the first two clauses of canon 1095. Therefore, as we study in this new chapter the scenario described in clause 3 of the same canon, we will be able to refer to the presentation of the matter there for many of the questions that arise.

Elements of substantive law

This norm establishes a principle that is logically and formally clear enough: those who cannot assume the essential obligations of marriage are incapable of contracting it. To this general principle the norm under consideration adds the prescription that said incapacity must originate in some cause of a psychological nature.

From a specifically formal perspective, canon 1095, 3°, appears to be extremely clear. So as not to let ourselves be fooled by appearances, however, it is advisable to subject its constituent elements to an analysis, albeit as simply as possible. Therefore, we will have to clarify (1) the concept and the type of incapacity intended by the norm, (2) the object of the incapacity itself, that is, what the "essential obligations" of marriage are, and (3) the proximate reason of the incapacity, in other words, the "causes of a psychological nature" to which the legal text refers.

1. In the first place, we must explain to what type of incapacity canon 1095, 3°, intends to refer.

The readers will recall that the first two clauses of this canon made reference to the intrinsic inadequacy of the matrimonial consent as a psychological act—in other words, its insufficiency as a human act in its subjective component, as a result of an insufficient use of reason or of an insufficient critical capacity, or else of insufficient internal freedom. In the present case, by contrast, the consent—while probably still sufficient as a psychological act, and therefore sufficient from the subjective point of view—is ineffective from the juridical perspective because of the lack of its object. In other words, inasmuch as it is not possible for the contracting party to fulfill those obligations that he may really intend to assume.

This, on closer inspection, appears to be exceedingly logical juridically and also consistent with the principles of marriage law—logical, above all, from a juridical perspective, since it must be considered a precept of the natural law that someone who is unable to carry out a particular promise is also incapable of making it in the form of a juridical obligation. This is also expressed in several classical maxims: *impossibilium nulla obligatio est* or *ad impossibilia nemo tenetur* [No one is obliged to do impossible things]. It is also consistent with the principles of the canonical system of marriage because, as the reader will surely recall, the object of the canonical marital covenant is the gift of oneself for the purpose of establishing a marriage (cf. can. 1057 §2). As was already remarked elsewhere, this rather abstract expression ("gift of self") finds its concrete juridical actualization when one assumes the burden of one's conjugal rights and duties with respect to one's spouse. Now, someone who is not in a position to guarantee that he will observe the rights and duties of marriage (or any one of them) must be considered a person incapable of validly establishing the (juridical) marital relationship.

From what has just been spelled out, it is rather obvious that the canonical system intends to take into consideration the profound personal involvement that occurs in the institution of marriage. It takes into consideration the person in his aptitude for marriage (albeit from the specific perspective of the essential obligations of marriage) and also marriage inasmuch as it is not only a covenant but also a state of life, or what classical canonists expressed with the effective expression *matrimonium in facto esse* [marriage in the act of being lived out].

It is also clear that the type of incapacity that canon 1095, 3°, intends to regulate is the inability to "assume" (inasmuch as the party is unable to fulfill) the essential obligations of marriage. Even the preparations for the new Code and, now, recent doctrine and jurisprudence too are largely in agreement in this sense. Clause 3 of the canon represents a scenario of incapacity distinct from the first two clauses, and is substantiated by the impossibility of achieving the object of what ought to be the obligatory essential content of the marital covenant. Nevertheless—as some commentators have carefully pointed out—the legislator has designated this type of incapacity *incapacitas assumendi* and not *incapacitas adimplendi*, to indicate, first, that it concerns not the mere fulfillment in fact of an obligation but the very prerequisites for its coming into being; and second, that the vantage point from which to evaluate whether or not the subject is capable of marriage in this regard can only be the point at which consent was given, in other words, at the historically definite moment in which the juridical relationship did or did not come into being.

Having clarified from a systematic viewpoint the concept of incapacity intended by the legislator in this case, it is necessary to spell out the same concept from the substantive point of view. In simpler terms, when should a specific person be considered incapable of fulfilling, and therefore of assuming, one or more of the essential obligations of marriage?

In this connection, we can only refer back to what was explained [in chapter 10] with regard to the topic of consensual incapacity. According to the standard of the authoritative instructions of the Pope commented on there, one can speak of true incapacity only when the subject's behavior (in this case, failing to fulfill or else positively violating one of the essential obligations of marriage) substantially escapes the control of his natural faculties of intellect and/or will. Otherwise, the subject—even though experiencing difficulties that have a psychological basis—can not be considered incapacitated in the proper sense.

In this regard, it is necessary to consider what some authors have noted, in the light of both the redaction history of this norm (initially, the various subjects were called *impotentia moralis*), and the traditional principles of moral theology, in which *magna difficultas* is equated with impossibility. Said authors, guided by these arguments, assert that such incapacity would be not only the physical impossibility of observing a particular obligation but also the moral impossibility, including precisely the concept of grave difficulty. One cannot but agree with the position of these scholars, such is the rational basis of their arguments. However, even when the question is framed this way, there is still a need to find an objective criterion for distinguishing between capacity (even in the presence of difficulties) and incapacity, or—otherwise stated— between "simple" difficulty and the "grave" difficulty of moral theology. This objective, rational criterion seems to be the one explained above: the substantial impairment (which does not necessarily mean the total failure) of the natural faculties of the person, intellect and/or will, the functioning of which is the basis for the subject's freedom and for the (juridical and moral) imputability of his actions to him.

2. The matrimonial incapacity we are dealing with is clearly correlated with the "essential obligations of marriage" by the norm that establishes it in positive law—or one might say, from a formal perspective—with those behaviors (actions or omissions) that can be required as a legal obligation and that relate to those aspects of the institution of marriage on which its very existence and its practical success depends. As we sometimes find it effectively explained, essential obligations are ones related to the very *esse* [being] and not just to the *bene esse* [wellbeing] of marriage.

Once this has been spelled out from a logical-formal perspective, it is still necessary to ask: But what, concretely, are these essential obligations of marriage? Can a list of them be made, perhaps an explicit, exhaustive enumeration?

To be perfectly clear, this is not possible at present. Indeed, the legislator did not produce a list defining explicitly what the essential obligations of marriage are, nor have canonists and tribunal judges arrived at common, constant positions in this regard.

This, however, does not mean that it is not possible to derive valuable guidelines in this regard from the legislation currently in force, from jurisprudence, and from canonical scholarship. Particularly persuasive is the approach that sees the determination of the essential obligations of marriage as something resulting from the very "essence" of marriage as a state of life (*in facto esse*), from the "essential" properties of that state described in canon 1056 and from the institutional ends described in canon 1055 §1.

Thus, included among the essential obligations of marriage would be those behaviors (here and in all the cases summarized below: both actions and omissions) necessary for the establishment of the partnership of conjugal life, those behaviors that necessarily result from the properties of the unity and indissolubility of marriage; and those behaviors that are necessary for the potential achievement of the institutional ends of marriage: the procreation and upbringing of children and the ordering of the marriage itself to the "well-being of the spouses". Canonical tradition has already studied some of these aspects in depth from the point of view of their content, even though presently they could be developed and researched further (think, for example, of the topics of marital fidelity and openness to procreation in relation to the development of methods of technologically assisted reproduction). Other aspects seem instead to be only hypothetically the object of incapacity, since one would have to consider it much more likely that possible shortcomings in their regard are to be traced back to voluntary choices (e.g., in cases concerning the indissolubility of the conjugal bond). Along this line of inquiry, the topics that appear to deserve further research are those pertaining to the establishment of the partnership of life and to the ordering of the marital institution to the well-being of the spouses.

In developing such research, it is necessary to be very careful and prudent, avoiding stereotypes and slogans. It will indeed be necessary to pay close attention both to the proper sense of the concepts that are employed and also to the context in which this reasoning is carried out (in this case, the context of canon law), in order to avoid ambiguity detrimental not only to the actual significance of the discussion but —even more seriously—to respect for the truth with regard to those whose state of life must be verified based on the application of the conclusions that are drawn.

Therefore, if in order to investigate the concepts "partnership of their whole life" and "well-being of the spouses", one tried to use the concept of capacity/incapacity for interpersonal relationships, one would have to keep in mind that the latter, belonging originally to the psychological disciplines, should in the first place be understood correctly in that context and then transferred to a canonical context in a way that not only is plausible and comprehensible from the logical perspective but also carefully verifies its compatibility with the very principles of canon law. If the concept of capacity/incapacity for interpersonal relationships were not clear in the context of psychology (and taking into account the sometimes-marked differences between the various schools of psychology whose studies are cited), and if the criteria for transposing this concept to a canonical context were not clarified, and the compatibility of this psychological approach with the fundamental principles of canon law were not verified, then the whole procedure—notwithstanding the good faith and right intention of the one initiating it—would be more harmful than helpful, both from the scientific viewpoint and from the perspective of enforcing justice.

To develop this concept along juridical lines (since the interdisciplinary developments just mentioned seem too complex for this context), it seems possible to say that the "partnership of life" described in canon 1055 §1 is rendered specifically conjugal in connection with its institutional ends and with the properties that characterize it. From this perspective, in order to explain in more detail the typically interpersonal aspect of this partnership, the institutional end of the "well-being of the spouses" deserves particular consideration. It is necessary therefore to try to identify a possible and plausible meaning of this term.

It is necessary to remark that canon law, in taking into consideration the well-being of the spouses as a possible factor of the subject's marital capacity, does not refer strictly speaking to the actual attainment of that well-being. The nonattainment of that well-being can in fact occur for reasons that are independent of the subject and conflict with his goodwill and aptitudes. The canonical norm envisages instead the capacity, in principle, that a particular subject possesses to order his own marriage to that well-being as its end and purpose. To make an analogy with regard to the other institutional end of canonical marriage: in determining the validity of a marriage, the juridical system does not assign direct relevance to whether children are born of it but rather to the subject's ability (or to his deliberate will) to perform the action (the natural sexual act) from which conception normally results.

That being said, the nature of this well-being that the spouses must be able to foresee as being at least possible in their union must be delved into. It appears indisputable that the well-being in question cannot be measured exclusively by subjective parameters, which in practice coincide with the mere personal satisfaction derived from the actual marital experience. If that were the case, we would be confronted with not only the impossibility of verifying anything whatsoever, given the extreme variety of people's personal characteristics and subjective preferences, but also the possibility of paradoxical situations. For example (anticipating some of what will be said below), two morally twisted persons who committed acts of sexual abuse violating the duty of fidelity would have to be regarded as fostering the "well-being of the spouses" within the scope of a valid canonical marriage, because they were subjectively satisfied with their behavior.

Then too, elaborating what is already partially contained in the example just given, this well-being of the spouses cannot be thought of in a way that obviously contradicts the principles of the Christian (Catholic) view of the human being and of marriage. Thus, to maintain that the well-being of the spouses is the possibility of reaching a satisfactory emotional and sentimental agreement of compatible characters, while the absence of such agreement and subjective satisfaction would be sufficient reason to dissolve or to declare null their own marital commitment, would mean to argue on the basis of presuppositions that are difficult to reconcile with the fundamental principles of the system of thought and values within which canon law is situated.

In developing a juridical argument that aims to maintain the continuity of the canonical system of marriage, clarified and deepened by sensitivities that the conciliar and postconciliar Magisterium have undoubtedly developed, it seems advisable to avoid unproved slogans such as talk about a "new" vision of marriage derived from the Council, or about "overcoming" a "legalistic" view in favor of a "personalistic" vision, etc. Rather we must take as our starting point what the previous legislation presented in canon 1013 §1 as the interpersonal ends of the institution of marriage. These ends were described by the 1917 Code as "secondary" not (according to some commentaries) to set up a hierarchy of value and dignity among the ends belonging to marriage (as was affirmed by the Magisterium of Pius XII but not further repeated by the Council or by the subsequent papal Magisterium and canonical discipline) but to indicate the specifically interpersonal aspect of genital sexuality that immediately (and therefore "primarily") characterizes the conjugal union between a man and a woman. As is well known, these secondary ends of marriage were called *mutuum adiutorium et remedium concupiscentiae* [mutual help and remedy for concupiscence].

Now, the fact that the legislator in the 1983 Code noted the interpersonal end of marriage with a different, fuller terminology (precisely in terms of *bonum coniugum*, "the well-being of the spouses") does not mean that the ends noted by the previous legislation have been abolished or rejected—not in the least! On the contrary, they must be included among the interpersonal ends of marriage, not merely because of the principle of positive order that establishes a line of interpretive continuity between the two Latin Codes of Canon Law of the [twentieth] century (cf. can. 6 §2), but rather for a substantial reason, since the aforesaid conceptualizations are surely qualified to give a useful and appreciable meaning to the more comprehensive concept of the "well-being of the spouses". Does this concept imply greater respect for the things that can be expressed by the formulas "mutual help" and "remedy for concupiscence"? We must wait for the legislator himself, or else a constant doctrinal and jurisprudential agreement, to clarify the question. Meanwhile, it is no small thing to identify a sure meaning that is to be attributed to the expression "well-being of the spouses", which can be considered truly essential to the valid constitution of a marriage and is not already included among the other acknowledged ends and essential properties of marriage.

Certainly, the formulas in question must be understood correctly, particularly in light of the Council's sensitivity (but not change of doctrine) in marital matters. Thus, by the expression "remedy for concupiscence" we must understand the possibility of exercising genital sexuality in a way not only respectful of the procreative end of conjugal union but also conducive to an at-least-minimal psycho-affective and psychosexual integration. Such integration is certainly impossible when sexuality can be experienced only in a violent or seriously immoral way, or when the exercise of sexuality decreases quantitatively, for reasons that cannot be imputed to a voluntary choice by both spouses, to a level far below what is normal. In this connection it is evident which elements in the above-mentioned examples could more clearly illustrate what has been stated.

The expression "mutual help" should be understood as the person's ability to offer his spouse at least minimal help—both moral and material—with regard to the circumstances of life, especially in their intimately personal aspects (e.g., help in the event of an illness) or the aspects closely involved in the common duties that result from marriage (e.g., the help in the upbringing of children, albeit with a reasonable division of responsibilities).

It is obvious that what is required of persons with regard to matters affecting the very validity of marriage can only be a minimum. It is clear that this minimum is the measure just sufficient to establish a valid conjugal bond and not, in contrast, what is to be hoped for in order that that same marriage might have a good outcome and the spouses might be better equipped to overcome the weariness and inevitable difficulties that occur in every vocation and walk of life, including married life. It is also clear that pastoral assistance, both in pre-nuptial preparation and post-nuptial pastoral care, must aim to encourage and to support the maximum potentialities present in the spouses (cf. can. 1063) toward that objective. Nevertheless, what is advisable and desirable cannot be assumed as a criterion of matrimonial capacity and hence of the validity of the marriage itself without contradicting the vision of the human person and of marriage underlying the legal system and without contradicting in practice certain principles of that same system that have been clearly affirmed, for example, the common presumption of a person's juridical capacity to contract marriage (cf. can. 1058).

3. The third clause of canon 1095 states that the type of matrimonial incapacity for which it offers a juridical regulation must result from causes "of a psychological nature". It is necessary to elaborate several clarifications concerning this normative provision.

In the first place, we need to recall that quite a few eminently trustworthy experts have criticized the legal provision that we are commenting on. Their argument can be summed up as follows: clause 3 of canon 1095 expresses a precept that can be considered to be of natural law. It affirms that someone who cannot in fact fulfill an obligation cannot make the commitment to do so; in other words, the transactional will is ineffective if its object is unattainable. These experts remark that this is true whatever the reason for that impossibility may be. Therefore, stipulating that the matrimonial contract is null if the impossibility of its object results from "causes of a psychological nature" should be considered superfluous on the one hand and unduly restrictive on the other.

This reasoning should be considered correct and generally acceptable, of course, and the principle of natural law that it expresses should be considered operative even if it is not canonized in a regulation of positive law specifically about marriage. It remains to be seen why the legislator decided to highlight the cause "of a psychological nature" at the basis of the type of matrimonial incapacity that he regulates in canon 1095, 3°. By way of argument there appear to be grounds for supposing that the legislator's choice is the result of reasons essentially related to the redaction history of the legislative text. For one thing, it started by postulating a "moral impotence" resulting from a psychological or psychosexual anomaly. Furthermore, since the norm in question went from being an autonomous norm to being part of a single canon regulating the consensual capacity of a party contracting marriage, it seems obvious that attention remained focused on the psychological aspect in particular. Finally, the need to find a formulation that would meet with the greatest possible consensus within the commission that prepared the legal text meant that the causal description itself progressively acquired an increasingly general and comprehensive meaning: from the initial phrase "psychosexual anomaly" to the serious "psychological anomaly" and finally to the very general description, "causes of a psychological nature".

In the second place, we must ask what, at a general level, these causes "of a psychological nature" are to which the norm refers. It is in fact obvious that the adjective "psychological" covers a rather vast spectrum of meanings, describing everything that has to do with the spiritual dimension of the human person. Thus, it could refer to cultural or educational factors, or even to moral and (therefore) voluntary factors. We must not forget, however, that the immediate context for this to the human psyche is that of matrimonial incapacity. Therefore, "causes of a psychological nature" must be understood in this context as those aspects of the person's spiritual dynamic that make him unable to place the specific act that is matrimonial consent, and for the specific reason of being unable to assume some one of the essential obligations. Within these parameters, it seems clear that the only "psychological" factors that come into consideration here are the ones that correspond to the genuine criterion of incapacity. What this criterion is has been repeated several times already: the essential unavailability to the subject of his intellect and/or will in carrying out his own behavior, when this is detrimental to some essential obligation of the married state.

Thus, it seems to follow that "causes of a psychological nature" in the sense understood by the norm do not include something that is under the control of the subject's deliberate will, whether fully (an aspect that possibly could involve the phenomenon of simulated consent), or incompletely, if the subject is somehow "conditioned" in his actions by educational, cultural, and/or environmental factors. These circumstances, indeed, can make the subject predisposed to act in a certain way, particularly inclined toward a certain behavior, yet not incapable of acting differently. To give a clearer example: an individual with little moral training, in a social and cultural setting marred by the worst sort of "machismo", could be particularly inclined to violate the essential obligation of marital fidelity, exploiting every occasion to do so. To maintain, however, that this proclivity makes the subject incapable of acting differently would mean to contradict one of the cardinal principles of the Christian view of the human being, the principle of personal freedom and responsibility to the extent that true incapacity has not been proved. To extend the boundaries of this "incapacity" by an extensive interpretation of the concept of "psychological" as it refers to the causes of said incapacity appears to be inconsistent with the way in which incapacity itself must be understood and, above all, with the fundamental principles of canon law in marital matters. Besides—even from a pastoral perspective—interpretations of the norm and jurisprudential practices that in fact undermine personal responsibility would be rather debatable from the perspective of the person's upbringing and with regard to the witness that canonical discipline must give to Christian values.

From this, we can conclude, in summary, that the notion of a cause of a psychological nature—with respect to incapacity for the essential obligations of marriage—cannot be other than what corresponds to the general criterion of matrimonial incapacity. It follows that we cannot talk about incapacitating causes of a psychological nature except in the presence of a serious form of anomaly relative to some essential aspect of conjugal life, however it may be described and classified from a clinical perspective.

In the third place, we must point out what these anomalies are in fact, at least the ones that have been recognized most frequently in jurisprudence as causes (of a psychological nature) of the incapacity to assume the essential obligations of marriage.

As was said already in connection with consensual incapacity in the proper sense, it is not possible to make a complete, exhaustive, and definitive list of all the anomalies that can cause incapacity to assume the essential obligations of marriage. However, apart from consensual capacities strictly speaking, we should point out, among the reasons most often proposed for inability to assume the essential obligations of marriage, several sexual disturbances and personality disorders.

The former may in fact preclude the possibility of finding in one's spouse the prerequisites for an at-least-minimal psychosexual integration, through an exercise of genital sexuality that respects the human person and the moral norm, or indeed that does not deviate greatly from the statistical norm. Among these are forms of sexual hyperesthesia (satyriasis and nymphomania), some serious conditions of sadism and sadomasochism, some degrees of homosexuality, full-blown situations of transsexualism (whether or not surgical modifications of the anatomy have taken place), and other serious sexual dysfunctions.

The latter, that is, personality disorders, may seriously compromise the possibility of an at-least-minimal psycho-affective integration, as far as this concerns the mutual moral and material help that one may legitimately expect from a spouse. For example: those affected by extremely serious forms of narcissism, which precludes at the very least the possibility of conjugal love that is not mere sentiment but also "benevolence" toward the other, since the narcissist loves only himself; antisocial personalities or those particularly prone to violence, which places at risk the physical integrity of the spouse and of the children, precluding also any proper sort of upbringing; and particularly weak personalities who allow themselves to become heavily involved in taking toxic substances such as alcohol or drugs or in expensive habits that are dangerous for family life, such as gambling, which can jeopardize the family's very means of subsistence and lead to dangerous contacts with nefarious persons and the criminal underworld.

4. As we mentioned earlier, the type of matrimonial incapacity regulated by canon 1095, 3°, was initially called "moral impotence". Perhaps also because of this analogy with the norm referring to copulative impotence (cf. the current can. 1084 § 1), canonists have debated, and still are debating, several characteristics of canon 1095, 3°, that in their opinion would be proper to it: antecedence, perpetuity, and relativity.

In this connection—and remaining at the level of maximum simplicity that ought to characterize this book—we should observe first of all that, unlike what happens when the norm related to copulative impotence is applied, canon law does not require these characteristics in order for there to be the type of incapacity described in canon 1095, 3°. Although this exegetical, literal argument cannot definitively decide the question, nevertheless it is important in guiding our interpretation of the norm. And so, subjecting the three characteristics mentioned above to further critical analysis, we consider it necessary to explain the following.

As for the antecedence of the incapacity to assume matrimonial obligations, we must consider how this squares, in practice, with the requirement that the incapacitating circumstance already effectively exist in the person at the moment of consent, although it may not already have manifested itself in its full set of symptoms. This is true also for latent incapacity: what may be latent, indeed, are only the symptoms of that incapacity and not the basic personal condition that makes people incapable. Some authors have claimed that the incapacity must be, at the moment of the marriage ceremony, present *in actu primo proximo*, in other words, in such a way as to emerge also at the factual and symptomatological level in contact with everyday married life. This perspective seems acceptable, since it does little to change the general requirement that the personal situation at the root of the incapacity for one of the essential obligations be present at the moment of consent. If things are considered in this way, it appears after all that the characteristic of antecedence is implied in the very concept of matrimonial incapacity in the proper sense (i.e., the sense relevant to the validity of the marriage). Indeed, not only for incapacity but also for every other cause of matrimonial nullity, it is necessary for the factual circumstance that is the empirical basis for the situation that the law considers invalidating or incapacitating to exist at the moment when matrimonial consent is given. Therefore, it seems to be irrelevant to insist on the antecedence of the incapacity: it is enough to require that the incapacity itself exist as such at the moment when the marital covenant is made.

As for the perpetuity of the incapacity to assume marital obligations, the discussion seems more complex. Indeed, besides the fact that perpetuity is not a normative requirement for incapacity, it is necessary to point out several distinctions.

First of all, although they are materially similar, the concept of juridical perpetuity must not be confused with the concept of the clinical incurability of a specific anomalous situation. So it is also in the case of copulative impotence, where the morality and actual feasibility of the means that would have to be used in order to remove the impediment are considered in the specifically juridical, nonmedical concept of perpetuity.

In the second place, it is necessary to distinguish, among the essential obligations of the married state, some obligations that are binding, as canonists say, *semper et pro semper*, in other words, at every moment, and others that instead bind *semper sed non pro semper*, in other words, obligations that are permanent in principle yet admit of suspensions in their fulfillment. An example of the first type, which are also called negative obligations (inasmuch as they consist of "not doing" something), is the obligation of conjugal fidelity, which is contravened by even one single violation. An example of the second type, which are also called positive obligations (inasmuch as they consist of "doing" something), is the obligation of mutual help. Although as an obligation it is permanent, there are in fact, however, situations (e.g., illness, physical separation) in which the subject may be temporarily excused from fulfilling it.

Taking into account the distinctions made above, we can draw the following conclusions. Surely for negative obligations, which bind *semper et pro semper*, it makes no sense to require the perpetuity of the incapacitating situation, since even one single violation of the obligation, if it was beyond the subject's deliberate control, would be sufficient to constitute a situation of incapacity. In contrast, it would make sense to require perpetuity of the incapacity with regard to positive obligations, which oblige *semper sed non pro semper*, among other reasons because one would have to ask whether a temporary subjective unavailability with regard to this type of obligation could conceivably constitute a situation of true incapacity. This provides a point of view rather than a principle. From a practical perspective, on the other hand, taking especially into account probative requirements, one must argue that if a specific subjective situation is clinically incurable (or curable only with difficulty), it may be considered an indication of a serious condition, and therefore, it more likely corresponds to the concept of incapacity.

To conclude our discussion on this point, we can emphasize that, in a careful assessment, the characteristic of the perpetuity of the incapacity essentially ends up being reduced to that of the "authenticity" of the same sort of incapacity.

Several things weigh against the admission of a "relativity" of the incapacity described in canon 1095, 3°: the silence of the law on this topic; the fact that the incapacity in question appears to relate to the essential obligations of marriage rather than to the person of the spouse; and the fact that the criterion of incapacity expounded, for example, also in the two addresses of the Pope to the Roman Rota (1987 and 1988), points rather clearly to a manifestly individual condition.

In favor of the admission of a "relative" incapacity to assume marital obligations is essentially the argument that although it is true that the incapacity regards the essential obligations of marriage, it is nonetheless true that these obligations are assumed not in the abstract but rather in reference to a specific person.

In the estimation of this author, the first position seems more persuasive; moreover, it is the one more commonly found in rotal jurisprudence, which is a reference point for the application of the juridical norm. Indeed, this position appears to offer greater security regarding the verification of the constitutive elements of the concept of incapacity: both in connection with the subjective situation of "anomaly" at the root of the unsuitability for marriage and also in connection with the actual correlation of the incapacity with the essential obligations of marriage, as distinct from a maladjusted character, which in contrast does not instantiate the concept of incapacity that we have sought to spell out.

This does not mean that the person of the spouse of the allegedly incapacitated party should not be taken into consideration in assessing the latter's situation. The spouse, however, must be regarded not as the cause of his incapacity or as one variable in an addition problem that adds up to the [relative] incapacity of two persons who are individually capable, but rather as a circumstance that may merely have contributed to the emergence on a symptomatological level of the signs of the individual situation of the one party's incapacity.

To conclude this discussion of the characteristics of the incapacity to assume the essential marital obligations along the lines of canon 1095,

3°, it seems possible to say, in the wake of several lucid scholarly opinions as well, that the fundamental question on which to focus is the question of the authenticity of the incapacitating situation at the moment of consent. Antecedence and perpetuity appear to be included in said authenticity, and relativity is a prior question that belongs to the definition of the very concept of marital incapacity.

Guide for the counselor

As for suggesting several points of investigation for the counselor of couples with intractable marital problems who is considering the possibility that at least one of the spouses was incapable of assuming the essential obligations, it is good to recall substantially what was already explained with regard to consensual incapacity properly speaking (can. 1095, 1° and 2°). Indeed, although formally they should be carefully distinguished, the three scenarios have quite a few points of contact: both theoretical, in other words, as far as the criterion of incapacity is concerned, which is the substantial impairment of the intellect and/or the will in making a decision (can. 1095, 1° and 2°) or in fulfilling the obligations assumed with the decision (can. 1095, 3°); and also practical, inasmuch as the same anomaly sometimes may cause more than one type of incapacity among those envisaged by canon law.

Therefore, we refer the reader to the ten areas of inquiry set forth in chapter 10 of this book, which is dedicated specifically to the incapacity to consent, while noting that—for the purpose of investigating a possible incapacity to assume the essential obligations of marriage—it will be necessary to investigate particularly area no. 8 relative to the possible violation of some specific obligation of the married state. In other words, it will be necessary to determine clearly which essential obligation or obligations of the marital state have been violated by the subject who declares himself incapable. Indeed, it would be altogether inconceivable to declare a person incapable of assuming the essential obligations of marriage if it had not been shown that any one of said obligations had been violated. Moreover, it would be profoundly unjust and contrary to the right of defense of the parties in the case to rule in favor of incapacity without determining which obligation the person proved incapable of fulfilling. Therefore, even in the preliminary investigation, it is necessary to examine whether some sort of serious neglect was committed by one of the interested parties, either as spouse or as parent. In the absence of serious and specific failings or neglect in these areas, the counselor would have to refrain from suggesting the possibility of a case due to psychological incapacity and, if anything, refer the individual to another expert who was professionally more qualified. Above all, the counselor must not allow himself to be fooled into giving immediate opinions by generic expressions such as, "There was no dialogue"; "He (she) never cared about me"; "He (she) thought only about himself (herself)"; "He (she) did not really love me." He should have the patience to ask for some example illustrating the sort of remarks just recorded, so as to verify whether there is in fact behind them something precise that may be relevant.

Examples

In keeping with our predetermined methodology, a few examples may hopefully help to clarify further the more abstract discussion in the previous sections of this chapter.

First example

George and Lucy were engaged for several years, preparing for their planned marriage. During the engagement there were no particular problems, even though they were occasionally sexually intimate. During their honeymoon trip, however, some problems became evident: George wanted to travel to Amsterdam during their honeymoon, and he was particularly interested in visiting the districts of that city that are sadly infamous for their overt prostitution, both male and female. Furthermore, during that same trip, George confided to Lucy that in the past he had had homosexual relations, at least one of them an ongoing relationship. Lucy was upset by this revelation; nevertheless, since she loved George and since he had told her about these incidents with a sense of sorrow and suffering, she considered it right to stay with him and forgave him for admitting them so late.

Their married life continued for a few years but was never happy. Their marriage was consummated, and there were some (infrequent) intimate relations between the spouses. Most times, however, George was disinterested in Lucy, or else altogether incapable of maintaining an erection for conjugal relations with her. Lucy, a rather simple person with little education and a very reserved character, did not dare to turn to anyone for help. Instead, she just bottled everything up inside herself, allowing only a sense of dissatisfaction and sadness to seep through.

In order to earn a degree that might lead to career advancement, George began to attend evening classes, staying after to study with several fellow students, in particular with one of them, another man. Besides, his presence at home and the time that he dedicated to Lucy were very limited anyway, in spite of the fact that his work schedule was much less demanding than that of Lucy, who was an employee in a commercial office. Later it turned out that George in his free time (or rather in the hours that he did not spend with his family) was visiting districts of the city that were notorious as homosexual meeting places.

Increasing the sense of estrangement between the spouses, George told Lucy about a new homosexual experience of his. George related the matter in very vague terms and made little of it as an occasional episode. Many facts, however, suggested that that was not the case. One particularly convincing sign of this was that George began an openly homosexual lifestyle. Lucy left him after this new development. He then became well known in the city where they both resided. George himself, who proved to be very cooperative and sincere during the trial, clearly admitted these facts.

The cause, which was initiated on the grounds of George's incapacity to assume the essential obligations of marriage, was rather complex, especially in point of law, since it was not easy to frame a situation like George's in juridical terms.

On the factual level, besides the reconstruction of the sequence of events briefly summarized above, it was possible to conduct an expert examination, with which George cooperated thoroughly and honestly, although he did not initiate the cause and was not particularly interested in it.

Here too, however, there was no lack of difficulties. Indeed, a first official expert report proved to be altogether insufficient. Among the various reasons for the inadequacy of the expert report was its obvious inconsistency with the principles of Christian anthropology. Indeed, the expert concluded his hasty presentation by saying that George proved to be a "bisexual, therefore normal" person. A further, more serious expert examination showed that George was affected by a serious personality disorder, characterized by a state of considerable uncertainty with regard to his sexual identity. He "is not a homosexual exclusively, but an extremely fragile person who allows himself to get involved in disordered sexual relationships in which his own weakness and the seriously disordered state of his own personality manifest themselves. He is profoundly uncertain about himself and incapable of deciding his own future, even with regard specifically to his psychosexual orientation." The expert prognosis too, in this case, seemed rather unfavorable toward George.

The judges of the case—although aware of the extremely delicate nature of the question—ruled that George, although capable of physically consummating the marriage on some occasions, was incapable of guaranteeing minimal psychosexual integration with his spouse and incapable even of observance of the obligation of fidelity. Indeed, they judged that George—who was not even sure about his sexual identity or about what choices he wanted to make concerning it—could not assume the obligation to carry out the responsibilities of a husband toward his wife, or present to her the possibility of a minimal psychoaffective and psychosexual integration. Furthermore, manifesting his personal fragility especially in his proclivity to let himself become involved in disordered sexual relationships (predominantly with members of the same sex), he was unable to guarantee the other party an exclusive right to acts of genital sexuality. In these terms, George was not able to guarantee in principle the institutional ordering of marriage to "the well-being of the spouses".

This example intends to highlight how—appearances notwithstanding—it is particularly complicated to apply the norm under consideration to the scenarios of real life, both by determining the type of essential obligation of marital life that would be involved in a specific case and also by detecting an anomaly of such importance as to fulfill the criteria for identifying an authentic incapacity for marriage. It may be of interest to note that the approach taken in resolving this case was confirmed by a sentence of the Roman Rota, which heard the case on appeal.[1]

---

[1] Cf. *coram* Funghini, December 19, 1994, in Apostolic Tribunal of the Roman Rota, *Decisiones seu sententiae* 86: 764–83.

Second example

Wilma was adopted by a good family—a couple without children—in which she got along rather well. She was grateful for the adoption and the affection of her adoptive parents; therefore, she willingly and often followed their advice, even in less important matters, and regretted it if she caused them displeasure in any way.

Not highly endowed intellectually—although good-natured and affectionate—Wilma led a tranquil life between home and school, where she had changed her course of studies after her first year at a high school that was too demanding for her (resulting in failure). At about the age of eighteen, Wilma happened to become acquainted with a certain Philip, an assistant manager of a business. Philip began to court Wilma persistently, and she agreed to engage in sexual relations with him, through which she became pregnant. After explaining the matter to her parents and discussing her lamentable situation with them, Wilma agreed that marriage would be the most advisable solution. No pressure was exerted on Wilma to marry. Her adoptive parents, although not very enthusiastic about the marriage in itself, inasmuch as they had guessed the unreliability of Philip's personality, offered to help the two young people, both with the wedding and in setting up a household afterward, allowing them to live temporarily in their large house.

After the wedding was celebrated, their life together lasted only a few months. When Wilma gave birth, the two were actually living apart and had already applied for a legal separation. The unfortunate course of their married life was due to Philip's behavior. After the wedding (unlike before) he turned out in fact to be rude to Wilma and his in-laws, violent and selfish toward the young pregnant woman, and interested instead in material possessions. Indeed, Philip himself was the one to leave the house of Wilma's parents where the two were living as guests, having understood that the young woman's father (wisely enough) was unwilling to give him money immediately for a new automobile and for the rather adventurous start of his own business.

The canonical cause was framed in terms of Wilma's lack of discretion of judgment and her incapacity to assume the essential obligations of marriage. Emphasis was laid in particular on the young woman's presumed inability to make decisions, influenced by her adoptive parents, who held traditional opinions in moral matters.

Two expert reports, one commissioned by the party and the other official, affirmed that the young woman was remarkably immature. These opinions notwithstanding, the judges did not deem it necessary to draw from the expert assessments the conclusion that Wilma was incapacitated, since they found no proof of true facts demonstrating such immaturity and not even an anomalous dependency of Wilma on her parents but only attitudes that could be explained by the life story of an affectionate, grateful young woman who found herself in an unexpected, embarrassing situation. Among other things, no outside pressure was exerted to limit her freedom or to influence, as an aggravating factor, her hypothetical lack of internal freedom. Then too the judges found that no failure to fulfill the essential obligations could be imputed to Wilma, and this persuaded them—circumstantially with regard to defect of discretion, and directly with regard to the incapacity to assume the obligations of marriage—to render a negative decision. Indeed, Wilma, during the few months of living together with Philip, sought to be a good wife and to bear with the situation as it worsened, trying to give no sign of it to her parents so as not to sadden them and hoping that Philip would go back to treating her as he had done during their engagement. Once their child was born, she dedicated herself maturely and affectionately to his care and upbringing, as all the persons examined in the case agreed in testifying. Since no deficiency could be found in Wilma, either as wife or as mother, it was therefore impossible to demonstrate her incapacity to assume the essential obligations of marriage.

This example is meant to highlight, in the first place, the possible concurrence of two hypotheses: consensual incapacity properly speaking (here, lack of discretion) and incapacity to assume the obligations. They can be taken into consideration together or else subordinately, by dealing eventually with the inefficacy of consent for lack of its object (can. 1095, 3°) only after ascertaining the existence of an intrinsically sufficient consent as a psychological act (can. 1095, 1° and 2°).

In the second place, this example points out that proving an allegation of incapacity must above all else take into consideration concrete facts while evaluating expert opinions on the basis of their consistency with those same facts. In particular, in the absence of actual violations of some essential obligation of married life, generic statements about immaturity will not be enough to issue a sentence in terms of incapacity.

This is not to deny that—in Wilma's case too—there might be a certain degree of immaturity and lack of preparation for marriage. It is simply the case that a tribunal cannot declare incapable of assuming the essential obligations of marriage someone who, although affected by some difficulties of a psychological nature, has not violated those obligations or who perhaps has fulfilled them quite well even in difficult conditions.

Third example

Patricia was a young woman from a good, traditional family that was fairly well off. She met and fell in love with John, a young man known in their little town and the surrounding area for his unruly life. Not a very steady worker, without a diploma, violent, irritable, and a drug user, John (or rather, Patricia's relationship with him) met with a very bad reception from the young woman's family. Patricia, however—on the one hand emotionally and physically attracted to John, and on the other hand stubbornly opposing the attitude of her own relatives—wanted to get married. She was urged to do so by John himself, who had taken the negative attitude of Patricia's relatives toward him as a sort of personal challenge.

The married life of this couple can truly be described as a disaster because of John's actions, which were not at all in keeping with the duties of a husband. Already on their honeymoon trip, he proved to be inclined to infidelity and sought to involve his wife in the same behavior. Indeed, when he met a couple of strangers who offered drugs and the opportunity for group sexual experiences, John promptly joined in. When Patricia finally understood where it would all end and rebelled, John was deeply resentful because of the lost opportunity, something for which he later reproached Patricia several times. To him it seemed that he had suffered a wrong and not that he himself had failed to fulfill one of his duties as a spouse.

Nor did his behavior in this respect improve after they returned home. John was repeatedly unfaithful, having quickly tired of his wife after achieving his victory in the "challenge" from her parents. In other respects too John's behavior proved to be lacking. He never held down a regular job, and because of absences, poor results, and insubordination, he lost several positions obtained for him by Patricia's parents, who were aware of the difficulties the young couple were having and wanted to help. Indeed, since funds were short for maintaining John's deadbeat lifestyle, he ended up moving in with a band of thieves. The couple's house became a meeting place for these persons and for those who purchased stolen goods from them. If Patricia tried to protest— which she did less and less often—the only argument that John knew was physical abuse.

The chief need for money on John's part resulted from his habitual, daily use of drugs. He also introduced Patricia to drug abuse. Initially out of curiosity and defiance of the rules against it, then as an apparent but illusory relief from the disordered situation to which she had willingly banished herself, Patricia too became a habitual drug user, to the point where it compromised her health. A treatment program she entered following this abuse is precisely what led to their actual separation, since Patricia found people ready to help her to get away from the source of her problems. It turned out, indeed, that John arrogantly continued in the same disordered lifestyle, untroubled by the outcome of his marriage, except for resentment toward Patricia for having left him.

When the canonical cause was initiated on the grounds of John's incapacity to assume the essential obligations of marriage, it was possible to conduct an expert examination of the young man. Even during the expert examination he reasserted the guiding principles of his own way of life, presenting himself in attire and with an attitude that were entirely inappropriate. Since it was hot he showed up at the expert's office with his shoes in hand, having just stepped into a fountain to cool off. Then, noticing several handsome pieces of furniture in the waiting room of the clinic, he offered to obtain others, obviously referring to stolen goods. The in-depth, direct contact in the diagnostic dialogue with the psychologist and the reconstructed facts of the case allowed for the diagnosis of a serious personality disturbance, with antisocial traits.

On the basis of these results, the tribunal judged John incapable, in principle, of ensuring that his marriage would be ordered to the good of the spouses. The tribunal's decision was based on a series of facts: his continual infidelities and his urging his wife to act the same way; his involving his wife in drug use and his initiation into circles where crime was a way of life; and his violation of his wife's physical integrity, knowing and using no other argument than blows and intimidation (to say nothing of other specifics that prudence and decency demand not be repeated). The assurance that these facts were symptoms resulting from John's distorted personality structure, which was clinically acknowledged and deemed serious, led to the conclusion that an authentic matrimonial incapacity on his part was well founded. This case was not about generic immaturity, different characters, or misunderstandings that originated or intensified after a few years but rather about specific, serious, continual violations of the other spouse's personal dignity, in the form of attacks on her physical integrity, lack of fidelity, failure to provide economically except through illegal means and for shameful ends, and involvement in practices harmful to health and in settings of depravity. Psychosexual integration worthy of Christian marriage (e.g., respect for the exclusivity of the sexual gift of self) or the prospect of an at-least-minimal mutual help, both moral and material, with regard to the necessities of life and the duties of the married state, were not within John's powers.

This example intends to draw attention to the fact that, even in apparently more extreme cases, before suggesting a canonical cause it is necessary to make certain that there is, at least at the initial level, the possibility of tracing the facts of the case back to some specific essential obligation of the married state and the cause of the non-fulfillment back to a reason that is independent of the subject's deliberate will.

Fourth example

Claude and Marina had been seeing one another for some time. After choosing to have intimate relations before marriage, Marina became pregnant—hence their plans for marriage, which beforehand the couple had not yet discussed concretely. Marina proved to be a not very attentive or faithful wife, and after a few years of married life she left Claude. He, wishing to regain his own freedom so as to marry another young woman whom he had met after being abandoned by his wife, initiated a cause of nullity on the basis of simulation on Marina's part. The instruction produced little evidence on this ground. Some witnesses, however, within the context of an overall description of Claude as a good guy, asserted that he was "immature" and "not ready for marriage". On the basis of these generic opinions (not supported by facts to prove them or by any indication of the criteria on which they had been based), Claude was advised to abandon the ground of nullity that had been advanced at the start of the cause and to introduce the same cause in terms of his incapacity to assume the essential obligations of marriage.

The tribunal therefore investigated the question by way of an expert report. It turned out to be entirely inconsistent with the alleged grounds. The objective examination revealed nothing anomalous in Claude; however, it declared that he was immature, seriously so, on the basis of two facts that he declared to the expert. One was his viewing of a sports event on television with friends before his wedding ceremony, which was held in the late afternoon. The other was his having been scheduled to see the expert at a certain hour on each of two days, and his arriving around an hour earlier than appointed; he was seen by the expert himself standing around on the public square below. These facts, in the absence of other clinically relevant data, could be explained otherwise: the first by the tension of the moment, which was relieved by watching sports with friends; and the second by the fact that Claude, aware of the importance of these sessions for him, and having to travel from a distance to the city where the expert resided, had been unable to take a later train without arriving late, and so politely waited for the hour of his appointment with the expert.

Upon the publication of the acts—which, as noted, were devoid of facts verifying Claude's alleged incapacity—and of the unsatisfactory expert report, which was illogical and deduced disproportionate conclusions from rather unsubstantial facts and offered a psychopathological explanation that did not necessarily appear to be cogent, Marina was summoned (until then she had been absent from the trial) to the tribunal to read the acts of the case. On that occasion the judge urged her to make a deposition of her own. In it, Marina declared very serious facts and reproached Claude for incurring gambling debts, beating her to get money, and showing no interest in her and their daughter on the occasion of a serious illness and a long recovery in the hospital. It is clear that these facts—if true—could have provided important corroboration of Claude's hypothetical incapacity and a minimal basis for the expert judgment (notwithstanding certain methodological reservations). It is clear, moreover, that these facts had to be verified and that Marina's statements when she was summoned could not be considered proved *eo ipso* [by that fact alone], since all the witnesses in the case—even those who thought that Claude was immature and not ready for marriage—portrayed Claude as a good guy, respectful, hardworking, nonviolent, and without serious vices. As it turned out, the verification that was carried out enabled the defender of the bond to refute Marina's statements, which were obviously motivated by resentment toward Claude. This refutation enabled the tribunal to confirm the weakness of the case, which could only be concluded with a negative decision.

This example is meant to exhort counselors of couples with intractable marriage problems to consider very prudently the possibility of causes based on psychological incapacity, recalling that it must correspond to real facts and to the criteria explained above. The counselor should not let himself be influenced by generic declarations of immaturity or unpreparedness but should demand specific examples. Then, given an account of precise facts, he should not fail to recall that they must be subjected to evaluation by the tribunal, which can render its judgment only on the basis of verified facts. Above all, the counselor should recall that psychological incapacity to marry is the exception, not the rule, much less a pretext for resolving the outcomes of unfounded cases. It is not good pastoral practice to create false expectations that the tribunal, which must base its work on proven facts and judge according to the common criteria for interpreting the law, will later then have to disappoint.

XII

Conditional Consent

In this new chapter of our book, we must deal with a rather complex case of matrimonial nullity, that of consent subject to a condition. The complexity of this question makes it advisable to avoid technicalities and the consideration of secondary aspects of the problem and to limit ourselves instead to a plain exposition of the fundamental knowledge—at the level of substantive law and of probative principles. Such knowledge may prove useful for an initial investigation by pastors of souls who have the impression that they are facing a case of matrimonial nullity of some member of the lay faithful who has turned to them for counsel and spiritual guidance. In presenting these elements of knowledge and reflection, we will proceed according to the tried and true expository outline used thus far.

Elements of substantive law

1. It is good, in the first place, to identify immediately what is to be understood by the term "condition", or indeed to offer a definition, a concept of it. It is clear that, in the present context, this concept must be understood with reference to conjugal consent, which as we know constitutes the essence or the "efficient cause" of the matrimonial covenant. In this context, "condition" must be understood as the correlation of the consent to a specific circumstance that is future and uncertain, upon whose existence or absence the person giving consent intends to make the juridical efficacy of his consent dependent, either by suspending said efficacy at the level of juridical relations until he ascertains that that circumstance has been verified, or else by intending to deny that efficacy upon ascertaining that the circumstance has not been verified.

To use an idea derived from civil law scholars as a further clarification of the concept of condition in the field of canon law, one could describe the phenomenon of conditional consent in these terms: it is a phenomenon of the will of a subject who, wishing to place a particular juridical act (in this case, matrimonial consent), finds himself confronted with a sort of conflict of interests. On the one hand, the subject intends to place this act and wants it to produce the effects that the legal system attributes to it. On the other hand, he wants to do this "only if", "provided that", there will be other particular circumstances, not envisaged by the law as necessarily being correlated with that act but that are, in his personal judgment, extremely important in order for the placing of that same act to be justified and to occur in what he considers optimally convenient conditions. If these circumstances or conditions do not materialize, the subject intends to deprive the act that he has performed of its efficacy, or to revoke the effects that, according to the standard of the juridical ordinance, he had agreed to attribute to it.

If the concept of condition is understood in this way, it becomes easier both to identify what can be considered its most proper and typical aspect and to distinguish this phenomenon from others that merely resemble it and must instead be differentiated in order to avoid dangerous confusions. This presentation is relatable to experiences and cases in everyday life, as the examples in the third part of this chapter well demonstrate.

The most typical and most proper aspect of the phenomenon of a condition is the connection, which derives from the subject who places it, between the object of the condition itself (the particular circumstance that is wanted or unwanted) and matrimonial consent, from the specific viewpoint of its efficacy. It is a very close connection whereby —to express the matter figuratively—one can say that the condition "affects" the consent, "enters into" the consent. Consent exists as an act of the subject's will, and as such it cannot be annulled or canceled (according to the reasonable classical principle whereby *factum infectum fieri nequit* [what is done cannot be undone]). However, the subject intends to "block" its efficacy, the production of its proper effects, or else to "interrupt" that production depending on the coming to pass (or not) of the circumstance that has been "tied" in conditional form to the consent itself.

In other words, the subject makes one of two things dependent on the circumstance that is the object of the condition (1) either the coming into existence of the marital bond (which is the proper effect of the consent, once given) or (2) the fact that he himself remains bound by that same bond.

This allows us to distinguish a true and proper condition from other figures that can be found in the reality of human relations (and therefore also of law) and are merely similar to condition. And the criterion for this distinction consists precisely of that peculiar connection between condition and efficacy of consent that we have sought to clarify thus far and that does not exist in the phenomena that only resemble condition.

Thus, it is necessary to distinguish condition from a presupposition or a prerequisite. In this case, indeed, the desire for a particular circumstance (e.g., a certain individual quality of the person chosen as spouse) does not "enter" into the consent, jeopardizing its efficacy, but is only a motive, a presupposition of the consent, which is given without establishing such a strict connection with that particular circumstance. To illustrate by a concrete example, there is a mere prerequisite in the case of a woman who married Tom because (among other reasons) she observed that he shared her religious, social, and political ideals. Her assessment is only a presupposition of her choice of Tom as a husband, since it does not imply per se and necessarily that she intends to subordinate the effects of her own matrimonial consent to the actual sharing of these values on the part of Tom.

Thus, condition must be distinguished from a "mode" or "obligation", in other words, a commitment that the subject believes that the other part has assumed simultaneously with matrimonial consent, although the consent is given independently (as to its efficacy) of the sincerity of that commitment and of its actual fulfillment. Thus, Harry, who married Kay with the understanding that she would help him run his business, merely intended to propose a particular obligation to his future spouse, without it necessarily and per se prejudicing the efficacy of the consent to marry that they intended to give.

These distinctions, obviously, have an importance that is not only speculative but also practical, since canon law connects conditional consent alone to nullity of marriage.

2. Having sought to clarify the concept of condition in itself and by distinguishing it from other scenarios that are merely similar to it, it is now necessary to explain briefly the types of conditions that can occur. As we will see, canon law also takes these possible figures into consideration:

a. In the first place, we must recall what a condition is in the proper sense, that is, the condition *de futuro*, inasmuch as the circumstance implied in the condition (or its object) is constituted by a future, uncertain fact. This type of proper condition normally has the effect of suspending the effects of the consent. The subject, in other words, does perform the act of matrimonial consent but intends to suspend his effective commitment to the bond of marriage until the fact that he sets as the condition of his own marriage is accomplished. This is easy to understand and to imagine concretely when the future fact is an event that happens at a point in time. Thus, for example, Tom might marry Kay while intending that his own commitment, even though manifested externally, should start effectively only when her father dies and Kay inherits the possessions that Tom wishes to have.

When the object of the condition is, by contrast, a fact that, although beginning at a point in time, is supposed to be perpetuated over a subsequent period of time, especially when it is a reality that is not desired but rather feared by the subject who sets the condition, the condition itself can appear in a resolutive form of the marital commitment. This would be the case of Tom, who in marrying Marcia, intended to break the marital bond in the event that Marcia did not give him an heir within a specified time.

Two important clarifications must be made in connection with what has just been said.

Condition in the proper sense and par excellence must be considered not only a condition *de futuro* but also and more precisely one that suspends the effects of the consent. On closer inspection, indeed, a resolutive condition ends up being nothing but a case of simulation of consent, specifically in the form of a rejection of the irrevocability of consent and of the indissolubility of the matrimonial bond once it has been established. Concerning this we will have to go back and explain the conditions that the 1917 Code called contrary to the substance of marriage.

Again, it is necessary to make a clarification in connection with those conditions *de futuro* that the scholarship and jurisprudence customarily call "potestative". These make reference to a future fact (normally to a series of facts, in the form of an attitude or a behavior) that is indeed uncertain as to its actual occurrence yet is within the control of the subject to whom the condition is proposed. For example: continuing an activity that is so highly appreciated by the subject who sets the condition that he binds to it his own matrimonial commitment ("I marry you on the condition that you will always live in my father's house and will take care of my parents when they are old and sick"); or else abstaining permanently from a behavior that the subject who sets the condition considers harmful, especially with regard to the conduct of married life ("I marry you on the condition that you will not go back to using drugs; or on the condition that you will not start gambling again"). This potestative condition was the object of special treatment on the part of canonists and jurists and needs to be explained right away. This special treatment was essentially a result of taking into account practical and moral problems that follow from having to consider matrimonial consent "suspended" indefinitely in time and dependent on someone else's behavior and decision. Think of the serious incongruity of the prolonged lack of conformity between the substantive and formal situations in such an important matter as the state of life of two persons; or of the moral problem of the illicitness of marital relations engaged in by the parties when the consent of one of the two is pending—in other words, when the parties are not yet effectively spouses. Therefore, the canonical scholarship and jurisprudence proceeded to establish a *fictio iuris* [legal fiction] by virtue of which the "purification" of the condition (or rather, of the will of the subject who sets the condition to produce the effects of the consent that he has given) was related not to the actual behavior of the one in whose power lay the fulfillment of the condition (e.g., continuing to help the spouse's parents, or abstaining from the use of drugs) but rather to the sincerity of that person's commitment, at the moment of consent, to ensure the fulfillment of the condition proposed to him. This solution certainly resolved the incongruities mentioned above. Indeed, it avoided a situation in which the consent remained suspended as to its efficacy in bringing the conjugal bond immediately into existence. Nevertheless, it was still a highly artificial

solution (precisely a *fictio iuris*) that was often quite far removed from
the actual reality of things. Indeed—to clarify this with an example
—it is obvious that someone who proposes the condition to her
future spouse that he not go back to using drugs intends not merely
that he should be sincere at the moment when he promises not to
do that anymore but rather that her husband-to-be should not go
back to using drugs as long as they are married. It must be said,
however, that canonical jurisprudence always was well aware of the
artificiality of this solution, recognizing that the proposed reasoning
would have to yield to the reality of the facts, or rather to proof
that what was intended as the object of the condition was not the
sincerity of the possible promise made at the moment of consent
but rather the effective fulfillment of what was required under the
form of a condition.

It must finally be mentioned that the discipline established by the
current Code (both Latin and Eastern) overcomes this entire set of
difficulties in practice. Indeed, the new discipline attributes force
that invalidates consent to every condition *de futuro*, regardless of its
type and content, and therefore also to a potestative condition.

b. Canon law also takes into consideration the conditions that
were traditionally called "improper". These indeed do not refer to
a future, uncertain fact, correlating the efficacy of the consent to
its verification. Rather, they refer to a fact that was past or present
at the moment of consent (hence to a fact that had already come
to pass), the exact knowledge of which, however, eludes the person
who places a condition in that regard.

Traditionally, these juridical figures are called conditions *de praeterito* (inasmuch as they refer to a past event) and *de praesenti* (inasmuch
as they refer to an event that is present with respect to the moment
of consent).

By their very nature, the influence of these types of conditions on
the efficacy of matrimonial consent is profoundly different from that
of a condition *de futuro*. Indeed, it is clear that the efficacy of matrimonial consent cannot remain suspended or possibly be retracted.
On the contrary, that efficacy will or will not be real immediately,
depending on whether or not the fact on which consent is conditioned actually exists. In the final outcome, even for the subject who

places the condition himself, that objective reality will be unknown until there is certain knowledge about the fact that is the object of the condition.

To offer some examples here too, by way of explanation, we can suppose the following cases. A woman who said to her fiancé, "I marry you, but on the condition that you were not in fact the one who caused the death of my father"; or the man who said to his fiancée, "I marry you, but only if the child that you are carrying in your womb is truly mine", would thus subject her or his matrimonial consent to a condition (respectively *de praeterito* and *de praesenti*). Now, being or not being the murderer of his fiancée's father, and being or not being the mother of the child of one's fiancé are facts that in themselves are certain and objective at the moment when a condition referring to them is placed. Hence the efficacy that the parties intend to give to their own consent (and therefore also the validity or invalidity of the matrimonial bond that results from it) are also facts that are in themselves certain and objective at that same moment. They are uncertain only relative to the knowledge of the one who places the condition and, normally, of third parties as well. More complex would be the discussion—which is not worth entering into here—about the certainty of the knowledge on the part of the person to whom the condition is proposed. Indeed, in this regard such a one could find himself in a position of considerable uncertainty, both as to the reality of the fact that is made the object of the condition and also as to the resulting validity or invalidity of the matrimonial bond. But that person could also be essentially in a position of certitude, knowing, for example, that he was the suspected murderer, or knowing that her current pregnancy in reality resulted from relations with a person other than the husband-to-be.

These examples certainly help to understand the logical structure of conditions relative to a present or past fact. The marriage to which they are correlated is or is not valid depending on whether or not the fact that is the object of the condition actually exists. And it is so, obviously, from the very moment when consent is given. Do not forget, however, that once consent is given, the marriage must be presumed valid and that therefore its invalidity is what must be demonstrated, and not the contrary. Hence, knowledge of the possible invalidity can be had only when the factual situation on which the possible original nullity depended has been demonstrated with moral certainty.

3. We must ask ourselves now why canon law attributes invalidating force to the imposing of conditions on matrimonial consent. In other words, we must ask about the foundation, the *ratio*, of this normative provision.

This question is certainly not pointless or purely academic. Indeed, if we keep in mind the fact that other legal systems (cf. art. 108 of the Italian Civil Code) assign no importance to conditions that may possibly be imposed on matrimonial consent, we can easily understand how this peculiarity of canon law can help bring to light some specific aspect of this same discipline.

Making reference particularly to the law of the Latin Church (although later on the Eastern Catholic discipline will also be taken into consideration explicitly), we can develop the following considerations. The invalidating force of conditioned consent must be considered a logical requirement of the "contractual" nature of the marital covenant. This statement must be understood correctly in order to avoid the pointless oversimplifications of dumbed-down popularizations. It certainly does not intend to depreciate the personal aspects of the nuptial covenant by comparing it, for example, to a legal transaction over property. On the contrary, in light of the canonical tradition, this statement expresses the role of the sole "efficient cause" (in the proper sense) that must be assigned to consent in terms of the production of the matrimonial bond. This statement highlights the unique role of consent as the "efficient cause" (in the proper sense) that brings into existence the matrimonial bond. It is precisely to guarantee the actual will of the subject that canon law does not consider it possible to ignore a condition that the subject may have imposed on his own consent. To put it more simply, canon law, which regards marriage as resulting from the consent of the parties, logically has an interest in ascertaining what the parties actually willed. If one of the parties of the conjugal covenant intended to deprive his own external consent of any substantial efficacy by conditioning it on the existence or nonexistence of a particular fact, the law cannot help but take note of this, nor can it presume (without intrinsically contradicting itself) to disregard or even to make up for that essential lack of matrimonial intention.

When things are explained this way, it is easy to see that the attribution of relevance (and even of invalidating force) to a condition imposed on consent is not a merely logical or technical-juridical requirement. It draws on higher moral principles that inform all of canon law, especially the substantive discipline of marriage law. And it does this, most particularly, in a twofold way:

(1) By respecting the freedom of the contracting party in his own self-determination, especially with regard to the choice of his state of life. This principle is sanctioned as one of the common rights of the faithful (cf. can. 219) and is confirmed in the acknowledgment, on the level of the will to marry, of what each of the contracting parties has actually willed, even if they subordinated their manifest will and its efficacy to some condition.

(2) By underscoring (and, in part, by penalizing) a certain dissonance that one cannot help but detect between the conditioning of one's own consent and the "purity" that ought to be found in the gift of self to the other in marriage. Indeed, imposing a condition (whether it suspends the effective establishment of the marriage, or ends in the possibility of revoking the consent, or subordinates the efficacy of consent to a past or present fact) does indeed make the gift of self in the matrimonial covenant less pure, less complete.

Finally, upon closer inspection, the two moral principles just mentioned cannot be considered mutually contradictory. Indeed, the exercise of individual freedom and its recognition necessarily entail a corresponding recognition of the individual's responsibility in connection with his actions and decisions, especially when these involve—in an extremely important matter—third persons and the whole ecclesial community.

4. Now that we have sought to clarify the concept of condition in relation to matrimonial consent and explained its possible typologies, and suggested the reasonableness of canon law's treatment of condition, we must move on to explain the positive discipline that canon law sets forth for conditional matrimonial consent. We will have to consider, although briefly and very simply, the discipline of the 1917 Code, that of the Latin Code currently in force, and that of the Eastern Catholic Churches.

a. It is indispensable to consider the discipline established in the 1917 Code concerning conditional matrimonial consent, in order to understand the content of the current discipline of the Latin Code and also to point out the changes in this matter between the one codification and the other. The previous discipline is contained in canon 1092 of the 1917 Code, a rather complex ordinance that begins with an introduction and then goes on to regulate the juridical effect of various types of conditions.

The introduction to this canon expresses an important principle, even on the probatory level. It declares that the juridical effects that are established in the following clauses must be referred to a condition that is "imposed and not revoked"—in other words, to a condition that, having been placed by a voluntary act at a determinate moment previous to the manifestation of consent (and therefore not necessarily at that moment), has not subsequently and before the giving of consent been retracted by a new act of the will. Two things are therefore taken into consideration: (1) that an act of the will that places conditional consent persists virtually unless a contrary will supervenes; and (2) that once the placing of a condition has been proved, its persistence must be presumed and the contrary cannot be presumed but only positively demonstrated (hence the reference to the additional probative importance of the principle).

Having made this important introductory statement, the 1917 Code considers the effects of several types of conditions concerning matrimonial consent, dividing the presentation into four clauses: the first three dedicated to conditions *de futuro*, the fourth dedicated to conditions *de praeterito* and *de praesenti*.

—Clause 1 considers the effects of some particular conditions *de futuro*, specifically those that, while not contradicting the "substance" of marriage (that type of condition is contemplated in clause 2 of the canon), fall into one of these three categories: necessary conditions (e.g., "I marry you only if the sun rises tomorrow"); impossible conditions (e.g., "I marry you only if the sun does not rise tomorrow"); and conditions of turpitude (e.g., "I marry you provided that you will be my accomplice in this criminal activity"). For these types of condition, the 1917 Code states that they have no effect on the efficacy of matrimonial consent, it is as if they had not been placed (*pro non adiecta habeatur*). It is not difficult to understand the reason for this normative provision. For the first two types of conditions being considered here, necessary and impossible conditions, the reason is a logical one. It is unthinkable that someone might seriously have wanted to condition his own commitment on something that either would certainly materialize or else would never materialize. In that regard there can be no doubt or uncertainty, and logically, there is no room for the serious placing of a condition. For the third type of condition, described as a condition of turpitude, the reason for the discipline is rather of a moral character. Indeed, it is repugnant that a marriage should be so closely correlated to a criminal practical agreement between the two contracting parties that they would mutually bind themselves to the purpose of committing actions that are contrary to morality and/or to the law.

This regulation of the 1917 Code—while understandable from the perspective of the commonsense logic and the moral requirements that it manifests—was nevertheless subject to a particular criticism, which was probably the reason for its disappearance from the current Code. The criticism was that in the cases envisaged (even though they are statistically rather rare) the law supplies in practice the consent of the subject, disregarding his actual will and overlooking the condition he set. This "supplying" was, from a systematic perspective, an inconsistency with respect to the cardinal principle of matrimonial law: the principle of the sole causality of the personal consent of the contracting parties in establishing the marriage.

—In clause 2 of canon 1092, the 1917 Code takes into consideration a second type of condition *de futuro*, which it describes as being "against the substance of marriage" (*contra matrimonii substantiam*). The "substance" of marriage must be understood to mean the totality of juridically relevant and protected values that correspond to that which—according to the classical terminology—is the essence, the institutional purposes, and the essential properties of the institution of marriage.

Proposing a view that is not inapplicable to the 1917 norm, it must be said that the essence of marriage consists of a partnership of their whole life between a man and a woman, the constitutive moment of which was raised by Christ the Lord to the dignity of a sacrament. This partnership of life is institutionally ordered to the procreation and upbringing of children and to the mutual perfecting of the spouses, which is to be accomplished through moral and material assistance in the vicissitudes of life and in the fulfillment of the duties of the married state. This state then entails an indissoluble and exclusive bond between the spouses. The latter "note" or feature of marriage [i.e., exclusivity] finds its particular expression in the duty of conjugal fidelity. These contents are (in a way not essentially different from the current legislation) the "substance" of marriage, and the 1917 Code ascribes invalidating force to any condition contrary to this substance, or contrary to any qualifying aspect. Nor could it be otherwise, inasmuch as such a will would be totally or partly contrary to the genuine plan of Christian marriage and intrinsically contradictory to what ought to be authentic conjugal consent. And indeed, on closer inspection, such a condition *contra matrimonii substantiam* is nothing but a particular type (characterized precisely by the "conditioned" form) of total or partial simulation of matrimonial consent, which is already in and of itself relevant for purposes of the validity of the marriage. For this reason it may be considered unnecessary to have a separate provision of its own (with respect to simulations) as the cause of nullity of consent. This is the basis—together with the choice of the new discipline as a whole in terms of conditions *de futuro*—for the fact that this figure of conditions "contrary to the substance of marriage" is no longer envisaged in the present Code.

—In clause 3 of canon 1092, the 1917 Code takes into consideration the condition *de futuro* that it describes as "licit" and decrees that placing of such a condition entails the suspension of the validity of the marriage (*valorem matrimonii suspendit*). Several clarifications are necessary.

What are we to understand by a "licit" condition about the future? The contents of this concept can be specified only in reference to the other types of condition *de futuro* that have already been regulated. Thus, we are to consider "licit" any condition whatsoever that is not necessary, impossible, of turpitude, or contrary to the substance of marriage.

What does it mean, then, that the placing of a condition of this type "suspends the validity of the marriage"? And until when does it suspend it? Strictly speaking, the aforesaid expression does not mean that the matrimonial consent or the marriage is invalid. Properly speaking, rather, it means that the consent, albeit manifested, is nevertheless voluntarily ineffective and that the marriage—by the will of the person who places the condition—is not constituted until the fact that is the basis of the condition has been verified. This simple overview already shows how complex and thorny are the problems raised by suspensive conditions, especially when they are further complicated by the presence of "potestative" conditions. These suspensive conditions create uncertainty in juridical relations, introducing a discrepancy between the external appearance and the actual situation of the persons, and they raise moral problems—for example, with the use of marriage until the "purification" of the condition, or until the confirmation of the fact that is the object of the condition. Since we already pointed out earlier the artificiality of the scholarly and jurisprudential solution devised for potestative conditions, at this point it is not difficult to understand the choice of the legislator of the 1983 Code as far as all possible conditions *de futuro* are concerned: in other words, the decision to attribute invalidating force to them—regardless of the type and of the effects that they might per se intend to produce on the consent. In this way, effective recognition is given to the conditioning will of the subject, and at the same time certainty concerning the state of the persons and whether or not their marriage is valid is obtained from the moment when consent is given.

—In clause 4 of canon 1092, the 1917 Code regulates the juridical relevance of improper conditions to the validity of marriage, in other words, conditions *de praeterito* and *de praesenti*.

The normative precept points out the effects that *de praeterito* and *de praesenti* conditions have in common: marriage subjected to this type of condition must be considered valid or not, according to whether or not the fact that is the basis of the condition exists. To return to the examples already cited earlier. In the case of a fiancée who imposes on her own consent the condition that her fiancé was not the murderer of her father (condition *de praeterito*), the marriage will be invalid in the event that the fiancé really was the murderer but valid if the fiancé was not the perpetrator of that crime. In the case of a fiancé who imposes on his own consent the condition that the child is really his (condition *de praesenti*), the marriage will be invalid if the pregnancy was another man's doing but valid if it was caused by the fiancé who places the condition. As was already mentioned, in this type of condition there is no suspension, or any possibility of revoking the consent. The marriage immediately and irrevocably comes into being or not, depending on whether or not the object of the condition exists. This is true on the objective plane, in principle. On the other hand, on the level of fact—more precisely on the level of knowledge of the possible invalidity of the specific marriage (for the one imposing the condition as well as for the community)— there can be moments or situations of uncertainty, depending on uncertain information about whatever is the basis of the condition. Canon law offers the possibility of a canonical trial, with its public form and characteristics, as a way to attain certainty in such matters.

b. In canon 1102, the 1983 Code presents a very simplified discipline concerning conditional consent, both in its form and its substance. The reasons that led to this disciplinary modification have already been stated in part, in the explanation of the older discipline. Now it is necessary, however, to set forth completely the main lines of the new legislation.

Unlike its counterpart in the 1917 Code, canon 1102 no longer has an introduction that is then developed in four clauses but instead presents three distinct paragraphs. Gone is the introduction from which it was necessary to deduce the presumption of the perseverance (as to the substance and as to the proof) of a condition that has been set and not revoked by a new act of the will. This, however, must not be thought of as an actual disciplinary change in this matter, since the principle enunciated is a logical requirement, corroborated by scholarship and jurisprudence, and therefore has no need of a normative iteration in order to be operative.

Canon 1102 is composed of three paragraphs, which are dedicated as follows: the first to conditions *de futuro*; the second to conditions *de praeterito* and *de praesenti* as to their substantive discipline; and the third to the rules that render licit the placing of a condition relative to the past or to the present. From the quantitative viewpoint alone, we already see a significant simplification, especially with regard to the space dedicated to conditions *de futuro*.

—The first paragraph of canon 1102 is dedicated to "proper" conditions, that is, to conditions *de futuro*. It formulates an extremely clear and simple precept: "A marriage subject to a condition about the future cannot be contracted validly." (*Matrimonium sub condicione de futuro valide contrahi nequit.*)

As a consequence of this very clear statement it must be affirmed that, from the moment when it came into force, any marriage (subject to the rules of ecclesiastical positive law; cf. cann. 11 and 1059) that is subject to a condition *de futuro* is by that very fact invalid. In other words, the invalidity of such a marriage depends on the very fact of the placing of a condition *de futuro*, regardless of its content or of the effects that the subject intended to correlate with it.

This new rule appears altogether reasonable—above all because it eliminates the drawbacks and the grounds for criticism that were occasioned by the earlier norm: (1) the incoherence of allowing the law to "supply" in practice the efficacy of the consent in the case of conditions that were necessary, impossible, and depraved; (2) the fact that it was not strictly necessary to provide that conditions *contra matrimonii substantii* [against the substance of marriage] —in particular resolutive conditions—have an invalidating effect, inasmuch as they are nothing but a simulation of consent; and (3) the complexity of the juridical and moral problems resulting from the concept of the "suspension" of the efficacy of consent in conjunction with licit conditions about the future, which is still further complicated in the case of potestative conditions.

In the second place, this new rule seems reasonable inasmuch as it appears to correspond correctly to the reasons why canon law devotes space to the phenomenon of the possible conditioning of matrimonial consent, outlining its various requirements. On the one hand, the law acknowledges (and does not supply) the effective will of the contracting party who sets a condition (i.e., that the marriage should not come into being substantially except in the presence of that particular fact). On the other hand, it simultaneously punishes—through a general declaration of nullity—the fundamental inconsistency that must be observed between spousal consent, which has as its object the gift of oneself that is achieved by assuming the rights and duties of spouses (cf. can. 1057 §2), and the placing of a condition, which makes that interpersonal gift less pure, less whole, and precisely less "unconditional".

—The second paragraph of canon 1102, in contrast, regulates the effects of improper conditions, in other words, conditions *de praeterito* and *de praesenti*. In this matter there is no need to point out any disciplinary change or innovation. Indeed, entirely in keeping with what was established in the earlier norm, the canonical legislator decrees that a marriage subjected to these types of conditions should be considered valid or not according to the existence or nonexistence of the fact that was made the object of the condition. Therefore, on this topic, we can only recall what was already observed in the context of the explanation of the discipline of the 1917 Code.

—Finally, the third paragraph of canon 1102 decrees—in this case by introducing a rule that was not previously codified—that for the licit imposition of a condition *de praeterito* or *de praesenti* on matrimonial consent, written permission from the local ordinary is necessary. What is the justification for this disciplinary innovation? It should be recognized in the need to stress the extraordinary nature of imposing conditions on matrimonial consent, by having the ordinary intervene for the obvious purposes of supervising and (at least implicitly) discouraging such conditions. The ordinary could indeed refuse his authorization, or else by his authority help to clarify any possible obscure points and doubts that exist at the basis of the intention to place a condition on one's own consent. Indirectly, this provision may also play an important probative role in the case of a trial (e.g., concerning the validity of the marriage) whose object is to prove (among other things) the placing of a condition. Indeed, it is clear that the written permission of the local ordinary must be considered a public ecclesiastical document (cf. can. 1540 §1) that serves as proof of what it directly and principally affirms (cf. can. 1541)—in this case, precisely the placing of and the type of the condition.

c. As far as the discipline of the Eastern Catholic Churches is concerned, it is necessary to point out that—in keeping with their constant disciplinary tradition and as a clarification of what was already codified by Pius XII[1]—canon 826 of the CCEO [*Codex canonum ecclesiarum orientalium*, Code of Canons of the Eastern Churches] decrees that a marriage subjected to a condition cannot be celebrated validly. (*Matrimonium sub condicione valide celebrari non potest.*)

As the CCEO makes clear, for the Eastern Catholic Churches a marriage subjected to any type of condition whatsoever is invalid. Hence, not only conditions relative to the future render the marriage invalid *eo ipso* (as is true also in the present Latin discipline) but also those relative to the past and to the present, regardless of whether or not the fact that is made the object of the condition exists. There is therefore, in regard to these last two types of conditions (*de praeterito* and *de praesenti*) a difference between the common legal systems of the two great traditions of the one Catholic Church.

We might wonder whether this difference between the two normative systems is also a contradiction that cannot be reconciled from the logical, systematic perspective and can be justified only on the basis of historical reasons involving the respective disciplinary traditions. Without trying to diminish the normative diversity, it nevertheless seems possible to understand the noncontradictory character of the regulations under consideration. Indeed, by comparing the two normative systems on the topic of conditional matrimonial consent, we can give an account of their essential consistency.

In neither case do the two systems supply the consent of the contracting party by disregarding his matrimonial intention, which may possibly be conditioned. For a condition in the proper sense (a condition *de futuro*) both systems immediately establish the nullity of the marriage. For conditions in the improper sense, the CCEO also declares the nullity of the marriage. The CIC does so only in the case of the reality of the fact to which the contracting party intended to correlate that effect.

One can speculate that this difference in discipline (apart from the principles on which both hinge: consent cannot be supplied, and consequently it is impossible simply to regard a deliberate condition as though it had not been placed) expresses two sensitivities that are somehow present in both normative systems and that receive,

---

[1] Motu proprio *Crebrae allatae*, can. 83 (February 22, 1949).

in this matter, emphases that are only different but not contradictory. In particular, the Eastern law could be said to take to an extreme the necessity of the "purity" of matrimonial consent, sanctioning with nullity any consent subjected to a condition, even when it is "purified" in fact. Western or Latin law could be said to pursue the concrete analysis of the consent, verifying, at least in the case of improper conditions (which, as we said, do not lead to the uncertainties of suspending or revoking consent), whether or not the conditioned will expressed by the contracting party corresponds to reality. With all due caution about using generalized ways of speaking (based on slogans and catchwords), one could say that the differences described here correspond to the more "spiritual" emphasis (in the East) and to the more "concrete, historical" emphasis (in the West) of one and the same substantially consistent disciplinary system.

5. Moving on, finally, to a consideration of several probative guidelines for conditional consent, it is necessary to recall that, considered in itself, the placing of a condition on matrimonial consent should be considered an act of the will. Therefore, in demonstrating condition, it is possible to employ—with due adaptations or additions—the probative schemes developed by jurisprudence to facilitate and guide the reconstruction of a voluntary act that must be proved in court. Having stated this in advance, suggestions on this topic of proof can be elaborated as follows:

a. In the case of conditions *de futuro* according to the Latin law (can. 1102 §1), or in the case of any type of condition whatsoever in a marriage to be judged according to the Eastern Code (can. 826 CCEO), the sole object of proof is the fact that the condition was placed. Indeed, it is from the placing of a condition that the nullity of the marriage follows immediately. According to the guideline recalled a little earlier by way of introduction, it is possible to obtain proof of this fact by a twofold method, which should almost always be pursued concurrently.

—Thus, the imposition of a condition can be proved by the direct method, starting from the judicial declaration by the party who asserts that he placed the condition (especially if it is credible in terms of canons 1536 §2 and 1679)—but above all by gathering testimonies that attest to some extrajudicial statement concerning the placing of the condition. Such testimonies will be more significant the more numerous they are, and the more circumstantial and internally consistent, consonant with other testimonies, and chronologically close to the moment in which consent was given.

—Moreover, the placing of a condition can be proved by the indirect or circumstantial method. Among the kinds of evidence that go to prove condition indirectly, two should be singled out as being of particular importance. First the subject's assessment (whether positive or negative) of the thing that is made the condition (the so-called *criterium aestimationis*). This is in fact a motive that makes the placing of a condition credible. It is easier to think that a condition about a particular thing was placed by someone who desires or abhors that thing in a special way than by someone who had no particular interest in that thing. In other words, a strong motive makes it more credible that a true and proper condition was placed.

Second, another particularly relevant indication—which belongs rather to the category of motives—is the doubt about the fact that is made a condition. The placing of a condition would indeed be rather difficult to square—from a psychological and therefore from a probative viewpoint—with certainty (positive or "negative", if you will) about that fact. If so-and-so already knew with certainty that a particular fact existed or did not exist, what sense would it make to postulate it as a condition for his own consent? This is a given. He has already learned of its existence or nonexistence, and it would make little sense to push it back again, so to speak, into the context of uncertainty, which is, by contrast, typical of condition. Therefore, the stronger the proof of a subjective doubt, the more plausible will be the fact that a true and proper condition was placed on the consent. This, obviously, is to be understood at the level of proof and starting from the consideration of *id quod plerumque accidit* [what commonly happens] in the psychology of human persons. Doubt, on the other hand, is not essentially a constitutive element of the juridical concept of condition and therefore cannot be required as absolutely necessary in proving it, even though—as was said—it will ordinarily be an important circumstantial element of that proof.

Among the circumstances that will have particular weight, is how the subject who is alleged to have conditioned his consent acted (the *criterium reactionis*) at the moment when he ascertained that the condition was not met—specifically, that the desired thing did not materialize or that something feared did materialize. Clearly, a humble, persevering attitude in one's marital situation is evidence that would go to disprove the placing of a true condition, while on the other hand a hypersensitive attitude that finds the marital situation intolerable is evidence of the fact that one's own entrance into or perseverance in marriage depended substantially on the fulfillment of a true condition that has been placed.

b. According to the Latin discipline pertaining to conditions *de praeterito* or *de praesenti* (cf. can. 1102 §2), there are two objects of proof: both the placing of the condition and whether or not the condition has been fulfilled. Indeed, in this case the nullity of the marriage depends not on the mere placing of a condition on consent but rather on the lack of correspondence between the condition that was placed and the reality of the object of the condition.

As far as proof of the fact of the placing of a condition is concerned, we can only recall what was said in the section (a) immediately preceding this one, merely adding that the possible existence of the original or of an authentic copy of the written permission of the ordinary described in canon 1102 §3 is proof positive of the placing of the condition.

On the other hand, as far as proof of the fact that is the object of the condition, the practical principles of this demonstration will follow from the nature of the fact itself. Thus, evidence from the testimony of witnesses, documents, expert reports, and logical arguments based on presumptions may be combined and reinforce one another depending on the nature of the fact. To stay with the examples mentioned several times already, the possibilities of proving paternity (at least negatively, by exclusion) will be different from those relative to the demonstration of responsibility for a murder.

Guide for the counselor

The pastor of souls who, in view of an account of the marital situation of a couple with serious marital problems, suspects that he may be dealing with a marriage that is null on the grounds of conditional consent, could prudently investigate along the following lines of inquiry:

1. First of all, the counselor would have to clarify the basic idea being expressed by the person who is consulting with him, asking him to recall and to formulate as accurately as possible what he was thinking and what he had decided at the moment of his marriage. Indeed, it is very easy to devise reconstructions a posteriori—even in good faith—or to call a "condition" something that in reality is only a similar but essentially different figure. The cardinal point to be clarified is whether the subject made the beginning of his marriage or its continuance (and of his commitment to it) dependent on some particular fact or circumstance.

2. Once he has understood as accurately as possible the idea that the person with whom he is consulting means to express, the counselor would have to insist on asking him whether this same idea was already clear to him at the moment of the wedding, and in what terms. If so, he would then have to inquire whether, how, when, and to whom this idea (or better, this intention, since subjecting consent to a condition is an act of the will) was expressed, and also whether these persons can be found and are willing to testify. It is clear that this research aims to investigate the possibility of a direct proof of the condition.

3. In terms of indirect proof, on the other hand, the counselor would first of all have to investigate the reason why the person's intention to subject his own marital commitment to a condition came about. This is, in other words, an inquiry into the motive, circumstantial evidence of the placing of a condition. In particular, the counselor will have to inquire as to the assessment that the subject had of the fact that was made a condition, recalling that there is a relation of direct proportionality between that assessment and the likelihood that the subject placed the condition. Moreover, the counselor will have to weigh the presence and the intensity of a possible doubt about the fact that was

made a condition, since that same relation of direct proportionality exists between the intensity of the doubt and the likelihood that the subject placed a condition.

4. Some circumstances preceding the wedding (which are to be carefully distinguished from motives) could also have indirect probative value. Therefore, it is a good idea for the counselor to devote a careful investigation to these too. Thus, by way of example, were there inquiries and insistent demands aimed at overcoming the state of doubt that was at the basis of the condition? Were there previous engagements or relationships broken off precisely because of the fact that is allegedly the object of the condition? For example and for the sake of clarity, if a young woman had to break off a previous engagement because her fiancé was addicted to drugs, it is more credible that she wanted to marry a young man who did not take drugs and that she even made this a condition for her consent.

5. Among the circumstances that could be described as "concomitant" to the wedding, the counselor could investigate whether some traces of the possible conditional intention were left in the preparations leading up to the marriage, especially in the context of the premarital inventory or in the form of permission from the ordinary along the lines of canon 1102 §3, in a case of conditions relative to the past or to the present.

6. Finally, among the circumstances subsequent to the wedding one would have to investigate the efforts that may have been made by the person who allegedly placed the condition to discover the truth of the matter (for conditions *de praeterito* and *de praesenti*), or to attain the desired object or to avoid something that is feared (for conditions *de futuro*), as well as the subject's reaction once he discovered the truth (that the desired object did not materialize, or that he now faces the thing that he feared).

Only after having positively—albeit initially—verified the above-mentioned points would the counselor (when there is no hope for saving the marriage) begin a discussion of whether or not to initiate a canonical examination concerning the validity of the marriage.

Examples

For the usual didactic purpose of illustration, the following pages offer several examples, each one highlighting the specific teaching that it can provide.

First example

Philip was a young enlisted man in the army, full of zeal and goodwill but very rigid in his way of seeing things and in his character. On the occasion of a ceremony in which the soldiers' families also participated, he met Mary, the daughter of one of his superiors. This very attractive young woman was several years older than he and more experienced romantically. They immediately felt a mutual attraction, and they began a relationship that was rather intense in every respect. Philip became very emotionally involved, since it was practically his first romantic experience.

Within a short time the two were considering marriage. Philip, however, while visiting the house of Mary's parents—with whom the young woman was living—noticed the strong ties between her and her parents. He spoke about it to her and was worried by the fact that she suggested to him that they should go to live with her parents. Philip respected them both but feared a living arrangement that could be one more difficulty at the beginning of married life and wanted to avoid the embarrassing situation of settling down, of all places, in the household of his superior. The discussion between Philip and Mary about this question became rather tense at several points. Philip mentioned the possibility of postponing their wedding plans, and at that point Mary said that she was willing to renounce her desire to continue living with her parents and was ready to set up an independent household with Philip after their wedding.

Something in Philip had snapped, however, and now he found himself full of suspicions and uncertainties about Mary. He took her to her pastor, who was already making preparations for their forthcoming wedding, and he asked the priest to make Mary swear that she would be willing to follow him, according to the terms that they had agreed on. The priest also spoke individually with the young woman. He did not require a formal oath from her but addressed the problem with her, emphasizing Philip's doubts and the seriousness of his intention to have a household independent from that of her parents. (The priest later confirmed all these things before the tribunal.) Philip (convinced, on the other hand, that Mary had taken a formal oath) was not yet persuaded and, having found a house for the couple in a different town from the one where Mary's parents resided, asked the young woman —an elementary school teacher—to request a job transfer to the town where he had found a house for them. Mary assured him of having made a request for a transfer.

Their wedding day approached, but Philip was upset, among other reasons because he saw that Mary was rather disinterested in getting the new house ready, putting off the purchase of furniture and buying only a few household items. Philip began to talk to Mary in very clear terms. He would marry her, but on the condition that she was sincere in her commitment to separate from her parents and to be willing to start with him a family life that was entirely independent of them. Mary once again and repeatedly assured Philip of the sincerity of her commitment. After the wedding was celebrated, their marriage failed within a few weeks. Mary decided not to start living together with Philip, making various excuses, among them the sparsely furnished house, which she herself had neglected before the wedding and which she had done nothing to remedy afterward. Philip, now suspicious, turned to the competent school district and managed to find out that Mary had submitted a request for a transfer but that a few days later she herself had retracted it, unknown to him.

For Philip that was the end of their marriage. From then on he would not agree even to meet with or see Mary. She tried to convince him to forgive her, even in a rather melodramatic way, showing up with a suitcase at the barracks where Philip was serving and declaring that she was ready to start their life together. But Philip, who no longer trusted her, refused even to speak with her. As far as he was concerned, it was all over now.

The marriage of Philip and Mary (celebrated while the 1917 Code was in force and therefore to be judged, as to its validity, according to that discipline) is a clear example of a licit condition *de futuro* and of the type described as "potestative". It is therefore to be decided according to canon 1092, 3°, of the 1917 Code. Indeed, Philip maintained that he had contracted marriage on the condition that Mary would be truly and sincerely willing to start an independent married life with him. His consent would be effective only in the presence of Mary's sincere commitment. In this case the object of the condition set by Philip is not only the fact of an actual common life with his wife but her very sincerity in promising to be willing to begin it (note Philip's insistence that the pastor make Mary swear an oath and her initial request for a transfer, which she made at Philip's insistence). Therefore, in this specific case, the connection between the future, uncertain fact (the beginning and continuation of an independent married life together) and the sincerity of the promise made to carry out that resolution proved to be less artificial than on other occasions.

The proof of the condition placed by Philip was accomplished by the tribunal not so much on the basis of the direct method (since few persons had heard Philip speak about a "condition" in the proper sense and since Mary admitted very little during the proceedings themselves, being worried chiefly about not making too bad an impression) as on the basis of the indirect method, in other words, on the basis of logical proof, based on the evidence and on the circumstances of the case. Along these lines the decisive factors were Philip's strong, rigid character; the certain proof of the intensity of his prenuptial decision not to live with Mary's parents but rather with her alone, and also of his strong doubts about the matter; the immediate and irrevocable nature of his reaction the moment he realized that Mary's promise was not sincere and that she did not intend to start a common life as husband and wife, as they had agreed on before the wedding.

This example—besides illustrating a case of potestative condition *de futuro*—is intended to highlight the probative weight of the indirect elements of proof, especially of the motive (concern about a specific reality and doubts about the matter) and of the reaction to the nonfulfillment of the fact that was made a condition (his swift and conclusive repudiation of the marriage). These are elements that, when verified, make it extremely credible that the subject truly wanted to give efficacy to his consent only on certain conditions (or else reserved for himself the right to revoke it).

Second example

Lucy was a nice young woman from the country. She fell in love with Richard and made plans with him to marry. A few days before their wedding, Lucy's pastor received a telephone call from Bridget, who claimed that she had had a child by Richard. The pastor summoned the young engaged couple to clarify the question with them. Lucy and Richard declared in writing that they had aired all possible doubts and dark secrets between them and that they firmly intended to marry.

The facts of those troubled days were really not very clear, both because Richard failed to appear at the canonical trial, and also because of quite a few contradictions between Lucy's story and those of her own witnesses. It appears, however, that Richard had assured his fiancée that for some time he had been "stalked" by Bridget, whom he once used to see regularly in a group of young adults, and that he had even filed a complaint against her. In fact, it appears, from the accounts of Lucy's witnesses, that Lucy herself had firmly believed her fiancé, despite the warnings from members of her own family.

The wedding was celebrated, and the couple began their life together. Lucy quit her job and began to work with Richard and his parents in the family business. Since their life together and her work-related activities did not develop according to Lucy's expectations—which had been fed also by Richard's rather unrealistic schemes—the young woman ended up leaving her husband.

Lucy therefore challenged the marriage, alleging, among other things, that she had gone through with the wedding on the condition that Richard's denial of Bridget's claim was true, in other words, that he was not the father of Bridget's child. From this perspective the marriage was challenged because of an improper condition. It is not easy at all to say whether it should be considered a condition *de praeterito* (that Richard in the past did not have that child by Bridget) or *de praesenti* (that Richard is not the father of Bridget's child), but from the practical viewpoint the question was not an insurmountable difficulty, both because the same norm is to be applied in either case (the current can. 1102 §2, since the marriage was celebrated while the present Code was already in force), and also because the factual terms of the question were clear, namely that Lucy maintained that she had intended to give truly efficacious consent depending on whether or not Richard was the father of Bridget's child.

In the present case, therefore, there are two proper objects of proof, two principal facts to be demonstrated: (1) that Lucy really had imposed said condition; (2) that Richard really was the father of Bridget's child. The evidence adduced in this matter by Lucy, however, was not such as to persuade the tribunal. Indeed it was very weak on the first point and entirely nonexistent with regard to the second.

Among other things, Lucy was not altogether transparent about important details, and so it was not demonstrated that she had truly placed a condition, either by the uncertain depositions of her witnesses or, most importantly, by the facts. She trusted her fiancé blindly and paid no attention to the doubts that her relatives were trying to instill in her. She took no practical steps following the meeting with her pastor, except to repeat for him in writing her decision and intention to marry. She did not ask for any serious guarantee from Richard (e.g., to see a copy of the complaint that he had filed, or to investigate Bridget's claim with clinical tests) before the wedding, nor was she in any hurry to investigate the question afterward. Only when the marriage went bad for other reasons did Lucy respond to Bridget's talk attributing paternity to Richard and introduce the argument about a condition that she had imposed in that regard. And so, for these reasons, it did not appear to the tribunal that the placing of a condition on Lucy's part had been proved. On the contrary, the evidence had demonstrated her absolute adherence to Richard, notwithstanding what she had come to know.

Then there was no proof whatsoever that Richard was the father of Bridget's baby. Lucy said that she had seen the little boy during her separation and that she had noticed a strong resemblance to her husband, which statement is certainly not a proof. Bridget came to make a deposition, saying that she was sure that the child was Richard's but without being able to adduce objective evidence to prove it. On the contrary, she had to admit that, at the time of the conception, she was having intimate relations with other young men as well (the information gathered by the tribunal confirmed that Bridget was a rather "free and easy" young woman). For lack of other serious evidence —even circumstantial—any assertion of Richard's paternity would be altogether irrational and arbitrary.

This example intends to warn counselors to be very circumspect about the possibility of matrimonial nullity on the grounds of condition, venturing to make such a suggestion only after recognizing—provisionally and summarily, of course—the likelihood of proving the basic facts at the foundation of the possible judicial petition. Otherwise, steering persons toward a cause of matrimonial nullity could be no help to them at all but only the setup for a new and painful disappointment.

Third example

Valerie was an inexperienced but clear-thinking young woman. She was a student and helped her parents in a family business in a rural town. While she was going to school she met Vladimir, "Mirko", from a nearby town. He was a timid, sensitive young man who was experiencing an unhappy family situation. His parents had separated after major disagreements, and his mother had become a zealous member of the Jehovah's Witnesses, carrying out her fervent proselytism even with regard to her son.

Valerie and Mirko started spending time together, and they fell in love. Both were rather young, and it was their first love. They became physically intimate and Valerie became pregnant. The young woman did not lose heart. She immediately considered marriage and spoke about it to her parents. They, although displeased, did not make a scene and were willing to help the couple, offering to provide for them both a house and a secure job in the family business. Even Mirko seemed content with the prospect. All the preparations were made for the wedding, and Valerie—who was still a minor but rather mature—obtained court approval to marry.

In the course of the wedding preparations, however, a problem arose. Several friends reported to Valerie that they had seen Mirko frequenting the Kingdom Hall, the place where the Jehovah's Witnesses met, and now Valerie realized that Mirko's stories about some of his activities elsewhere did not add up. Despite her age and the moral failing already mentioned, Valerie was a clear-thinking young woman with rather solid religious convictions. She told Mirko very explicitly, and not just once, that she liked him very much and that she was happy to marry him but that she would not agree to marry someone belonging to a different religious faith. Moreover, she stated that in order more fully to share important aspects of their life, and also with a view to bringing up the children that she expected to have, she wanted him to be Catholic. Valerie clearly told Mirko to tell her immediately whether he was or intended to become a Jehovah's Witness. If so, she would certainly give birth to the baby, but she would call off the wedding.

Every time Valerie mentioned the subject, Mirko hastened to reassure her. He said that he was subjected to his mother's proselytism but had no intention of belonging to the Jehovah's Witnesses. On Sundays he went to Mass with Valerie, and no difficulty arose concerning the marriage preparation sessions that were conducted by the girl's pastor. Valerie, however, was not sure (because the rumors that she heard from her friends were repeated). Therefore, she had the same discussion again with Mirko, but in the presence of her own family. In the final days leading up to the wedding and also on the day before it, Valerie argued as follows with Mirko: "Look, I do not want to marry a Jehovah's Witness. Tell me right away if you are one or if you plan to become one, so that we can call off the wedding. And you can be sure that, even after we are married, if I ever discover that you are a Jehovah's Witness or that you plan to become one, I will leave you and act as if I had never married you." Mirko repeated to her his reassurances.

After the wedding was celebrated, already on their honeymoon trip, Mirko proved to have a large supply of literature from the Jehovah's Witnesses, maintaining that there was nothing wrong in reading them and trying to persuade Valerie to do so as well. When the baby was born, he tried, in vain, to prevent the child from being baptized Catholic. Over the course of a few months, he confirmed by his actions to Valerie's pastor, to whom the girl had turned for help, that he belonged to the sect, and he even made clear his intention to assume ever more demanding responsibilities in it. At that point, unhappily but very resolutely, Valerie put her threat into action and told Mirko to leave, since her commitment to the marriage was over, as she had forewarned him.

Valerie then challenged the validity of the marriage. Among the grounds of nullity that she alleged she proposed the condition that she herself had placed, that Mirko was not and/or had no intention of becoming a Jehovah's Witness. The facts in this case were very clear, and Valerie's position too was well represented—both by the persons who had heard her statements and also by the facts, which were perhaps more eloquent than the words themselves: the prenuptial doubts, the clear manifestations of her intentions to Mirko, Valerie's swift and decisive reaction upon discovering the real intentions. More difficult was the juridical classification of those same facts. Was it a condition *de praesenti* ("If you are a Jehovah's Witness, my consent is not effective")? Was it a condition *de futuro* properly speaking ("If you ever become a Jehovah's Witness, my consent, which in the meantime is suspended, will never take effect") or maybe of the potestative type ("If already at this moment you have the intention to become one and your promise to me about this matter is not sincere, the consent that I give is not effective")? Did it involve the simultaneous presence of several types of conditions? Upon closer inspection, it seemed to the tribunal easier (in the probative sense), but also more in keeping with the reality, to understand the condition that Valerie set for Mirko as a condition *contra matrimonii substantiam*, precisely as an intention to dissolve the bond if she ever discovered that he was a Jehovah's Witness or that he intended to become one. Recall, moreover, Valerie's own words: "And you can be sure that, even after we are married, if I ever discover that you are a Jehovah's Witness or that you plan to become one, I will leave you and act as if I had never married you." This is, practically speaking, a "resolutive" condition, which in itself would be a form of condition *de futuro*, but one that in practice ends up being an intention excluding (although in a possible, "conditioned" way) the indissolubility of the matrimonial commitment. And in fact the tribunal decided the case on the basis of Valerie's exclusion of indissolubility (which was also among the grounds being examined), claiming that by their ruling they had already dealt with the point about the condition, which in substance was included in it.

This example is meant to call to mind both the difficulty of classifying the facts that can be traced back to the phenomenon of conditional consent in light of the (necessarily abstract and generalized) categories of canon law. Secondly, it illustrates the necessity of distinguishing carefully the phenomenon of condition from other scenarios that are only similar but in reality cannot be reduced to it. This may be because they are not relevant to the validity of the marriage, or because they are but should more fittingly be described in terms of other scenarios of matrimonial nullity foreseen by canon law.

XIII

Convalidation of an Invalid Marriage

At first glance it may appear strange that this book should deal with the possibilities of convalidating—in canon law—marriages that for well-founded reasons are to be considered null.

In reality, careful reflection shows that the procedure of convalidating a marriage is just one of the possibilities for the Church's counseling and pastoral action when faced with an invalid marriage. And that there should be more than one possible way to respond is quite logical, since pastoral ministry should enjoy a reasonable range of flexibility so as to be able to apply to various personal situations those prospective solutions that appear more equitable and effective. In pastoral ministry too, which cannot prescind from respect for justice, the principle holds true that justice itself does not consist of treating everyone in the same way, according to rigid, predetermined schemas, but rather consists of "giving to each his own"—in other words, that which is pertinent to an individual situation when compared with the general rules of ecclesiastical discipline.

Considered along these lines, the possibility of convalidating an invalid marriage is further evidence of the pastoral character of canon law, whereby "pastoral" means an attentive concern to individual situations that proposes solutions that are not vague and sentimental but rather that correspond as much as possible to the objective reality that canon law confronts.

To be clearer about what has been said thus far: What could the Church's responses be to an invalid marriage? Essentially the following four:

1. The dissimulation—on the part of the ecclesial authority—of that situation. This should occur in a case where the two "spouses" (not really) are in good faith about their status and when bringing the

nullity of their bond to their attention could cause them serious harm, especially of a spiritual sort. If the factual situation at the basis of the nullity was irremediable and if there were no reasonable risks that their situation (and therefore the invalidity of their marriage) could become known, the authority that has come to learn of it can dissemble what it knows, so as not to disturb the pseudospouses in their good faith. Certainly, such a case is rare (think, for example, of a degree of consanguinity that cannot be dispensed that is discovered after the parties —perhaps in a mission territory or among populations troubled by wars and migrations—have contracted marriage in good faith), but it cannot be ruled out a priori.

2. Tolerance, again on the part of the ecclesial authority, of an apparent marital situation of persons who are aware of the canonical nullity of their union for a reason that even the authority itself cannot dispense. When there is no reasonable risk of divulging such a situation (with resulting scandal) and when the pseudospouses sincerely promise to abstain from properly conjugal acts (living "as brother and sister", as we say), the authority can tolerate the continuation of their cohabitation. This solution is similar to the one applied in the case of a second marriage contracted—obviously only in the eyes of the civil authority—on the part of Catholics who are bound by a previous conjugal bond. Such a union is invalid not only and not so much because of the omission of the canonical form but rather because of the presence of a bond that, if valid, is beyond the power of the interested parties and of the Church to dissolve. Under the aforesaid conditions, and also given serious reasons of expediency (e.g., the presence of children from the second union who need material and educational assistance from the parents), the ecclesial authority may tolerate the continuance of said cohabitation without insisting on the separation of the couple because they are in an invalid union.

3. A declaration of nullity—the formal recognition by the entity set up for that purpose (the tribunal), through procedures determined by law, of the original nullity of the conjugal bond that is impugned as to its substantial validity. It is clear that this solution normally follows the actual end of married life between the parties involved, even though the reason for the invalidity of the bond does not always coincide with the reason for the rift between the spouses. It is also clear, consequently,

that this route should be suggested above all when a peaceful common life between the spouses can not as a matter of fact be restored.

4. The convalidation of a marriage—the application of those procedures that allow for the passage from a situation of marital invalidity to one of validity should be carried out with respect for the truth of the facts and for the fundamental principles of matrimonial law. The purpose of this chapter is precisely to show how this can happen. The convalidation of a marriage is clearly the Church's most natural reaction in the case of a marriage that is null but for which there is a founded hope—based on the expressed desires or behavior of the spouses—to persevere in their common life.

Canon law plainly shows that it does not overlook the possibility of convalidating a marriage that is null. Consider, for example, two procedural norms that express this intention clearly. In establishing the conditions for actively authorizing the promoter of justice to challenge the validity of a marriage, the Code decrees that this authorization (the possibility of initiating a cause of action) does not obtain when it is technically possible and also expedient to convalidate the marriage (can. 1674, 2°). Then, in defining the specific duties of the judge in cases of matrimonial nullity, the Code likewise decrees that, among others, there is an obligation—before accepting the case and when, even during the course of it, possibilities of success in this regard are discovered —to employ "pastoral means" (conversations, exhortations, referral to counselors or experts who can be of help) that may lead the parties to convalidate their marriage and to resume their life together (can. 1676).

Therefore, a counselor of couples with marital problems is not faced with the sole question of whether to propose a canonical cause of nullity. Even when that would theoretically be possible, he must not overlook the other possibilities that exist, among them the convalidation of the marriage, when these appear to be better suited to the actual situation of the parties.

But what is the basis for the possibility of convalidating an invalid marriage? In what sense is this possibility consistent with the fundamental principles of matrimonial law? This is what we must analyze by following our usual outline, which starts by taking into consideration the elements of substantive law.

Elements of substantive law

1. The fundamental principle underlying the procedure of convalidating a marriage is the principle at the basis of matrimonial canon law as a whole: the principle that identifies the consent of the parties as the genetic cause, the "efficient cause"—as the classical terminology puts it—of marriage.

Canon law itself ratifies this principle, declaring that the consent of the parties is what brings marriage into being (*matrimonium facit*), as is clearly repeated in canon 1057 §1. This consent—which the law considers as a highly personal, irreplaceable act—consists in the act of the will by which the contracting parties mutually give and accept one another for the purpose of establishing the marriage (can. 1057 §2). This gift of self comes about specifically by assuming with regard to the other party the obligations of the married state and by granting to the other party the rights belonging to the legitimate spouse and to him alone.

The act of the will—considered from the viewpoint of its psychological analysis—is perfect in itself when it is deliberately directed toward an object that is suited to be the terminus of the matrimonial will, even if that object is not in fact available to be concretely the object of that will. To illustrate, consider the following examples, which are commonplace, certainly, but hopefully apt, abstracting for a moment from the topic of marriage. Tom could have a will that in itself is perfectly formed to purchase the automobile that he thinks is Dick's property, even though Dick in reality is not the owner of an automobile. Harry could have a will that in itself is perfectly formed to acquire for himself the *Mona Lisa* painted by Leonardo da Vinci, even though that work of art cannot in fact be sold or acquired by a private individual.

These examples may perhaps help the reader to understand a distinction that can be expressed in terms that have become customary among canonists, so much so that they were included in earlier legislation. Indeed, the 1917 Code, in dealing specifically with convalidation, distinguished in canon 1139 between the kind of consent that it called "naturally sufficient" and the kind of consent that it called "juridically effective".

"Naturally sufficient" consent is in itself perfect as a psychological act. It is consent having within it all the potentialities to be true conjugal consent, because, for example, it is not intrinsically defective by distorted intentions (cases of simulation) or vitiated by extrinsic causes (such as constraint or errors of fact). In contrast, "juridically effective" consent is consent capable of producing its fruits effectively in the legal world, both because it is in fact directed toward an object capable of marriage and because it is expressed in the forms that the law considers essential in order for it to come into being.

We can seek to understand these concepts even better by returning to the aforementioned fundamental norm expressed in canon 1057, § 1. This norm declares that the efficient cause of marriage is the consent of the parties (consent that is perfect in itself, or "naturally sufficient") but adds nevertheless that this consent actually produces its effects ("juridically effective") only if it is exchanged between two persons who are legally capable and in the manner foreseen by canon law.

If we want to consider this regulation "negatively", we can conclude that a marriage could be null either for lack of naturally sufficient consent, or else—even if naturally sufficient consent were present—because of the juridical inability of at least one of the contracting parties, or else by the illegitimate manifestation of that same consent. In the last two cases the consent, although naturally sufficient, would be juridically ineffective.

The convalidation of a marriage—assuming that a wedding was celebrated invalidly—is precisely the possibility of assigning juridical value to the bond that it ought to have created: either (1) by making sure that the possibly missing consent of the spouses (or of one of them) does come into being; or (2) by attributing juridical efficacy to consent that in itself is naturally sufficient but so to speak paralyzed in its efficacy by some personal inability or formal irregularity.

2. Hence, an objectively invalid marriage, in other words, one that can morally be considered such, is the prerequisite for applying the procedure for convalidation of a marriage. Now, a marriage can be invalid for three sorts of reasons:

a. We have seen that the most radical cause of the invalidity of a marriage is the natural insufficiency of the consent. In that case, convalidation can consist only of a renewal of the insufficient consent, obviously with the fulfillment of the conditions for its juridical efficacy at the moment in which the convalidation occurs. Thus, for example, if between the giving of naturally insufficient consent and its renewal a nondispensable impediment arose in one of the parties (e.g., copulative impotence), the convalidation could not take place.

b. In the second place, a marriage could be invalid through the juridical incapacity of one or both of the parties being affected by one of the matrimonial impediments in canons 1083–94. It is clear that, when an impediment is not dispensable (inasmuch as it derives from the codification of a precept of divine right, a positive or natural precept), the convalidation can take place only when the impediment has ceased. Take the case of the bond of a previous valid and consummated marriage, which can be dissolved only by the death of one of the spouses (cf. cann. 1141 and 1085 §1).

c. Finally, a marriage can be null because of a defect of the form prescribed for the validity of its celebration. Since in this case the reason for invalidity is based on incapacitating norms of a purely ecclesiastical nature (cf. can. 10), it is clear that a convalidation of the marriage would always be theoretically possible. This is obvious and undisputed as far as possible formal defects of a canonically celebrated marriage are concerned (e.g., by reason of an insufficient number of witnesses; or because it was celebrated in the presence of a pastor who was suspended from his office by a sentence or a decree of his bishop; or for the reason explained in the fourth example given below [p. 268]). Not so obvious, on the other hand, is the case where canonical form was entirely lacking because the parties opted to be bound by a civil form of celebration instead or by a ceremony in a religious community whose celebration of marriage the Catholic Church does not consider substantially equivalent to her own (in practice, that of non-Catholic Eastern Christians; cf. can. 1127 §1).

It is obvious—especially in Italy and its pastoral context—that the commonest, and of greatest interest, is the case of civil marriage celebrated by two persons, at least one of whom is bound to the canonical form along the lines of canon 1117. Recall—among other things—Catholics are not permitted to celebrate, among themselves and with a dispensation from the canonical form, a marriage according to the civil rite, except in case of danger of death.[1] Even in the case of a mixed marriage canon 1127 §2 provides that the alternative form of celebration must generally have a religious character.[2]

Canonists debate whether a civil marriage of persons bound to the canonical form can be convalidated. The scholarly debate as well as administrative and jurisprudential practice are rather inclined toward an affirmative answer. Here it is not possible to analyze the arguments made in this regard, which can be examined in the literature for specialists.

3. Having grasped the fundamental principle and basis for why the convalidation of a marriage is possible, it is necessary now to ask how the mechanism established in law functions concretely.

Canon law in reality provides two forms of convalidation of marriage: the first, called simple convalidation, and the second, radical sanation. The Code itself adopts and uses this terminology.

Canon law does not set up an "automatic" form of convalidation of a marriage, as might happen in a case where the spouses continued in their common life for a certain amount of time after having learned about the invalidity of their marriage, thus implicitly confirming—with conclusive behavior consisting precisely of continuing their common life—that they wish to sanate, as far as it depends on them, their initial consent, whether it was naturally insufficient or merely ineffective. On the contrary, canon law requires several positive, specific interventions, either on the part of those directly interested or on the part of the ecclesial authority for convalidation.

4. The first form of convalidation of an invalid marriage, called simple convalidation, has as its characteristic and essential element the fact that it happens through the renewal of the consent. This renewal of consent is required by positive ecclesiastical law, even in the case of a marriage that is invalid not because of the natural insufficiency of the consent itself but only by its juridical inefficacy (cf. can. 1156 §2). It consists in an act of the will aimed at the establishment of the marriage,

---

[1] Cf. *AAS* 77 (1985): 771.
[2] Cf. art. 50.

which is known (with certainty) or at least thought (probably) to have
been invalid (cf. can. 1157).

The modalities of expressing this new act of the will can vary, depending on the cause of the invalidity of the marriage and on the degree
to which it was public knowledge. First, however, it is worthwhile to
explain and summarize the essential aspects characterizing simple convalidation by means of the renewal of consent.

From a substantial perspective, in order to have a simple convalidation of marriage there must be certain knowledge or at least the
opinion that one's own marriage is invalid. Consequently, there will
have to be also the awareness of giving a new consent. Insufficient for
the purposes of the substance of the convalidation, therefore, would
be the conviction that it was merely a matter of formally regularizing
consent that had already been given, or of confirming or reinforcing
it. The party bound to renew his consent must instead be aware that
he faces the necessity of an authentic renewal of his own matrimonial
consent and that the alternative to it is remaining in that situation of
the (known or putative) invalidity of his own marriage.

In the second place, at the moment of its renewal, the consent that
is given must be supplied with all the characteristics required in order
to be the efficient cause of a matrimonial bond. If it were intrinsically
defective or vitiated, it could not give rise to an effective convalidation. For example, suppose the case of two spouses who convalidated
a union from which they had already had four children and, in giving
their renewed consent, deliberately decided to exclude additional children. Their new consent would be intrinsically defective.

Finally, in the third place, all the prerequisite conditions of the contracting parties must be present at the moment of convalidation. If not,
the consent, although renewed, would be ineffective.

As was mentioned earlier, the modality of the renewal of consent depends on the ground of the nullity of the marriage to be convalidated
and on the extent to which it is public knowledge. Thus, the following
cases should be distinguished:

   a. In the case of a marriage that is invalid because of the presence
   of a diriment impediment, in order to proceed to convalidation, the
   impediment must have "ceased"; in other words, it must no longer
   exist (e.g., age, a previous bond), or if possible, it must be dispensed

(e.g., consanguinity, the perpetual public vow of chastity of a religious), as canon 1156 §1 decrees. In such cases the renewal of consent is a requirement of positive ecclesiastical law that derives the nullity from consent that is ineffective (because of the impediment) but naturally sufficient in itself.

As for the different ways in which consent can be renewed, if the impediment that is the cause of the nullity was public (i.e., demonstrable in the external forum; cf. cann. 1074 and 1158 §1), the consent must be renewed while observing the canonical form. On the one hand, when the impediment cannot be proved in the public forum, the consent may be renewed privately and in secret and solely by the party aware of its existence, provided, of course, that the other party's consent persists. If, however, the occult impediment is known to both parties, the consent must be renewed by both, even if privately and in secret—in other words, not in canonical form, and in a way unknown to others (can. 1158 §2).

b. In the case of a marriage that is invalid because of a defect of consent, its renewal is required by natural law insofar as the one whose consent is defective. As for the form of this renewal, it can be private and secret when the defect cannot be proved and when the consent of the other party persists (cf. can. 1159 §§1–2). It must however be expressed in canonical form when the defect of consent can be proved (cf. can. 1159 §3).

c. Finally, in the case of a marriage that is invalid because of a defect in canonical form, simple convalidation can take place only by a new exchange of consent that involves the regular observance of the form that was previously lacking.

5. The form of convalidation called "radical sanation" is characterized essentially by the importance that must be attributed to the persistence of consent as a psychological act. Radical sanation is in fact applicable to marriages that are invalid because of the simple inefficacy of consent that is in itself naturally sufficient but was rendered unproductive—that is, ineffective—by the presence of an impediment or of a defect in the form of the celebration.

In this particular form of canonical convalidation, the ecclesial authority, basing its action precisely on the persistence of the naturally sufficient consent, eliminates the reason that paralyzed its efficacy, by dispensing from the impediment or from the imperfectly observed ceremonial form, without, however, requiring a renewal of the consent itself. If we consider the definition that canon 1161 § 1 gives of radical sanation, we can correctly identify the essential elements of this juridical procedure.

It is clear that, since the argument hinges on the persistence of consent as a psychological act, this must be verified in order to be able to apply this remedy to an invalid marriage and, even prior to that, in order to propose to a Catholic couple its application. In this connection counselors must not forget a common principle of practice and several evidential criteria.

The common principle is the one whereby matrimonial consent, once given, must be considered ongoing. Its revocation is a fact, and facts must be proved, not just assumed. Certainly, the demonstration of a fact can also occur by means of a circumstantial proof. And in this connection, the criteria discussed a little earlier are helpful. Thus, the following sorts of circumstantial evidence would be considered insufficient to demonstrate the revocation of consent: a situation in which the spouses disagree; the refusal to agree to the simple convalidation of their marriage by means of renewing consent; personal separation, de facto or legalized; a request for a divorce. On the other hand, indications proving the revocation of consent are the dissolution of the marriage by the Roman Pontiff because of nonconsummation, or an executive sentence of matrimonial nullity. It must not be forgotten, however, that this is a question of evidential criteria that provide a presumptive proof. The actual will of the spouses must be carefully investigated and may prove to be different from what the provisional evidence would lead one to think.

Although the simultaneous and current persistence of the parties' consent is the necessary condition for the validity of the sanation, for liceity there must also be reasonable certainty that it can reasonably be foreseen that this consent will persist in the future as well, since the spouses in question have the intention to persevere in their common life (cf. can. 1161 § 3). Indeed, the sanation of a marriage whose actual failure could reasonably be foreseen would be rather imprudent.

The fact that the simultaneous persistence of the parties' consent is an indispensable condition for the application of radical sanation is stressed by canon 1162, the second paragraph of which must be understood correctly. Indeed, the first paragraph is easy to understand, since it limits itself to repeating that sanation cannot be applied if the consent of even one of the two is lacking, either from the beginning or because it was subsequently revoked. The second paragraph, however, indicates that as for its substance and as for its effects (which we will analyze further on) sanation can take place, in the case of consent that was originally lacking and was given later, only from the moment when that same consent came into being. To proceed otherwise—as to the substance and as to the effects of sanation—would mean to contradict the fundamental principle about the nature of the efficient cause of consent in relation to marriage.

Normally radical sanation entails a dispensation from an impediment or from the observance of canonical form. Given this dispensation, and if the persistence of the consent has been ascertained, nothing essential is lacking for the sanation (cf. can. 1163), and it is up to the authority to evaluate the expediency of granting it. However, as is well known, not all impediments can be dispensed, since some of them can be traced back to the natural law or divine positive law, and so do not fall under the power of the ecclesiastical authority to dispense. Concerning these latter impediments, the earlier legislator manifested his own respect toward the natural and divine positive law by decreeing the inapplicability of radical sanation even after the cessation of such impediments (cf. the 1917 Code, can. 1139 §2). The present legislator, without diminishing the respect due to the law inscribed by the Creator in the nature of things or manifested in revelation, decrees that sanation can be applied also to marriages that are invalid because of impediments of natural law (copulative impotence, consanguinity in the direct line, probably consanguinity in the second degree of the collateral line) or of divine positive law (the matrimonial bond) but only after said impediments have ceased (cf. can. 1163 §2). This decree is perhaps more consistent with respect to the logic of the sanation procedure, which appreciates the naturally sufficient consent in its reality as a psychological act (which can exist—as remarked above—even though its object in reality is momentarily unavailable).

Since it is fundamentally based on the importance of the naturally sufficient consent of the parties, which is rendered efficacious by the elimination (dispensation or cessation) of the impediment or by dispensation from canonical form by an intervention of the authority, it therefore seems obvious that radical sanation can be granted—for a grave reason, however—even in the case where one or both of the interested parties do not know about the procedure (cf. can. 1164).

6. What are the effects of the convalidation of marriage? From this perspective, both forms of convalidation that we have studied have an identical principal effect, that of establishing the marital bond. The marital bond comes into being at the moment of the renewal of consent in the case of simple convalidation, and at the moment when it is granted by the ecclesial authority in the case of radical sanation. As canonists usually say, the principal effect of both forms of canonical convalidation takes place *ex nunc* [from now on].

In radical sanation there is, moreover, a secondary effect, which is projected into the past and therefore usually said to take effect *ex tunc* [from then on]. Specifically, this means that the canonical effects of marriage (e.g., the legitimacy of the children who are born of it; cf. cann. 1137–38) are made retroactive from the moment of the wedding. As canon 1161 §2 very clearly puts it, distinguishing the two effects of radical sanation: "Convalidation occurs at the moment of the granting of the favor. Retroactivity, however, is understood to extend to the moment of the celebration of the marriage unless other provision is expressly made."

What may these contrary provisions be, and how are they justified? They are the provisions of canon 1162 §2 and of canon 1163 §2, and they are justified in relation to the ground of the nullity of the marriage that is to be sanated. The first case (can. 1162, §2), which refers back to the moment of the wedding the effects of a marriage that was invalid because of an impediment of natural law or of divine positive law, appears to be incongruous, surreptitiously asserting control that the Church does not have over those reasons for matrimonial nullity. The second case (1163 §2), which makes the canonical effects of consent given later refer back to the moment of the wedding, also appears to postulate surreptitiously that the law supplies the proper efficient cause of the marriage, which would contradict the fundamental principles of that same law in this matter.

7. To what authority should one turn for a simple convalidation or for a radical sanation of a marriage? Here it is necessary to make rather careful distinctions.

In one case, it is not necessary to turn to any authority. Specifically, when there is a need for the simple convalidation of a marriage that is invalid because of an impediment or else because of a defect of consent that cannot be proved within the context of the community's public relations (the external forum)—in this case it is sufficient that the party or parties aware of the nullity should renew their consent privately (without public formalities) and secretly (without witnesses): compare canons 1158 §2 and 1159 §2.

On the other hand, in the case where one must proceed to the simple convalidation of a marriage that is invalid because of a defect of form, a provable impediment, or else a provable defect of consent, it seems sufficient that the interested parties turn to the authority competent to assist at their marriage according to canon 1115—essentially, to their own pastor. It will then be up to him to request a dispensation from the possible impediment (if that is the cause of the invalidity) of the authority that can grant it: the ordinary, or else the Holy See.

Finally, in the case of radical sanation, the new Code—developing the conciliar sensitivity to and appreciation of the particular Churches and making permanent the habitual faculties that in fact had already been granted to diocesan bishops—broadened the options of the diocesan bishops to grant the radical sanation of invalid marriages. If we read carefully the regulation in canon 1165, we can conclude that the Holy See reserves radical sanation to itself only in three cases: (a) the case of general sanations, in other words, several cases having in common one and the same reason for nullity (e.g., a series of marriages celebrated by someone posing as an ordained minister); (b) the case of a marriage that is invalid because of an impediment whose dispensation is reserved to the Holy See (sacred orders; public perpetual vow of chastity in a religious institute of pontifical right; crime); and (c) the case of a marriage that is invalid because of an impediment of divine right—whether natural or positive—that has ceased to exist.

In all other cases, radical sanation can be granted by the diocesan bishop. By the decision of the bishop, one can refer by way of analogy to the norms of canon 1115, employing its criteria for identifying the pastor who is competent to assist at the marriage (the pastor of the domicile, of the quasi domicile, or of a month's residence of at least one of the two interested parties); or one can turn to the bishop of the place where the marriage to be sanated was celebrated, provided that it was celebrated in canonical form, even if defective, but not in the complete absence of canonical form.

Guide for the counselor

Rather than suggestions for lines of investigation, in this chapter we must point out to the counselors of couples who have marital problems a few simple prudential considerations:

1. In the first place, counselors must keep in mind the possibility of convalidation. The solution to be proposed when faced with a marriage that one suspects is invalid is not necessarily, not only, and not always the initiation of a cause of nullity. Indeed, it can happen that the spouses, although subjectively convinced that there may be a reason for the invalidity of their marriage, have no intention of challenging its validity. Even if they later do have that intention, it seems right to present to them the possibility of convalidating their marriage, so that their decision may be informed, as much as possible, by all the possibilities that the discipline of the Church offers in their case.

2. The possibility of convalidating a marriage should be presented particularly in the case where the common life of the parties is resumed after they abandon an intended cause of matrimonial nullity. As will be clear in the second example related below, it can happen that, during the delays in a cause of matrimonial nullity, the spouses may decide to resume their common life, either in the interests of the children or because they have given further thought to their decision or to their opinions. In the meantime, even though a verdict has not been reached, the proceedings of the case may have demonstrated the actual possibility of proving a defect of consent or an impediment in the external forum. In that case, one must propose to the interested parties the convalidation of their marriage.

3. That being said, the wise counselor will also have to exercise prudence so as not to introduce prematurely or inconclusively a discussion of (simple) convalidation of the marriage, in a case where he foresees that—for example, because the subjects are uneducated—the need to renew consent would not be understood or might be rejected outright. In that case, whenever the circumstances allow (in other words, when the nullity of the marriage depends on an impediment or on a defect of form), the counselor can turn to the competent authorities to obtain radical sanation, thus evaluating whether there is a chance of involving

the interested parties at least in this particular form of convalidation, which does not entail the need to renew consent.

4. Even when the interested parties are willing to have their marriage convalidated (even simply), the counselor should suggest that they themselves (and possibly also their pastors) not be hasty in undertaking convalidation. Among the examples related below, there is one (the first) of a convalidation that should have been avoided (and that in reality convalidated nothing, because there was a defect of consent), and another (the third) of a convalidation that was invalid for lack of its essential prerequisites. In both cases a certain haste and an inconsiderate "pastoral" anxiety to "regularize" the marital situation of the interested persons were harmful.

Examples

First example

Claudia was a good, very simple young woman. She had had an unfortunate family life: her parents fought a lot and she lost loved ones. She remained single, lived with an elderly aunt, and worked as a schoolteacher. She met Fredrick, an office worker. They proved to be mutually sympathetic and began to see each other regularly, even at events in the parish where Claudia was very active.

Fredrick was an educated young man, a bit affected in manner, lackadaisical, and not very assertive in his displays of affection for Claudia. She, however, being a simple, naïve, well-meaning young woman, did not worry and let the years go by, spending Sunday afternoons at parish socials, playing board games at home, having company over, and chatting with her old aunt.

When the aunt died, Claudia was left alone at home, and the two decided to get married. Claudia, however, was very disappointed by the fact that Fredrick, after the wedding, did not even try to approach her for conjugal relations, and even withdrew or sought to avoid her timid attempts. After a few months Claudia, who had married with the right intentions and also wanted children, summoned all her courage and confronted Fredrick for an explanation, and he confessed with tears and sobs that a few years before their wedding he had discovered that he was HIV positive. Fredrick told Claudia that he had contracted the disease during his military service. In a moment of sadness and loneliness—he told her—he had given in once to an invitation from two of his fellow soldiers to "get high". That was the only time that he had used drugs, but he had been infected by using the same needle as the other two. Fredrick also explained to Claudia that he had told her nothing about it before marrying her because he loved her and was afraid of losing her.

Claudia, very upset, turned to the priests of her parish, who had known her for a long time and were fond of her. The young woman was distraught but, since she was a devout Christian and still loved Fredrick, said that she was willing to forgive him. The parish and the assistant priest suspected that a marriage celebrated in that way could be invalid, and they asked for advice from the diocesan curia. The diocesan official in charge listened to the story, spoke with the interested parties, and—while stressing the probability of matrimonial nullity because of the deceitful error to which Claudia had been subjected along the lines of canon 1098—advised against convalidating the marriage, citing (1) the very short time that had elapsed since the discovery of the deceit, something that perhaps did not allow her to reason cool-headedly and to clarify the situation in depth, as well as (2) the objective difficulties, from a human and moral viewpoint, of married life with someone who is HIV positive (think of the problem of how to have intimate relations). Convalidation of the marriage was therefore discouraged, at least in the short term, but not forbidden. Claudia and Fredrick, however, insistently begged the parish priests, and thus—with the pastor assisting, and the assistant priest and a trusted female friend as witnesses—they proceeded to convalidate the marriage.

Their life together continued therefore for a few years. Fredrick's health, as far as his being HIV positive, remained stable. His behavior, however, worsened. Strange absences from home for unlikely work shifts; clumsy lies told to his wife; individuals who noticed him in dubious haunts and places of ill repute; unbalanced attitudes at home, with strange manias and real persecution complexes in dealing with colleagues and neighbors. Gradually, with the help of the family physician and of other specialists who were also consulted, the real story emerged. Fredrick, from his youth, had allowed himself to get involved in homosexual experiences, frequenting homosexual meeting places and engaging in more or less lasting relationships with homosexuals. He had never used drugs, and his HIV-positive status had resulted instead from homosexual relations. Even after his wedding, once the first few months had passed, he started frequenting those meeting places again regularly, unbeknownst to the generous, naïve Claudia, who had been deceived on her wedding day and at the time of the convalidation when—by a decision that was certainly imprudent but that others perhaps might not have had the courage to make—she had renewed her own consent with regard to an HIV-positive man who had already deceived her once so seriously.

It is clear that Claudia's consent—both at the wedding and at the convalidation—was vitiated by the error deceitfully induced in her by Fredrick about one of his personal qualities (first his HIV-positive status, then his homosexuality), which by its nature was likely to disrupt seriously their partnership of life, an error induced for the purpose of obtaining Claudia's consent. The marriage and the convalidation therefore had to be declared null, and Claudia could not be blamed for her generosity and her naïveté in believing Fredrick's story about becoming HIV positive as the result of using drugs on only one occasion.

It is, however, rather probable—and this is what the example is meant to show—that greater prudence in allowing the couple to have their marriage convalidated and greater resistance to their pressures and concerns about immediately "regularizing" their status could have helped to clarify the situation better. By weighing more critically Fredrick's account while having more time to notice his ambiguous behavior, which was revealed rather quickly once the marriage had been convalidated, those counseling the couple would have had a clearer picture of the situation.

Second example

Louise and Vladimir were two rather young adults. Each had a job. She was a sales clerk and he was a laborer. They met, fell in love, and after a short engagement, planned for marriage.

As the wedding day approached, though, Louise noticed that Vladimir was less attentive to her than before. She asked him whether there had been some change in his feelings, but Vladimir told her no. So they went through with the wedding.

Louise's impression was confirmed, however, by their married life. Vladimir was rather reluctant to stay at home, did not seek to have intimate relations with her, and seemed distracted, with his head somewhere else.

Louise was worried and spoke about it to her parents and to mutual friends. From two of them—Julian and Peter—she came to learn about something that Vladimir could no longer deny. During the engagement, while going to make preparations at the house recently purchased for the couple, Vladimir had met a young woman who lived nearby, Laurie, who was very young but already separated. He had given in to her charms and started a relationship with her. When Julian and Peter found out about it and advised him to call off the wedding, Vladimir declared that he did not think that he should burn his bridges. He intended to have a trial marriage with Louise without breaking off his affair with Laurie, such that if the trial marriage was a failure, or if he found that Laurie was actually more attractive, he reserved for himself the option of leaving Louise and marrying Laurie. Julian and Peter had harshly criticized Vladimir's intentions and had spoken about them with other friends (Joe and Maurice), but all four had been unable to bring themselves to warn Louise before the wedding.

When all this was discovered, Louise and Vladimir separated, only a few months after the wedding celebration. Louise went for counseling in her parish and—at the pastor's suggestion and after consulting with an experienced lawyer—initiated a cause of nullity on the ground of a twofold defect of consent on Vladimir's part: the exclusion of indissolubility and of fidelity on his part. The instruction made it possible to bring the situation fully to light. Vladimir, now repentant, came to admit his guilt; Peter and Julian made depositions as direct prenuptial witnesses of his intentions; Joe and Maurice did so as indirect prenuptial witnesses. Several relatives both of Vladimir and of Louise also appeared to report on what the two interested parties alleged as the justification for their separation: Vladimir had clearly told all these relatives how matters stood. Laurie appeared also, and since her affair with Vladimir was now coming to an end, she did not hesitate at all to admit her prenuptial relationship with him and their intention to continue it even after his marriage, while waiting to find out how his marriage with Louise developed.

The acts of the cause were published, and, it must be said, they proved rather clearly the twofold defect of Vladimir's consent. At that point, however, the advocate who was assisting Louise asked for a delay in the course of the cause, then another, and then presented a petition to renounce it, since Louise and Vladimir had started to see each other again, had been reconciled, and finally had resumed their life together.

A "happy ending", certainly. However, the defect of Vladimir's consent in this case was not only provable but by now had practically been proven in a judiciary proceeding, although it had not yet reached the sentencing phase. The need for a convalidation of the marriage became evident. The judicial vicar therefore wrote to the pastor who had counseled Louise and had recommended the cause of nullity. The good priest made an appointment with her and Vladimir and explained the matter to them, and the two interested parties willingly agreed to convalidate their marriage. The pastor prefaced the convalidation with a sort of renewed prenuptial inventory, which allowed him to put into words extensively the renewed intentions of the couple, in light of the events that had occurred meanwhile. Then, in the presence of two trusted witnesses, the priest proceeded to receive their renewal of consent.

This example intends to show a typical case in which simple convalidation must be applied: that is, in a case where the ground of nullity of the marriage was provable and where the invalidity of the marriage was unlikely to become common knowledge.

Third example

Peter and Marianne were second cousins, as is commonly said. More precisely—according to the 1917 Code, under which their marriage was celebrated (cf. cann. 96 §3 and 1076 §2)—they were consanguineous in the third degree in the collateral line. Even more specifically, they had a great-grandfather in common; their grandmothers were sisters; their mothers were first cousins. In this consanguinity, transmitted by the female line, the last names of the two young cousins were obviously different. Moreover, whereas Marianne had always lived in the little town in the mountains, the family's place of origin, Peter was born and had always lived in a large city rather distant from the town, to which Peter's grandmother—it should be noted—had moved when she married, in search of work and a good life.

The fact remains that the two young people met on the occasion of a local festival in which Peter had taken part, in the region of his family origins. They knew that they were distantly related, but they had almost never seen each other until reaching almost twenty-five years of age. They fell in love and decided to marry. The wedding was planned in the little town in the mountains. The couple had the requisite meetings with the pastor. As mentioned, they knew of their distant kinship, but they did not think that it was a problem (for the 1917 Code it was a diriment impediment) and therefore did not mention it to the pastor. This excellent priest—although, as the chancellor of the diocese would say later during the cause, an "administratively a colossal bungler"—conducted a rather superficial examination. The last names were different; she was from the country, and he was from the big city far away and had never been to the country before his engagement; etc. After asking practically no questions, the pastor concluded the premarital inventory and assisted at the wedding to the great joy of all.

The Saturday after the wedding, the pastor went to a feast day celebration in a neighboring town, to which all the priests of the rural vicariate were invited, and participated in a solemn procession. At the customary luncheon afterward, the pastor was approached by another priest of the vicariate, a distant relative of the newlyweds, who told him, "Last Saturday you married my cousins. Did you request the dispensation?" The pastor was dismayed, and he was alarmed by the umpteenth item of parish business that he had bungled. The next day, after Sunday Mass, he stopped Marianne's mother and told her that he urgently needed to speak with the two newlyweds. She contacted them in the city to which they had both gone to live. Despite considerable inconvenience (this story goes back several years), the couple traveled to the town the following weekend, and on Friday evening—not even two weeks after their wedding celebration—called on the pastor. Imagine their astonishment and consternation: the pastor scolded them for not saying anything about their distant kinship (forgetting his own superficial examination), said that he would have to consult the bishop about their case, and told them that the marriage had to be entirely redone. The couple were alarmed and did not understand—thinking that they had to reconvene all the invited guests—and objected that they no longer had the money for such an event. They calmed down when the pastor told them that two persons would be enough, the wife's sister and brother-in-law, and that they should come again to the parish late the following evening, without making the matter known.

And so on Saturday evening, at around eight, Peter, Marianne, and her sister and brother-in-law went to a lesson in canon law. The pastor welcomed them in his study, and after twenty minutes at most, after another scolding, it was all done. The couple (and the two witnesses also) do not even recall whether they were asked to renew their consent: the fact remains that they had to sign a form in which they declared that they had done so. Peter and Marianne—like their two chaperones—did not even read the form that they signed. In awe of the pastor who had scolded them, they were content to have resolved, without making an ugly scene and without unforeseen expenses, an issue that for them was already assuming tragic proportions, and to have done so promptly, exactly two weeks after their wedding.

So Peter and Marianne went back to the city and to their everyday work routine. Several years passed, and a child was born of their union, but things were not going well. Ultimately they separated, and Marianne decided to return to the town. The old pastor was now deceased, and Marianne, by attending Mass at the parish as usual, met the new pastor. She told him the story of her marriage. The new pastor became suspicious, checked in the archives, and discovered that the renewal of consent by the spouses (assuming that they truly had expressed it and had realized what it was about) had been carried out two weeks after the wedding, but that the dispensation from consanguinity had been requested and obtained—thanks to a rather hazy, summary presentation of the case—only afterward. The old pastor, in his haste to "regularize" the couple and to fix the clumsy mistake he had made, had committed an ever greater one.

The question was brought before the tribunal. By means of the depositions of the direct protagonists, of the witnesses of the (dubious) renewal of consent, and of another relative who knew about the second round with the pastor two weeks after the wedding, and also through the documents of the dispensation granted by the ordinary, the tribunal ascertained that when the couple (assuming the best) had renewed their consent, they were still juridically unqualified to marry (since they were related by a dispensable degree of consanguinity but had not yet been dispensed), and that therefore their consent was certainly at least juridically ineffective.

The example is meant to recall that it is not prudent (to counsel couples) to proceed to a simple convalidation of marriage with excessive haste without having an exact picture of the situation in law and in fact. Without intending to condemn the old country pastor, who, again, was an excellent priest but a "bungler"—he should have declared his mistake to the bishop and asked for a radical sanation of the marriage of Peter and Marianne instead of proposing a simple convalidation to two spouses who perhaps were not even capable of truly realizing (because of their simplicity and their fear) the need to renew their consent.

Fourth example

Having just been ordained, Father Richard was assigned as assistant priest to one of the two parishes in town, Saint Mary's. He dedicated himself to youth ministry and drew many young people to his gatherings. They liked him because of his enthusiasm and his good qualities.

There were young people of various ages. Among them were Martin and Christine, who had been engaged for several years and were about to be married. Of course, they asked Father Richard to conduct the marriage preparation sessions and to assist at their wedding. Everything was set. Father Richard took care of the spiritual and liturgical preparations, and the pastor of Saint Mary's made the canonical arrangements. The wedding was now imminent. Father Richard was alone in the parish because—since it was summer—he took turns with the pastor in leading various summer trips for adults and youth. Around ten days before the wedding—which Martin and Christine wanted to be small and intimate, with just a few relatives and friends—the engaged couple asked Father Richard, "There are just a few of us. Why can't we get married in the Chapel of Saint Isidore, which is near Christine's house? There is a woman next door who has the key, and she has already agreed to open it. We will do everything. We will bring the flowers, clean the place, and leave everything in order." Father Richard saw nothing wrong with the idea and was happy to comply with the request of the young couple, who were so dear to him. On the day of the wedding he took the marriage register, went with the few invited guests to the Chapel of Saint Isidore, and assisted at the wedding.

There was a problem, however. Father Richard, relatively new to the town, was not aware that the Chapel of Saint Isidore was located not within Saint Mary's parish but rather in Saint John's. Not knowing this, it never even occurred to him that the delegation from the pastor of Saint Mary's to assist at the wedding of Martin and Christine was valid only for the parochial territory and that he would have to ask for a delegation from the pastor of Saint John's instead. And so he celebrated the nuptial Mass and assisted at the wedding of the young couple.

When the pastor of Saint Mary's returned from the vacation trip with the adults of the parish, Father Richard told him about the pastoral activity that he had conducted in his absence. Quite enthusiastically, he told him also about the beautiful marriage of Martin and Christine. The pastor of Saint Mary's immediately noticed the trouble caused by Father Richard. Very paternally he explained the situation to Father Richard (reminding him perhaps of a bit of canon law that Father Richard had not studied in great depth at the seminary), and they both traveled to the chancery for advice on what to do. The applicability of supplied jurisdiction because of common error (cf. can. 144 §1) was ruled out, since many of the local faithful knew that the Chapel of Saint Isidore was located in Saint John's parish, where Father Richard had never carried out his ministry, and instead the possibility of radical sanation was suggested, presuming the persistence of the consent of Martin and Christine, which was only juridically ineffective because Father Richard had not been delegated to receive their vows. And, in fact, not only did the consent of Martin and Christine persist, but their marriage went well too, and in their Christian life they also benefited from the pastoral care and help of Father Richard, whose carelessness on that day is unknown to them even now.

The example is meant to show that radical sanation is a rather flexible solution for convalidating a marriage that is objectively null. It respects the naturally sufficient consent of the spouses and makes it possible to overcome—with due discretion too, if necessary—obstacles of a merely formal character to its juridical efficacy.

XIV

Pontifical Dispensation from a Ratified and Nonconsummated Marriage

Sometimes while questioning parties to a case or witnesses in the course of a case of nullity of marriage, one hears it said, "But how could this marriage possibly be declared null? It was certainly consummated, since there are children!" Sometimes—although rarely—it happens that an individual appears at the tribunal and says, "My parish priest told me to come to you because my marriage is null; as a matter of fact, it was not consummated!" It is clear, for these individuals, that there is the danger (if not the actual reality) of causing some confusion.

Therefore, it seems quite fitting that our discussion, which aims to offer advice to those who want to provide canonical consultation to couples in irremediable matrimonial difficulty, should offer some information as well with regard to the problems raised by the possible nonconsummation of the marriage and with regard to the legal means that canon law offers to address them pastorally.

In presenting this information one should remain, as usual, at the initial level of examination and at a very simple level of explanation, since there is no lack of scholarly texts that can help those who are interested in going more deeply into the whole subject.[1] As far as several

---

[1] Among the many works that could be cited, we limit ourselves here to the following suggestions. First of all, one cannot overlook the manual of matrimonial canon law by the late Dominican father Antonino Abate, which is noteworthy for its very clear and well-informed presentation of theological doctrine, substantive law, and procedures in relation to cases of possible dissolution of marriage in the canonical system. The entire second part of the manual is, in fact, dedicated to these problems; see A. M. Abate, *Il matrimonio nella nuova legislazione canonica* (Brescia: Paideia Editrice, 1986), 207–349. From the more specifically procedural perspective, but without omitting due reference to doctrine, we recommend the four articles by Oscar Buttinelli, Raffaele Melli, Raymond Leo

aspects connected to the question are concerned, namely, the topics of the indissolubility of marriage and the sexual capacity required for marriage itself, we refer the reader to the discussion of these matters earlier in this book.[2]

Elements of substantive law

1. Earlier mention was made to some confusion that may be encountered among the faithful with regard to the importance of the consummation of a marriage as far as its validity is concerned. In reality, at least for the Latin-rite matrimonial discipline, the fundamental elements of the solution of this question were already established long ago, in the twelfth century.

As the reader may know, right at that time particular attention was being paid to the problems connected with the constitutive moment of marriage and with the determination of its formal constituent element, or as the classical terminology puts it, of its efficient cause. At that time two schools of thought came into conflict on this matter. They were connected to the respective traditions of the two most important universities of the time—Bologna and Paris—and to the teaching of the jurists and theologians who worked at them. To simplify greatly, we could say that at Bologna the prevailing theory (with antecedents in Germanic law) maintained that, although the consent of the parties was necessary, their carnal intercourse was what actually and properly breathed life into the marriage. On the other hand, at Paris the prevailing doctrine (of more purely Roman origin) was that the constitutive moment of marriage was found in the exchange of consent, which was specifically the efficient cause that gave rise to the marital bond.

Distinguished pontiffs of the period who were canonists, and first among them Alexander III, enshrined the doctrine that regarded the

---

Burke, and Settimio Carmignani Caridi in *I procedimenti speciali nel diritto canonico* (Vatican City: Libreria Editrice Vaticana, 1992), 107–56. In these articles the obligatory procedures in cases of dispensation are carefully followed, from their diocesan phase to a final appeal to the Holy See, while looking more closely into the nature of the papal provisions in this matter and analyzing the delicate problem of how to treat the parties in the process, in particular as far as the right of defense is concerned.

[2] Respectively in the chapters dedicated to the exclusion of the indissolubility of marriage and to the impediment of sexual impotence.

consent of the parties as the sole efficient cause of marriage, the principle upon which, from then on and with no doubt whatsoever, the entire canonical system of marriage was gradually constructed.

It follows then that the consummation of marriage—which takes place through carnal copulation and by means of which the two spouses become what is described in the language of Scripture as "one flesh"—cannot be considered an element that essentially brings a marriage into being and that therefore has influence on its validity from the juridical perspective. The example cited by the classical authors is that of the marriage of the Virgin Mary and Saint Joseph. It was valid because of the consent of the two spouses although not consummated, according to the altogether traditional interpretation of Mary's virginity, not only in relation to the conception and birth of Jesus but also for the rest of her life.

If the validity of a marriage does not depend, therefore, on whether or not it is consummated, what possible juridical relevance does its consummation have? Catholic doctrine, including canonical teaching, certainly did not mean to ignore the importance of this fact, which is surely very important for the spouses from the interpersonal perspective and also symbolically, because of the value of their union as a sign of the very intimate and fruitful relationship between Christ and the Church. Indeed, over the centuries immediately following the doctrinal clarification in regard to the efficient cause of marriage, scholars little by little arrived at the conviction that the nonconsummation of marriage was a circumstance that permitted the supreme authority of the Church to derogate from the extrinsic indissolubility of a marriage, even if ratified, thus allowing the possibility of celebrating another.

Behind these few words there are rather complex concepts and formidable problems, including doctrinal problems that we must patiently seek to elucidate, without losing sight of the resolution to keep the presentation simple.

2. In the first place, there is the indissolubility of marriage. Everyone knows that Catholic doctrine considers this to be a property of marriage, that is, one of its characteristics, one of its peculiar notes. In this way, indissolubility is distinguished from the essence of marriage, which in its constitutive aspect is the consent of the parties, whereas in its existence as a state of life it is the partnership of the entire life

that is established between the spouses. This property, however, is traditionally called "essential" (cf. can. 1056) so as to indicate that, in principle, it characterizes marriage in its perfection, in its comprehensive identity.

As to its foundation, this property of marriage is said to go back to the natural law. This means that Catholic teaching maintains that indissolubility is a property of every valid marriage, however or by whomever it is celebrated. Marriage, in fact, is regarded by Catholic teaching as an institution of natural law, in other words, as the right and lawful way for a man and a woman to live out the union between them that involves also the possibility of a complete psycho-affective and psychosexual integration. Therefore, its essential characteristics as well cannot but exist whenever the reality itself of marriage comes to exist.

Nevertheless, a distinction is usually made between intrinsic and extrinsic indissolubility. Intrinsic indissolubility is then considered to be absolute, while there may be exceptions, albeit very rare ones, to extrinsic indissolubility.

Intrinsic indissolubility concerns the two contracting parties who, with their consent, brought the marriage to life, and it means that, once they have exercised their freedom in their act of consent, they must respect the bond that was created. In other words, they can in no way do away with it by dissolving the reciprocal bond that joins them. The permanency of this bond—from a substantial and therefore also a juridical perspective—is completely independent from their will.

Extrinsic indissolubility, on the other hand, refers to the powers over the bond belonging to an authority other than that of the spouses who brought it into being. In this matter, the law of the Catholic Church acknowledges the Roman Pontiff as the sole authority that has power to dissolve the marital bond. This implies that any other canonical, civil, or religious authority whatsoever is, by canon law, completely incompetent to dissolve the marital bond.

3. What is the basis of this authority of the Pope? And what is the extent of its exercise, or if you prefer, what are its limits? These are extremely complicated arguments, which we will try to simplify here.

As to the basis of the papal authority in this matter, it is customarily traced back to the particular authority of the Pope that is usually called "vicarious", inasmuch as he exercises it not as the successor of Peter and head of the Church (in other words, in his own name) but properly speaking as the Vicar of Christ. The reasoning in support of this affirmation would be roughly as follows: the indissolubility of the marital bond is a precept, a "law" given by God and confirmed by Christ; therefore, a lesser authority than this could not dispense from its observance, unless it were a special authority held and exercised in a specifically vicarious way in relation to Christ. Nevertheless, this kind of explanation and terminology does not appear to be well accepted, even by those who do not call into question this power of the Roman Pontiff. And so commentators sometimes prefer to explain the power of the Pope in this matter as a particular aspect of the unique sacred power entrusted by Christ to his Church, precisely the aspect by which the Pope would be authorized, in particular cases, to dispense from the divine law. It would be a question, then, of a very special aspect of the sacred power and of the Church's responsibility with regard to divine law (whether it is positive, deducible from revelation, or natural, that is, inscribed in the nature of things and so capable of being derived with the aid of rational reflection). This aspect of sacred ecclesial power—without intending thereby to undervalue the fullness of power that is received with episcopal consecration—is held precisely by the Supreme Pontiff and his primatial office.

As to the limits of this power, it must be said that they are strictly correlative to the sacramental nature of marriage, which—by virtue of its more explicit symbolic reference to the union between Christ and his Church—adds a special binding character to the natural precept of the indissolubility of marriage (cf. can. 1056). Thus, a nonsacramental marriage can always (albeit with due caution) be dissolved when there proves to be a true pastoral need for it, which can be traced back to the privilege of faith. A sacramental marriage, on the other hand—and called "ratified"—can be dissolved only if the fact of the nonconsummation of the same marriage accompanies the real pastoral expediency. Consummation, which brings about the "one flesh" between the spouses, confers an absolute indissolubility from the extrinsic perspective on the bond.

These doctrinal facts are also explicit precepts of the ecclesiastical discipline. The title of the Latin Code that is dedicated to marriage contains a chapter 9 entitled "The Separation of the Spouses", in which we find an article 1 entitled "The Dissolution of the Bond". The first two canons of this article summarize the doctrinal facts presented thus far while decreeing that a "ratified" and consummated marriage cannot be dissolved by any authority or for any reason, except by death. A marriage of two Christians on the other hand (even though "ratified" or sacramental inasmuch as it was contracted by two baptized persons) can be dissolved by the Roman Pontiff and for a just reason if it was not consummated. These are the principles of substantive law that summarize and presuppose the doctrine set forth thus far and that substantially find their counterparts in canons 853 and 862 of the Code of Canons of the Eastern Churches.

4. At this point, in order to understand the exact terms of the discipline that is being explained, it is necessary here to ask what is meant by the "consummation" of marriage and how the nonoccurrence of this fact could be proved.

While staying on a general level, suffice it to say that the consummation of marriage is that physical, genital union that is proper to spouses and that helps to bring about, in fact, the orientation of marriage to its institutional final ends: the interpersonal end, or the good of the spouses (which has the possible psychosexual integration of the spouses as one of its qualifying aspects), and the social end, or the good of offspring.

More concretely and from the physical, phenomenological perspective, the consummation of marriage is accomplished if the individual of the male sex penetrates with his male member, even if only partial, the vagina of his own wife, ejaculating into it. From the physical perspective, no more is required, and this suffices for the consummation of the marriage.

From a psychological perspective, it is required that the act take place in a human manner, as stated in canon 1061 §1. This specification in the present Code, which reflects the standard of *Gaudium et spes*, no. 49, can by its relative vagueness give rise to a rather complicated interpretative problem. At the present state [1998] of the debate we can say that the expression surely implies the following requirement: a sufficient, at-least-virtual act of the will by the subject, to which physical violence is certainly opposed. It is not certain that other intentional and psychological qualifications are required to establish the "human fashion" of consummating the marriage, at least for juridical purposes, as a constituent element of the fact itself.[3]

In the context of the present discussion, we mention only in passing that, in recent times, some authors have proposed a new concept of the consummation of marriage. In particular the French scholar Jean Bernard, from the canonical school of thought responsible for the *Revue de droit canonique*, proposed the concept of "existential consummation in the faith", which would be achieved whenever a profound interpersonal and spiritual union occurs between the spouses. In the absence of this existential consummation in the faith, their marriage would be dissoluble. It is obvious that this perspective aims in practice to eviscerate the present concept and discipline of the indissolubility of marriage. I say "in practice" inasmuch as the indissolubility of the bond is reaffirmed formally yet is in fact considerably attenuated by the breadth of the proposed concept of consummation. It does not seem, however, that this concept has met with widespread acceptance, nor could it find many adherents, both because it attributes an essentially foreign content to a traditional concept, without any evident reason to justify doing so, and also because the concept of "existential consummation in the faith" is extremely vague, the use of which in practice would end up rendering the marital bond uncertain. It is clear that this author will hold to the traditional concept of consummation, since neither rationally compelling motives nor directions from the legislator in this matter prompt us to change it.

5. In relation to the last point, the reader may wonder, "All right, the innovative concept of consummation is, among other things, extremely difficult to verify. But the traditional one does not seem very easy to prove either. How is it possible to prove a fact (and a negative

---

[3] The *Litterae circulares* of December 20, 1986, issued by the then Congregation for the Sacraments, recalls that a plenary session of the same Congregation held in April 1986 reached the conclusion that "ad habendam consummationem matrimonii oportet ut actus sit humanus ex utraque parte, sed sufficit ut sit virtualiter voluntarius, dummodo non violenter exigitus. Cetera elementa psychologica, quae actum humanum faciliorem vel amabiliorem reddunt, non attenduntur." [In order for there to be a consummation of marriage, it is necessary that the act be human on the part of both spouses, but it suffices that it be virtually voluntary, provided that it is not demanded violently. Other psychological elements that render the human act easier or more gratifying are not taken into consideration.]

one, at that) that usually happens (or more precisely, does not happen) in a situation in which the spouses are alone, without other persons present?" Such a question by the reader prompts us to confront the very delicate problem of proving nonconsummation of marriage.

Over the course of history, the canonical tradition has identified three ways, three probative methods, that assist in obtaining this proof. They are called the physical argument (from the Latin *argumentum*, "proof"), the moral argument, and the argument *per coarctata tempora*.

Let us start with the last one, which is the easiest to explain. There is proof *per coarctata tempora*, an expression that could be translated "for lack of sufficient time", when the spouses do not live together after the wedding. Canon 1061 §2 of the Code establishes the simple presumption of consummation of marriage if the spouses have cohabited. On the other hand, if the two spouses have never been able to begin an actual common married life, this is circumstantial proof of the nonconsummation of their marriage. Clearly, we are dealing with a rather exceptional situation, which can occur, for example, in a case of a marriage by proxy; or in the case of a marriage by proxy in which one of the parties is subject to incarceration. These are cases that occur very rarely yet are still possible. The fact remains that the canonical tradition of jurisprudence has developed the presumptive proof of nonconsummation whenever it is certain that cohabitation never took place in any way between two persons joined in marriage.

The physical argument likewise consists essentially in a presumptive proof, inasmuch as it deduces the nonconsummation of marriage from factual data, this time related to the physical state of the persons concerned. There are essentially two sorts of factual data that make up the physical argument: in the first place, the intact state of the hymen—in other words, the woman's physical virginity—which is considered conclusive evidence of the nonconsummation of marriage; in the second place, a malformation of the genital organs of one of the parties concerned (or a certain dysfunction, this time especially of the male party). These two types of evidence render certain the presumption that it is and was impossible to engage in the sexual intercourse essential to the consummation of marriage. As is obvious even from what is presented just in these few lines, the physical proof of nonconsummation of marriage can present particularly complex probative problems. Think, for example, of the case of particularly elastic hymenal tissue, or of a hymen that exhibits tears that could have had an origin other than coitus. Think of the difficulty of proving (for the entire time that his married life has lasted) the impossibility of ejaculating on the part of a subject who is nevertheless capable of penetrating his own wife. Here it is not possible (nor perhaps is it appropriate) for us to enter into the clinical problems related to the physical argument in proving nonconsummation of marriage. It is enough to have shown that it is possible and to have suggested the difficulties and pitfalls involved. It is not difficult to find appropriate in-depth treatments in specialized works in canon law or medicolegal matters.

Finally, the moral argument is based on the sworn testimony of the parties, backed by references vouching for their credibility and by the testimony of persons who—at a nonsuspect time—had a first-hand account from the parties themselves (or just one of them) as to the nonconsummation of their marriage, that is, of the total absence of any properly marital relations. In connection with this type of proof, it must be emphasized what it represents. Since long before the present Code introduced the general provisions of canons 1536 §2 and 1679 about the probative value (which by way of exception may even constitute full proof) of confessions and declarations of the parties at the tribunal, sworn testimony by credible witnesses has always been a particular instance of the attention the canonical system pays to the requirements of substantive justice. By taking into account the particularities of proving the nonconsummation of marriage, the canonical system showed that it was inclined to give credence to the declarations of those who had firsthand experience of facts that are the direct object of the investigation, as long as they proved to be completely reliable persons. As a guarantee of their trustworthiness, testimonies as to credibility of the parties were required from those whom the earlier Code called *septimae manus* ["seven-hand"] witnesses, who could swear to the honesty of the spouses and to the veracity of their declarations about the matter of the controversy (cf. can. 1975 of the 1917 Code). In the current legislation, it must be admitted, all formalism has been overcome with respect to proof based on the credibility of the parties (e.g., there is no predetermined number of witnesses to be called). Instead the judge can appraise the reliability of the parties' statements on the basis of testimonies concerning their credibility and on the merits of the case, as well as any other evidence or circumstance that may be useful. Thus, for example, the number of character witnesses will not assume a particular and almost autonomous importance, but rather what is important is the actual authoritativeness of a given witness, the extent of his acquaintance with the interested party, and the objective facts on which he bases his own judgment. Thus, in the case of witnesses who report statements by the interested parties about the nonconsummation of their marriage, it will be especially important to know the time of the statements that are reported, the amount of detail in them, and the extent to which they are consistent and analytical.

To conclude these brief observations about proving nonconsummation of marriage, it remains to be said that often the physical and moral arguments combine, both being present in the same case, and that not uncommonly, the moral argument helps to reinforce a weak or uncertain physical argument.

6. At this point of our presentation the reader might go on to wonder, "Is the mere fact of proof of nonconsummation of marriage enough to obtain the papal dispensation? And given that proof, is the Pope obliged to grant such a dispensation?"

It is possible to answer both questions simultaneously by recalling the nature of the measure under consideration. A dispensation is the authorization in a particular case not to observe an obligation resulting from a law (compare, by analogy, the concept of dispensation contained in canon 85, which per se refers to merely ecclesiastical laws). Now, in order to grant a dispensation, it is necessary for there to be a just and proportionate reason, such as to justify the exemption from the obligation of which one is being relieved. In evaluating this cause, the authority has rather broad discretion, even though the concept of "just reason" is interpreted rather broadly, since it is necessary to include in this concept anything opportune that might benefit the *salus animarum* [salvation of souls]. For example, the proximate danger that one of the interested parties could fall (or has already fallen) into an irregular marital situation is considered just reason for the dispensation. On the other hand, there would be no just reason for dispensation if the marriage was not consummated because of the spouses' intention contrary to the procreation of offspring, which was manifested, for example, in malicious abstention from sexual relations, or else through contraceptive devices that prevent ejaculation into the vagina.

Other chance elements too enter into the authority's discretionary estimation of whether or not to grant a dispensation. For example, the reasonable prospect that the provision could be harmful to third parties, in the form of scandal or confusion among the faithful. Such a reasonable and well-founded fear of that can be sufficient reason not to grant the dispensation, even if a marriage was not consummated, since a favor for the benefit of individual persons (one could say, of private persons) cannot cause harm to the community. This is an indirect confirmation of the public and not private nature of canonical matters pertaining to marriage and therefore of the impossibility—considering also the contemporary cultural and secularist legal sensibility in the area of marriage—of reducing the matter itself exclusively or even only tendentiously to the private sphere.

In conclusion, it should be said that proof of nonconsummation is not enough to obtain a dispensation, and that the authority, in the presence of the aforesaid proof, is not obligated to grant it. It is necessary to evaluate other circumstances—in the first place, the existence of a proportionate cause—to grant it. Note, among other things, that any dispensation granted because of an error about the existence of the alleged motive would be invalid (compare also by analogy can. 90, which per se refers to dispensations from positive ecclesiastical laws).

It is probably because of this discretionary intervention of the ecclesial authority that the dispensation itself is described as an "administrative" and not a strictly judicial act and that the procedure leading to it is described precisely as "administrative" and not as a judgment properly speaking (in terms of civil law one would say a proceeding and not a trial, at least according to widely accepted scholarship). Clearly this description of a dispensation (as an administrative act) is not intended to imply that the power the Church exercises in this regard and the ways by which she does so must be understood as being strictly analogous to the power and the *modus operandi* of the public administration of the state. This description simply means that the aforesaid measure is an act of the executive pastoral authority, directed toward individuals and having no properly judicial nature, even though the act itself is arrived at through a codified procedure and follows an evaluation of the matter and a deliberation on the part of the authority.

7. At this point we should turn to a summary presentation of the procedure that must be followed in cases of dispensation relative to nonconsummated marriages. This procedure is regulated today by canons

1697–706, which make up the third chapter of the first title ("Matrimonial Processes") of part 3 ("Certain Special Processes") of book 7 of the Code. However, we must not forget canon 1681 either. To these properly legislative norms must be added the *Litterae circulares* "De processu super matrimonio rato et non consummato" issued on December 20, 1986 (prot. 1400/86) by the Congregation for the Sacraments (henceforth LC). This circular letter has the technical force of an instruction (cf. can. 34), through which provisions of a law are rendered clearer and procedures to be followed in applying them are developed and defined, specifically for the benefit of those whose duty it is to execute the law.

Presenting this procedure very summarily, we can distinguish two phases of it: an instructional phase, which is normally conducted at the diocesan level, and a decision-making phase, which is conducted at the Holy See.

a. The chief purpose of the instructional phase is to collect the matters of fact that demonstrate the existence of the required qualifications for effectively proposing the cause of dispensation to the Holy See. In this diocesan phase particular prominence is assigned to the bishop of the requesting party (commonly called the "petitioner"), who is competent to admit the brief, to designate the one responsible for collecting the evidence, and possibly to admit a legal expert as an assistant to the parties, and finally to express his opinion as to whether the request is well founded and can be proposed to the Holy See.

Without going into overly elaborate procedural considerations that are of less interest to the readers for whom the present volume is intended, it seems appropriate, with respect to this first phase of the process, to emphasize the following points.

As already mentioned, the request for a dispensation must be presented to the bishop of the domicile or quasi domicile of the petitioner (cf. can. 1699 §1). It is up to him to admit the petition for consideration, after examining the possibility of a reconciliation of the parties (cf. LC, art. 4) and after consulting the competent Roman congregation in cases that present particular difficulties, for example, the alleged incapacity to ejaculate, or the conception of a child in the attempts to consummate the marriage and the birth of the child himself (cf. can. 1699 §2 and LC, art. 2).

By law, however, the bishop does not instruct the case personally in the instructional phase but delegates it to his own tribunal, or else to a tribunal of another diocese (in mission countries or where the judicial organization of the Church is not highly developed), or even to a priest who is considered qualified to carry it out (cf. can. 1700 §1). In a case where there is a transition, as described in canon 1681, from a cause of nullity to a cause of dispensation, the tribunal to which the cause of nullity was assigned pursues the possible instruction (see also LC, art. 7). In a case where a petition for a dispensation and a petition for a declaration of nullity of the same marriage are filed in two different tribunals, the instruction thereof must be assigned to the tribunal dealing with the cause of nullity (cf. can. 1700 §2 and LC, art. 5).

In carrying out the instruction, one must follow the rules concerning the acquisition of proof laid down for the contentious trial, whether ordinary or matrimonial, naturally wherever they are in keeping with the particular administrative proceeding of dispensation (cf. can. 1702).

As for the instruction and the evidence to be collected in it, two points should be made. First, the evidence can be of any kind, provided that it is licit and useful for the reconstruction of the truth of the facts (cf. LC, art. 14), even though there is likely to be a certain preponderance of testimonial and expert evidence, as compared with the moral and physical arguments that usually go to prove that a marriage was not consummated. (In fact, articles 8–20 of the LC refer specifically to these special methods of proof.)

Second, it must be pointed out that the instruction of the case itself, like all the rest of the administrative process of dispensation, is characterized by great discretion and confidentiality. In particular with regard to the instruction, there is no publication of the acts of the cause, although it is possible—either at the request of a party or of an official—to communicate some piece of evidence to the parties, especially when ignorance of such evidence would be seriously prejudicial to the petitioner's plea or to an exception raised by the respondent (cf. can. 1703). Leaving to scholars the technical evaluation of this solution, it is enough for the counselor to know that the legislator sought an effective balance between discretion and the interested parties' right to a defense and that the counselor can reassure the interested parties that any facts concerning their intimate private life that may come out in the canonical proceeding will be treated with the strictest confidentiality.

The collection of evidence, once completed, is then examined by the defender of the bond, who must always intervene in this type of process (cf. can. 1701 § 1). In this case his function is to propose reasonable arguments against the dissolution of the marriage (cf. can. 1432). Having obtained the observations of the defender of the bond, the instructing judge must draw up a report that will accompany the acts that are to be submitted to the diocesan bishop, who on the basis of the acts themselves composes an opinion *pro rei veritate* [on the veracity of the fact], in which he evaluates whether the necessary elements necessary for the dispensation are present and decides whether or not to transmit the petition and the instructional acts to the Holy See (cf. can. 1704 § 1). The writing of this opinion, in particular, calls for the exercise of the utmost pastoral prudence on the part of the bishop, who must be able to weigh carefully the evidence that has been collected, with a view to providing for the spiritual good of the individuals in regard to the truth of the matter and the general interests of the community entrusted to his care.

With the opinion of the bishop the diocesan phase of the process ends.

b. The decision-making phase of the process, by contrast, occurs at the Holy See. To it belongs the judgment on the fact of the non-consummation of the marriage and on the existence of a just reason for the dispensation from the marital bond (cf. can. 1698 § 1), without prejudice to the fact that the dispensation is properly a personal act of the Pontiff (§ 2). [In particular—as article 2 of the motu proprio *Quaerit semper*[1] (August 30, 2011) clearly states—the Roman Rota is competent, as of October 1, 2011, to make that evaluation and possibly to present the case to the Pope for the dispensation.]

Within this important dicastery of the Roman Curia, the case may be dealt with according to a procedure that varies, depending on the degree of the case's difficulty. We will not explain here analytically the various types of procedures but will mention only the one that is the ordinary way of examining and deciding cases that reach the Congregation.

---

[1] Cf. Apostolic constitution on the Roman Curia *Pastor bonus* (June 28, 1988), 67.

After an opinion by the defender of the bond at the Congregation, the acts of the cause are entrusted to a body that is made up of three members selected from among the consultors of the Congregation itself and is called a "commission". The members of this commission study the case and meet on an appointed day to respond to the *dubium* of whether there is sufficient evidence to propose to the Supreme Pontiff the dispensation from the marriage. If the three opinions agree on an affirmative conclusion, the cause moves on to the final phase. If only two votes are in favor, the vote of a fourth expert is sought, or else additional instruction is arranged. With two or more negative votes, on the other hand, the petition is rejected. The final phase of causes that receive favorable opinions on the part of the commission calls for a new opinion from the defender of the bond and the composition of a summary of the acts, in other words, a page that summarizes both the case and the procedure followed, to present to the Pope. Notice of his decision is then given to the interested parties by way of the diocesan bishop (cf. can. 1706), who will also see to it that the papal rescript is duly noted in the baptismal registers and the marriage register of the interested parties.

Because it less directly pertains to the counselor's concerns, we merely mention here the fact that the papal rescript may contain additional clauses limiting the exercise of the faculty to enter into a new marriage. The lifting of such restrictions may be reserved to the competent ordinary or to the Congregation itself. These prohibitions are added when it turns out that at the basis of the nonconsummation of the marriage that has been dispensed there was some reason of a physical or psychological nature (or else a distorted mindset with regard to marital duties) that, it is feared, could reassert itself in a new marital experience. Especially in the first case, said prohibition will be lifted after carrying out medical or psychological tests that make it morally certain that the obstacle to engaging in conjugal life, in its sexual aspect as well, has been overcome.

8. All that remains is to mention one question about which it is a good idea for the counselor to inform the interested parties as soon as there is any prospect of a cause of dispensation. Following a decision of the Italian Constitutional Court going back to February 1982, the Courts of Appeal of the state have ceased to recognize the civil effects of papal rescripts dispensing from a nonconsummated marriage. The

1984 revision of the concordat between the Holy See and Italy—which did not touch upon this question—in practice acknowledges this new disciplinary situation.

This is not the place to discuss the arguments of the Italian Constitutional Court and the merits of the pronouncement that declared unconstitutional the legislative provision that papal dispensations are to be recognized. It is, however, the place to emphasize that, given this situation that has been created, a possible dispensation by the Pope will not be able to have civil effects in Italy; therefore, if the interested Catholic laypersons were once united in a marriage under the concordat with Italy (that is, a canonical marriage with civil effects), now they would have to see to it that the bond was dissolved in a civil court by means of a request for the cessation of the civil effects of their marriage as recorded by the state. It is logical that, in this case, from a moral perspective the request for divorce would be morally justified, since the lay faithful resort to it only because the state in its own legal system does not attribute any juridical importance to the dissolution of the bond already declared by the Pope. From the strictly juridical perspective, the general decree of the Italian Episcopal Conference on canonical marriage that has been in force since February 17, 1991, regulated this case in article 44, paragraph 4; and articles 63–66. It is a good idea for the counselor to inform those who would like to undertake a cause of dispensation from the bond of their allegedly nonconsummated marriage about this problem. Recall, among other things, that the nonconsummation of marriage is one reason foreseen by Italian law to declare immediately the cessation of the civil effects of the marriage, without waiting an interval of three years from the presidential audience in the parties' process of separation.

Guide for the counselor

The following paragraphs offer some suggestions concerning the points that the counselor of couples in an irremediable marital crisis ought to examine—with due discretion and the utmost respect—when he suspects that he may have before him a case of nonconsummated marriage and before describing the possibility of asking the Pope for a dissolution:

1. In the first place, he should seek to find out as precisely as possible the crux of the matter. People, indeed, either out of timidity or because of incorrect information, often express themselves in ambiguous and confused terms: "My husband never approached me", "My wife never wanted to have full sexual relations", "We never lived as husband and wife", "Our marriage has remained chaste", "We only attempted to have marital relations", etc. These expressions are often heard, but plainly their meaning remains vague.

The counselor, therefore, keeping in mind the canonical concept of consummation explained above, should prudently and respectfully have the interested parties express as precisely as possible what in fact happened between them in their intimate relations. It may seem embarrassing, but if he clearly explains the reason why such questions need to be asked, and if he has the patience to guide the speaker gently as he explains the case, one can arrive, even at this level, at a substantial clarification of the question.

It is obvious, indeed—and it is a good idea to remind the interested party of it immediately—that it is worth the trouble of initiating a cause of dispensation only in the case in which the marriage was truly not consummated. Otherwise it would be useless and, especially if there were untruthful declarations about the matter, seriously harmful to the conscience.

2. It may happen that, in analyzing the testimony thus far, it will not be possible to arrive at a judgment, even an initial one, about the nonconsummation of the marriage, either because the woman does not have a clear awareness of her own physical state, or else because there are malformations that have never been observed and described by physicians.

In that case, it may be useful to suggest a visit to a gynecologist or other specialist who could shed light on the matter. It is good, in that case, to make a referral to experts who are capable of addressing the question with the appropriate delicacy and moral sensibility, as, for example, experts listed with ecclesiastical tribunals.

3. Whenever the counselor becomes convinced of the nonconsummation of the marriage, he should take the trouble to understand the causes of it. He should do so for three purposes:

First, so as to be able—if the interested parties desire it—to suggest persons whom they may consult for help in overcoming their problem. Indeed, especially if their common life is just beginning (it would be different if they had already spent several years without achieving intimate union; in such cases one observes that the situation becomes chronic and more difficult to remedy), one should not discuss immediately and exclusively the prospect of a cause of dispensation. It is prudent to suggest to the interested parties practical options for overcoming the difficulty and beginning a complete marital experience.

Second, so as to tell whether, behind the nonconsummation of the marriage, there might be a reason that could make one suspect that the marriage itself was null. There are various examples: a physical or psychological inability to copulate; a serious disturbance of sexuality, such as a homosexual orientation, that one of the parties had sought to disguise by marriage; the decision not to procreate since the subject knew that he was afflicted with a serious hereditary or contagious disease. From a logical and systematic perspective, indeed (although not always from the probative perspective), the cause of nullity prevails over the cause of dispensation.

Third, so as to determine whether it is possible to present a petition for dispensation. For example, if the nonconsummation of marriage were the result of a bilateral agreement not to have children, dictated by egotistical motives and implemented with contraceptive devices that prevent ejaculation into the vagina, it would be altogether useless to present a petition for dispensation, inasmuch as it would not have the qualifications to be accepted from the perspective of its just reason. The dispensation would in fact end up "rewarding" deceitful behavior in contempt of the duties of Christian marriage, duties that the spouses declared that they were assuming when they gave consent.

4. The counselor ought therefore to strive to examine the possible proof of the nonconsummation. It is easy to verify immediately whether or not cohabitation occurred between the spouses.

5. It is more difficult to investigate the physical state of the interested parties (normally this is a question of the intact hymen of the woman). It was already noted that sometimes even a woman who is per se in favor of initiating a cause does not know her own physical situation correctly, and it was also mentioned what is appropriate to advise in that case so as to clarify it.

There may also be the case, however, of a woman who resists the idea of submitting to the medical examinations and the investigations necessary for this type of cause. In that case it will be necessary, with great patience, to pursue the path of persuasion with a view to making the necessary assessments. If not, the only remaining option is to go on to verify the solidity of the moral argument.

6. For the purposes of evaluating the adequacy of that proof, it is a good idea to find out whether both spouses are willing to give a sworn deposition and whether their statements are (and will be in a canonical cause) in agreement on the point of the nonconsummation of their marriage. Above all, in the case of divergent statements, it will be absolutely necessary to clarify which of the two deserves greater credence.

This must be investigated also from an extrinsic perspective—for example, in relation to possible attestations of credibility that are truly certain and authoritative (the pastor, a nun, the bishop, a person disinterested in the outcome of the case and known as being above all suspicion).

Credibility, however, must be investigated above all from an intrinsic perspective—in other words, by means of credible witnesses who received, at a nonsuspect time, the confidences of the interested parties or of one of them about the nonconsummation of their marriage. Another means would be the reconstruction of the circumstances that testify to the verisimilitude of nonconsummation, as may be, for example, certification of an intact hymen at a time (long) after the wedding; a deposition by physicians who intervened specifically on account of the parties' sexual difficulties; or proof of treatments that imply the idea of difficulty in achieving intimate union, for example, a surgical incision of the hymen or a treatment for phimosis undergone by the man immediately after the wedding.

The combination of such evidence—as described in canons 1536 §2 and 1679 of the Code—can give a truly complete corroboration of the statement by the parties or even by only one of them, resulting in moral certainty about the nonconsummation of the marriage.

7. The counselor should make sure, furthermore, that there is a just reason for granting the dispensation, in other words, that several conditions are satisfied that make it suitable for the *salus animarum*. Thus,

for example, the fact of having entered (after the de facto end of the marriage that turns out to be nonconsummated) into a new pseudo-marital situation that is objectively irregular from the canonical perspective and could be regularized following a dispensation (although per se not something commendable) can be a reason that impels the ecclesial authority to grant the dispensation. Or again, by way of example, the fact of having lived in a nonconsummated marriage for which the other spouse was responsible (by condition or action) and having now the concrete opportunity to start a new family, which would have to be renounced in the absence of a dispensation. As was said before, with regard to the presence of a just reason, the ecclesial authority normally proves to be very benevolent and attentive to different personal situations.

8. Finally, the counselor will have to examine whether foreseeable circumstances could be obstacles—even with proof of the nonconsummation of the marriage—to the granting of a dispensation, for example, because of some foreseeable harm to third parties and/or to the community. This is the case, as we will see in one of the examples related below, with the presence of a child born of the marriage and still living within a rural setting that is very restrictive, both in terms of the small size of the community and culturally.

Only after having examined, if only summarily, the points listed above with positive results will the truly prudent counselor advise the persons who have confided in him to introduce a canonical cause of dispensation from the marital bond.

Examples

For the usual didactic and illustrative purposes of our study, we now propose several examples.

First example

This is the case of Lucy and Armand, two young people who had known each other since early childhood in a parish setting.

Ever since he was a boy, Armand had been in love with Lucy, and this sentiment had never left him. Lucy, on the contrary, a kindly but rather nervous and irritable girl, while fond of Armand, never really felt that she was in love with him. As the years went by, the two planned to marry, with an obvious lack of enthusiasm on Lucy's part. As the wedding day finally drew near, she on one occasion revealed to Armand her hesitation about this step and aired the possibility of abandoning their plans to marry.

For Armand this was an intolerable prospect, and he reacted with forceful expressions of his discouragement and sorrow, and even referred explicitly to desperate acts that he might commit. Lucy was disturbed and frightened by Armand's reactions and resigned herself to go through with the wedding plans, very reluctantly, yet sincerely taking upon herself the duties of a wife.

After the marriage was celebrated, however, and when the moment for intimacy arrived, Lucy, although she had intended to give herself to her husband, could not bring herself to let him come near her. When he approached her for intimacy, Lucy repelled him, saying that she was experiencing disgust and pain. Armand was patient at first but then began to manifest his disappointment with increasing vehemence; but Lucy's attitudes did not change. She refused also to consult physicians or counselors, saying that it was quite clear to her that the reason for her reactions was that she had never really loved Armand as a husband and that she had married him because he had pressured her.

After several years of life together, in one of Armand's frustrated attempts at intimacy, she became pregnant. This was a pregnancy caused by the absorption of the semen emitted by Armand onto Lucy's external genitals. It is a commonly occurring case that is well known to gynecologists. Lucy had an intact hymen despite her pregnancy, as shown also on clinical documentation of the medical examinations that she underwent at that time. She then gave birth by caesarean section, which became necessary because of a detached placenta and in order to save the life of the preborn child. Consequently, Lucy remained a virgin even after birth and remained such even though her life together with Armand lasted several more years after the birth of their daughter Camille.

However, since the problem of understanding between the spouses, about intimacy as well, was not resolved, Lucy decided after several more years of unhappy married life to separate. This time too she met with Armand's opposition, who again resorted to explicit threats of suicide. He even went so far as to stage several attempts for show. Lucy, however, was resolute and, at the recommendation of a priest, began both a canonical cause for dispensation and a civil cause [in Italy] for divorce on account of nonconsummation.

In both cases tests were carried out, and Lucy was found to be still a virgin. As far as the canonical cause was concerned, the aforesaid documentation relative to her medical treatment during pregnancy was also obtained, and there were judicial hearings of the parties and witnesses. The moral argument proved to be somewhat weak, since the parties confided in no one about their situation until rather late, when they spoke about it to two priests, and then only in veiled terms. Nevertheless, the physical argument seemed very strong, given Lucy's intact hymen.

The cause was therefore sent to the Congregation, which—after additional instruction consisting in a confrontation between the parties concerning several discrepancies in their stories—rejected the petition for dispensation. It should be explained, at this point, that no reasons are given for the rescripts sent in this matter, which simply note the judgment of the Congregation of the decision of the Pontiff. Because Lucy's case was not thought to merit dispensation, it is therefore necessary to deduce the reasons for it.

It is rather unlikely that the nonconsummation of the marriage was not considered certain: Lucy's gynecological situation was quite clear, in light also of the tests carried out both in the civil cause and in the canonical cause of nonconsummation. We should conclude instead that the reason for denying the papal favor depended on these facts: the birth of little Camille, after which the spouses still cohabited; the small rural and therefore still rather old-fashioned locality in which the two spouses had always lived and were still living; and a certain hesitation on the part of the pastor in giving his own assessment of the effects of a possible dispensation on the little farming community. It is quite likely that, because of this combination of reasons, a dispensation was considered inappropriate in this case. And this example is meant to emphasize precisely the fact that, in order to obtain the dispensation, it is not enough to prove that the nonconsummation of the marriage is certain; a just reason and the absence of contraindications as to its appropriateness are also necessary in order for it to be granted. Therefore, in recommending a similar cause, the counselor should pay attention to the presence of all the qualifications necessary for its effective proposal.

Second example

In the late 1940s, Arthur, a professional in his forties from a large city, the chief town in its province, was introduced to Dorothy, a romantic, fresh nineteen-year-old. The idea of marriage was mentioned, and approved by Arthur, who was established in his profession and looked favorably on the prospect of having a beautiful young wife in his life. Dorothy's parents, however, liked the idea even more. They, members of a good family from another important city in a different region, were going through not-so-good times from the perspective of the family's finances. Seeing their young daughter desired as a wife by a well-to-do, respected individual like Arthur was for them highly gratifying and an "opportunity" not to be missed. Indeed, the only one not that happy with the prospect of marriage was poor Dorothy. She would have to leave her hometown and move far away, to a place that was completely new to her, in the company of a man who in her eyes was already "old".

Dorothy in fact told her parents confidentially that Arthur was not the ideal husband she had longed for in her girlish dreams, but the consternation that they manifested, together with their speeches about the good of the family, about the girl's little brothers whose chances for a good education might be compromised if she were to refuse to marry, and so forth, overcame her resistance.

And so Dorothy got married and began her new life with Arthur. She was almost completely ignorant of the facts of married life, yet she very soon suspected that something was not happening in the usual way in her new home. Arthur, although courteous and respectful to her, never behaved toward her as she had even vaguely expected from a husband. On one occasion he delicately placed one hand on her genitals, saying that in this way he had "taken possession" of her and that therefore their marriage had now been consummated. From that moment on, nothing more happened.

While guessing the oddness of her situation, Dorothy, alone in a strange city, continued to lead her unhappy life for several years, conducting herself like a devoted wife and perfect lady of the house but disappointed in her womanly dreams and in her desire for mother-hood, which would at least partly have compensated for the affection that was not being given to her by her husband. Dorothy did not dare to confide even in her parents, of whom she was very fond. She feared that the revelation of her unhappy situation could cause them remorse for having pushed her into a wedding despite her lack of enthusiasm.

After a dozen years of married life led in the terms summarized above, Dorothy found herself about to turn thirty, with a fifty-year-old husband who, although he respected her, did not treat her as a wife and lived only for his work and his social connections. Now, after the death of her father, who had pressured her the most to marry, Dorothy found the courage to confide in her mother and in a trusted friend, Claudia. With the help of the latter in particular, who offered her hospitality and the opportunity of a job in a city in a third region, Dorothy decided to leave her husband and to move there. This was, in the early 1960s, a very difficult and painful decision for Dorothy, but she preferred to give up a life of ease and deep dissatisfaction for the sake of a life that was perhaps harder and more wearisome (she faced work for the first time) but certainly more free and authentic.

As often happens in cases of this sort, in the mid-1960s Dorothy, now thirty-five years old, became acquainted with Walter, an unmarried physician of the same age, with whom she fell in love, and he with her. Given Dorothy's previous marriage, the two lovers felt that there was nothing to do but start cohabiting. Then, in late 1970, when divorce became legal in Italy, Dorothy filed for divorce from her husband Arthur so as to contract a civil marriage with Walter.

Notwithstanding their morally questionable decisions to cohabit and to marry civilly, Dorothy and Walter developed a religious sensibility and even a certain practice of religion. During the 1980s they confided in a friar, to whom they explained their situation little by little. Upon hearing the story of Dorothy's marriage with Arthur, the religious advised her to initiate a cause of marital nullity. After she had sought the counsel of experts, her cause was introduced in the early 1990s in the competent tribunal in the region where Arthur's domicile was located (he had never moved from his native city), citing as the reason Arthur's copulative impotence.

The instruction of the cause of nullity, however, proved to be anything but easy. Dorothy gave her deposition, supported by those of her elderly mother and of her friend Claudia, as well as that by Walter, who, assisted also by the fact that he was a physician, could testify that he had found Dorothy a virgin when he joined with her for the first time. The friendly friar was able to vouch for the reliability and the religious motivation of Walter and Dorothy. Contrary to expectations, the now eighty-year-old Arthur appeared to give a deposition. He did admit that his marriage with Dorothy had never been consummated, although he remained very vague about his health-related conditions at that time and noted that he had recently undergone surgical operations in the genital area so as to correct his physical situation.

Given Arthur's vagueness about his health problems, his actual age, and the surgical procedures that he had undergone, proving that his copulative impotence was a condition already existing at the time of the marriage and, most importantly, was perpetual, was somewhat arduous. When the acts of the cause were published without arranging for any expert testimony (which was obviously useless at that point; cf. can. 1680), the advocate who was assisting Dorothy wisely recommended abandoning the cause of nullity and proposing (as is allowed by can. 1681) a petition for dispensation because of the non-consummation of the marriage. Having obtained Arthur's consent to this new petition and having completed the instruction according to the special requirements of the new procedure, the cause was presented to the Holy See, obtaining the papal dispensation.

The moral proof of nonconsummation was obviously considered sufficient; the quasi compulsion to which Dorothy had been subject with regard to her marriage, the anomalous married life that she had had to endure for a decade, and the opportunity to regularize her now long-standing union with Walter were considered just reasons for the dispensation. The amount of time that had elapsed and Dorothy's moves from one city to another—having resided now for thirty years in a place where her first marriage was completely unknown—evidently gave sufficient assurance that there would be no danger of scandal.

This example, besides recalling the procedural possibility allowed by canon 1681, is meant to draw attention to the fact that the moral argument alone, even at a considerable distance in time from the facts, can be decisive when it appears genuine and not artificial, even though there may not be a great quantity of evidence.

Third example

Miriam and John were engaged for several years and decided to marry. Miriam was a very idealistic young woman, but she was much inclined to worry and was extremely fragile psychologically. She suffered for years from anorexia and amenorrhea. She failed her high school final examinations several times, solely because of her emotional fragility, since she was otherwise diligent and studious. She had many complexes and was always fearful.

John, nevertheless, really liked her and wanted to help her. He came from an unhappy family situation. His father was a ladies' man and violent. One of his brothers had been sentenced to a long prison term for very serious crimes. He, however, was a sensible, sweet-tempered, respectful young man who practiced his faith.

And so, hoping that married life would have in store for both of them more joy than they had experienced until then, Miriam and John were married. They remained together for around fifteen years but without ever being able to consummate their marriage. In fact, no sooner would John come near Miriam to engage in sexual relations than the young woman would react vehemently and refuse. Despite John's patience and the treatments that Miriam underwent, including extensive psychological counseling, the situation did not change. If John so much as caressed her out of sexual desire, Miriam froze and became rigid and even became physically ill. Miriam's attitude toward food was still troubled as well; she was dissatisfied with her job too, which was not up to her potential and aspirations. There were also a few episodes of self-harm on her part.

After about fifteen years of patient waiting, John gave in to weakness. He fell in love with another woman and began a relationship with her. For both spouses this was the sign of a profound crisis in their marriage—a crisis, plainly, that was always part of it. They therefore decided to separate.

Miriam, however, who was always scrupulous and anxious, did not feel right about it and wanted some clarification about her situation from the religious perspective as well, a clarification approved by the Church too, since she had never stopped going to Mass. Fortunately, she met a lawyer who was also an expert in canonical questions, who gave her excellent advice. First she sent Miriam to a gynecologist whom she trusted, who after a complete, in-depth physical examination found that Miriam's hymen was intact. Then she patiently helped Miriam to find the witnesses with whom, over the course of her married life, she had confided about the nonconsummation of her marriage and about her own reactions to John's attempts to have conjugal relations. Miriam, in fact, being anxious and always in need of affirmation, encouragement, and reassurance, had told several persons at different times during her fifteen years with John how matters stood between them as far as marital relations were concerned.

After the cause had been well prepared, it was introduced. John too —besides Miriam and the witness that she introduced—came to confirm what had happened. The gynecologist confirmed under oath what she had ascertained in relation to the aforesaid physical examination. Miriam herself, although it cost her quite a lot of trouble, agreed to be examined also by a gynecologist appointed as an official expert by the tribunal. He too found with scientific certainty that the woman was still a virgin. On the basis of the aforesaid testimonies, the now-irreparable rift between Miriam and John (who, as was mentioned, was now in a relationship with another woman), and the reasonable unlikelihood of scandal (both of them still lived rather isolated lives, with few acquaintances, essentially those called by Miriam as witnesses who were therefore already in the know about the situation of the parties), the dispensation was granted.

This example is meant to highlight not only the agreement of the physical and moral arguments, and the need for careful preparation of the cause in advance, with thorough and conscientious consultation, but also the following circumstance. It might also have been possible for the marriage of Miriam and John to be challenged as invalid, for example, on the ground of Miriam's psychological incapacity. However, the mere likelihood of that (but without any materially available evidence of it) and the consideration that that type of proof, especially the expert testimony, would have been even more burdensome for the extremely fragile Miriam, suggested that it would be wise to seek a solution to this delicate human case by choosing the most economical path from the psychological, procedural, and probative perspectives: namely, the path of papal dispensation.

Fourth example

Richard and Josie—like many young people the same age, unfortunately—made a mistake in starting their relationship. Having just met, and mistaking mutual attraction for love, they launched into an intense emotional relationship that very quickly included complete intimacy as well. Just as quickly the two considered marriage, especially because Josie desired it. She was a very headstrong young woman, and at that time her relations with her own family were strained. The prospect of leaving home was very attractive to her.

After they found a place to live and set the date for their wedding, however, Richard and Josie found themselves in a completely new situation. Their initial infatuation had quickly faded and was replaced by increasingly heated arguments. Nevertheless, their wedding plans were confirmed. Josie was too eager to leave her family and too proud to admit that she had made a mistake. Richard, whose character was weaker, deluded himself, supposing that after the wedding Josie would be calmer and things would start to improve.

This illusion survived only a few hours after the wedding was celebrated. Already on the ride from the church to the restaurant, in the restaurant itself, and then in the newlyweds' house, after their friends and relatives had left, the quarrels started again, louder than before. Their wedding trip, which started the day afterward, was only partially completed, and their life together lasted only a few weeks. The two never slept together. On the few occasions when Richard, in an attempt to relieve the tension, tried to be affectionate with his wife, she lashed out at him furiously. She demanded that Richard always sleep on the couch in the living room of their house.

Richard was upset. Having a weak character, he went crying to his three older brothers, to his own parents and to Josie's, to several colleagues at work, and also to his pastor. None of these persons succeeded in coming into contact with the proud Josie. Only the wife of one of the aforesaid colleagues went to visit her on some pretense and received confirmation of the complete disaster, with regard to their intimate relations, which were completely absent after the wedding.

As was mentioned, not even two months after it was celebrated their life together fell apart and they suddenly initiated a process for their personal separation and a canonical cause for dispensation due to nonconsummation. All the above-mentioned persons appeared to confirm Richard's statements, and Richard's colleague's wife corroborated Josie's. The pastor, then, who had known Richard from when he was a little boy, gave extensive testimony to his credibility and to that of his parents and brothers. Then, after some effort, Josie too was convinced to give a deposition. She was a very tough young woman yet sincere and frank, and she too had no difficulty admitting the nonconsummation of their marriage.

The moral proof of nonconsummation appeared solid. The young age of the two parties and the certain impossibility of their resuming life together were a just reason. The fact that their married life lasted a few weeks and took place in a suburban bedroom community where Richard are Josie were and would always remain unknown guaranteed that there was no likelihood of scandal or other harm to third parties. One may conclude that precisely for these reasons the dispensation from the marriage in question was granted.

This example emphasizes not only the particular importance of the moral proof of nonconsummation (which can sustain the whole cause even by itself) but also the fact that only intimate relations (within the parameters elucidated further above) engaged in by the interested parties after the wedding are considered to consummate the marriage. Any premarital relations—as in the case of Richard and Josie—remain merely a morally unseemly fact and do not accomplish the consummation of a marriage that by definition does not exist, since no exchange of consent took place in the form required by canon law, and therefore cannot be "consummated" either.

www.ingramcontent.com/pod-product-compliance
Lightning Source LLC
Chambersburg PA
CBHW061129160726
48006CB00036B/1476